£10·00

DOMESDAY BOOK

Bedfordshire

History from the Sources

DOMESDAY BOOK

A Survey of the Counties of England

LIBER DE WINTONIA

Compiled by direction of

KING WILLIAM I

Winchester
1086

DOMESDAY BOOK

text and translation edited by

JOHN MORRIS

20

Bedfordshire

edited from a draft translation prepared by

Veronica Sankaran and David Sherlock

PHILLIMORE
Chichester
1977

1977

Published by

PHILLIMORE & CO. LTD.,

London and Chichester

Head Office: Shopwyke Hall,
Chichester, Sussex, England

ISBN 0 85033 149 8 (case)
ISBN 0 85033 150 1 (limp)

Printed in Great Britain by
Titus Wilson & Son Ltd.,
Kendal

BEDFORDSHIRE

Introduction

The Domesday Survey of Bedfordshire

Notes
Appendix
Index of Persons
Index of Places
Systems of Reference
Map
Technical Terms

History from the Sources
General Editor: John Morris

The series aims to publish history
written directly from the sources
for all interested readers, both
specialists and others. The first
priority is to publish important
texts which should be widely
available, but are not.

DOMESDAY BOOK

The contents, with the folio on which each county begins, are:

1	Kent	I	1	20	Bedfordshire		209
2	Sussex		16	21	Northamptonshire		219
3	Surrey		30	22	Leicestershire		230
4	Hampshire		37	23	Warwickshire		238
5	Berkshire		56	24	Staffordshire		246
6	Wiltshire		64	25	Shropshire		252
7	Dorset		75	26	Cheshire		262
8	Somerset		86	27	Derbyshire		272
9	Devon		100	28	Nottinghamshire		280
10	Cornwall		120	29	Rutland		293
11	Middlesex		126	30	Yorkshire		298
12	Hertfordshire		132	31	Lincolnshire		336
13	Buckinghamshire		143		Claims, Yorkshire		373
14	Oxfordshire		154		Lincolnshire		375
15	Gloucestershire		162		Yorkshire, summary		379
16	Worcestershire		172				
17	Herefordshire		179	32	Essex	II	1
18	Cambridgeshire		189	33	Norfolk		109
19	Huntingdonshire		203	34	Suffolk		281

Domesday Book is termed *Liber de Wintonia* (The Book of Winchester) in column 332c

INTRODUCTION

The Domesday Survey

In 1066 Duke William of Normandy conquered England. He was crowned King, and most of the lands of the English nobility were soon granted to his followers. Domesday Book was compiled 20 years later. The Saxon Chronicle records that in 1085

> at Gloucester at midwinter ... the King had deep speech with his counsellors ... and sent men all over England to each shire ... to find out ... what or how much each landholder held ... in land and livestock, and what it was worth ... The returns were brought to him.[1]

William was thorough. One of his Counsellors reports that he also sent a second set of Commissioners 'to shires they did not know, where they were themselves unknown, to check their predecessors' survey, and report culprits to the King.'[2]

The information was collected at Winchester, corrected, abridged, chiefly by omission of livestock and the 1066 population, and fair-copied by one writer into a single volume. Norfolk, Suffolk and Essex were copied, by several writers, into a second volume, unabridged, which states that 'the Survey was made in 1086'. The surveys of Durham and Northumberland, and of several towns, including London, were not transcribed, and most of Cumberland and Westmorland, not yet in England, was not surveyed. The whole undertaking was completed at speed, in less than 12 months, though the fair-copying of the main volume may have taken a little longer. Both volumes are now preserved at the Public Record Office. Some versions of regional returns also survive. One of them, from Ely Abbey,[3] copies out the Commissioners' brief. They were to ask

> The name of the place. Who held it, before 1066, and now?
> How many *hides*?[4] How many ploughs, both those in lordship and the men's?
> How many villagers, cottagers and slaves, how many free men and Freemen?[5]
> How much woodland, meadow and pasture? How many mills and fishponds?
> How much has been added or taken away? What the total value was and is?
> How much each free man or Freeman had or has? All threefold, before 1066,
> when King William gave it, and now; and if more can be had than at present?

The Ely volume also describes the procedure. The Commissioners took evidence on oath 'from the Sheriff; from all the barons and their Frenchmen; and from the whole Hundred, the priests, the reeves and six villagers from each village'. It also names four Frenchmen and four Englishmen from each Hundred, who were sworn to verify the detail.

The King wanted to know what he had, and who held it. The Commissioners therefore listed lands in dispute, for Domesday Book was not only a tax-assessment. To the King's grandson, Bishop Henry of Winchester, its purpose was that every 'man should know his right and not usurp another's'; and because it was the final authoritative register of rightful possession 'the natives called it Domesday Book, by analogy

---

[1] Before he left England for the last time, late in 1086.   [2] Robert Losinga, Bishop of Hereford 1079-1095 (see *E.H.R.* 22, 1907, 74).   [3] *Inquisitio Eliensis,* first paragraph.   [4] A land unit, reckoned as 120 acres.   [5] *Quot Sochemani.*

from the Day of Judgement'; that was why it was carefully arranged by Counties, and by landholders within Counties, 'numbered consecutively ... for easy reference'.[6]

Domesday Book describes Old English society under new management, in minute statistical detail. Foreign lords had taken over, but little else had yet changed. The chief landholders and those who held from them are named, and the rest of the population was counted. Most of them lived in villages, whose houses might be clustered together, or dispersed among their fields. Villages were grouped in administrative districts called Hundreds, which formed regions within Shires, or Counties, which survive today with minor boundary changes; the recent deformation of some ancient county identities is here disregarded, as are various short-lived modern changes. The local assemblies, though overshadowed by lords great and small, gave men a voice, which the Commissioners heeded. Very many holdings were described by the Norman term *manerium* (manor), greatly varied in size and structure, from tiny farmsteads to vast holdings; and many lords exercised their own jurisdiction and other rights, termed *soca*, whose meaning still eludes exact definition.

The Survey was unmatched in Europe for many centuries, the product of a sophisticated and experienced English administration, fully exploited by the Conqueror's commanding energy. But its unique assemblage of facts and figures has been hard to study, because the text has not been easily available, and abounds in technicalities. Investigation has therefore been chiefly confined to specialists; many questions cannot be tackled adequately without a cheap text and uniform translation available to a wider range of students, including local historians.

Previous Editions

The text has been printed once, in 1783, in an edition by Abraham Farley, probably of 1250 copies, at Government expense, said to have been £38,000; its preparation took 16 years. It was set in a specially designed type, here reproduced photographically, which was destroyed by fire in 1808. In 1811 and 1816 the Records Commissioners added an introduction, indices, and associated texts, edited by Sir Henry Ellis; and in 1861-1863 the Ordnance Survey issued zincograph facsimiles of the whole. Texts of individual counties have appeared since 1673, separate translations in the Victoria County Histories and elsewhere.

This Edition

Farley's text is used, because of its excellence, and because any worthy alternative would prove astronomically expensive. His text has been checked against the facsimile, and discrepancies observed have been verified against the manuscript, by the kindness of Miss Daphne Gifford of the Public Record Office. Farley's few errors are indicated in the notes.

[6]*Dialogus de Scaccario* 1,16.

The editor is responsible for the translation and lay-out. It aims at what the compiler would have written if his language had been modern English; though no translation can be exact, for even a simple word like 'free' nowadays means freedom from different restrictions. Bishop Henry emphasized that his grandfather preferred 'ordinary words'; the nearest ordinary modern English is therefore chosen whenever possible. Words that are now obsolete, or have changed their meaning, are avoided, but measurements have to be transliterated, since their extent is often unknown or arguable, and varied regionally. The terse inventory form of the original has been retained, as have the ambiguities of the Latin.

Modern English commands two main devices unknown to 11th century Latin, standardised punctuation and paragraphs; in the Latin, *ibi* ('there are') often does duty for a modern full stop, *et* ('and') for a comma or semi-colon. The entries normally answer the Commissioners' questions, arranged in five main groups, (i) the place and its holder, its hides, ploughs and lordship; (ii) people; (iii) resources; (iv) value; and (v) additional notes. The groups are usually given as separate paragraphs.

King William numbered chapters 'for easy reference', and sections within chapters are commonly marked, usually by initial capitals, often edged in red. They are here numbered. Maps, indices and an explanation of technical terms are also given. Later, it is hoped to publish analytical and explanatory volumes, and associated texts.

The editor is deeply indebted to the advice of many scholars, too numerous to name, and especially to the Public Record Office, and to the publisher's patience. The draft translations are the work of a team; they have been co-ordinated and corrected by the editor, and each has been checked by several people. It is therefore hoped that mistakes may be fewer than in versions published by single fallible individuals. But it would be Utopian to hope that the translation is altogether free from error; the editor would like to be informed of mistakes observed.

The map is the work of Jim Hardy.

The preparation of this volume has been greatly assisted by a generous grant from the Leverhulme Trust Fund.

Conventions

*	refers to a note to the Latin text.

[ ]   enclose words omitted in the MS.   ( )   enclose editorial explanations.

BEDEFORDSCIRE.

BEDEFORD. T.R.E. p̄ dimidio hund se deꝼdeƀ.
7 m̄ facit. in expeditione 7 in nauibȝ . Terra
de hac uilla nunꝗ fuit hidata. nec m̄ eſt. p̄ter
unā hid quæ jacuit in æccła Ꞩ Pavli in elemoſina
T.R.E. 7 m̄ jacet rećte. Sed Remigi eꝑs poſuit eā
ext elemoſinā æcclæ Ꞩ Pauli injuſte ut hōes dicuꞇ.
7 m̄ tenet. 7 quicqd ad eā ꝑtinet. Valet. c . ſolid.

BEDFORDSHIRE

B BEDFORD answered for a half Hundred before 1066, and does so now, in (military) expeditions, (by land) and in ships. The land of this town was never assessed in hides and is not now, except for 1 hide, which lay in (the lands of) St. Paul's Church before 1066, in alms, and now rightly so lies. But Bishop Remigius wrongfully placed it outside the alms (lands) of St. Paul's Church, as the men (of the Shire) state. He holds it now, and whatever belongs to it.
Value 100s.

.I. Rex Willelmvs

.II. Eps Baiocensis.

.III. Eps Constantiensis.

.IIII. Eps Lincoliensis.

.V. Eps Dunelmsis.

.VI. Abb de S Edmundo.

.VII. Abb de Burg.

.VIII Abb de Ramesy.

.IX. Abb de Westmon.

.X. Abb de Torny.

.XI. Abbatissa de Berching.

.XII Canonici de Lundon.

.XIII Canonici de Bedeford.

.XIIII. Ernuinus pbr.

.XV. Eustachius comes.

.XVI. Walterius gifard.

.XVII. Wills de Warenna.

.XVIII. Wills de Ouu.

.XIX. Milo crispinus.

.XX. Ernulf de Hesding.

.XXI. Eudo dapifer.

.XXII. Wills peurel

.XXIII. Hugo de belcap.

.XXIIII. Nigell de albingi.

.XXV Wills Spech.

.XXVI Robt de Todeni.

.XXVII. Gislebt de gand.

.XXVIII Robt de olgi

.XXIX. Rannulf fr Ilgerij.

.XXX. Robt Fasiton.

.XXXI. Aluered de Lincolia.

.XXXII. Walter Flandrensis.

.XXXIII. Walter fr Seiherij.

.XXXIIII. Hugo Flandrensis.

XXXV. Hugo pincerna.

XXXVI. Sigarus de Cioches.

XXXVII. Gunfrid de Cioches.

XXXVIII Ricard fili Gislebti comitis.

.XXXIX. Ricardus pungiant.

.XL. Wills camerarius.

XLI. Wills Louet.

.XLII. Wills

.XLIII. Henricus filius Azor.

XLIIII. Osbn filius Ricardi.

.XLV. Osbn filius Walterii.

.XLVI. Osbn piscator.

.XLVII. Turstin camerarius.

.XLVIII. Gislebt fili Salom.

.XLIX. Albt Lothariensis.

.L. Dauid de Argentom.

.LI. Radulf de insula.

.LII. Gozelin brito

.LIII. Judita comitissa

.LIIII. Adeliz fem. H. de grent.

.LV. Azelina fem. R. talgeb.

.LVI. Burgenses de bedeford.

.LVI. Pfecti regis 7 bedelli

7 elemosinarii.

[LIST OF LANDHOLDERS IN BEDFORDSHIRE]

1 King William
2 The Bishop of Bayeux
3 The Bishop of Coutances
4 The Bishop of Lincoln
5 The Bishop of Durham
6 The Abbot of St. Edmund's
7 The Abbot of Peterborough
8 The Abbot of Ramsey
9 The Abbot of Westminster
10 The Abbot of Thorney
11 The Abbess of Barking
12 The Canons of London
13 The Canons of Bedford
14 Ernwin the Priest
15 Count Eustace
16 Walter Giffard
17 William of Warenne
18 William of Eu
19 Miles Crispin
20 Arnulf of Hesdin
21 Eudo the Steward
22 William Peverel
23 Hugh of Beauchamp
24 Nigel of Aubigny
25 William Speke
26 Robert of Tosny
27 Gilbert of Ghent
28 Robert d'Oilly
29 Ranulf brother of Ilger
30 Robert [son of] Fafiton
31 Alfred of Lincoln
32 Walter of Flanders
33 Walter brother of Sihere
34 Hugh of Flanders

35 Hugh Butler
36 Sigar of Chocques
37 Gunfrid of Chocques
38 Richard son of Count Gilbert
39 Richard Poynant
40 William the Chamberlain
41 William Lovett
42 William
43 Henry son of Azor
44 Osbern son of Richard
45 Osbern son of Walter
46 Osbern Fisher
47 Thurstan the Chamberlain
48 Gilbert son of Solomon
49 Albert of Lorraine
50 David of Argenton
51 Ralph de L'Isle
52 Jocelyn the Breton
53 Countess Judith
54 Adelaide wife of Hugh of
    Grandmesnil
55 Azelina wife of Ralph Tallboys
56 The Burgesses of Bedford
[57]The King's Reeves and Beadles
    and Almsmen

TE꞉RA REGIꞅ.

Ⓜ *Lꞔ̄STONE* dn̄icū Maneriꞇ Regis

p.xLvii.hiđ ſe defđ modo.T.ℝ.E.n̄ eraꝗ niſi.xxx.hiđ.

De his.xLvii.hiđ ſuꝗ in manu regis.xL.iii.hiđ.

Tra.ē ad.Lii.caꝝ.In dn̄io ſunt.vi.caꝝ.7 uiꞔꞔi hn̄t

xLvi.caꝝ.Ibi ſunt q̄ter x̄x̄ 7 ii.uiꞔꞔi.7 xxx.borđ.

7 ii.ſerui.7 ii.molini de.xxx.ſoꞇ.Ptū.xL.caꝝ.Silua

c.porc.Theloneū de mercato redđ.vii.liꞇ.Inꞇ

totū redđ p annū.xxii.liꞇ ad pensū.7 dimiđ diē

ad firmā regis.in frum̄to 7 melle 7 aliis rebꝫ ad firmā

ptinentibꝫ.Ad oꝑ reginæ.ii.uncias auri.7 p.i.sūmario

7 c̄ſuetuđ cañ.Lxx.ſoꞇ.7 c.ſoꞇ ad pensū.7 xL.ſoꞇ de

albo argento.Hoc miſit de crem̄to Iuo tallieboſc.

7 i.unc auri ad oꝑ uicecomitis p annū.

De huꝩ Ⓜ tra tenuit Weneſi camerari̇.x.hiđ de

rege Edw.quas Radulꝰ tallieboſc appoſuit in Leſtone

ubi n̄ adjacebant.T.R.E.Et iterū iſđ Radulꝰ appo

ſuit alias vii.hiđ huic Manerio quæ ibi n̄ eraꝗ.T.R.E.

Has.vii.hiđ tenuit Starcher teigñ.R.E.

Æcc̄lam huꝩ Ⓜ ten Rem eꝑs.cū.iiii.hiđ quæ ad eā

ptinent.7 Hæ.iiii.cōputanꞇ in.xLvii.hiđ manerii.

Tra.ē ad.iii.caꝝ.In dn̄io.ē.i.caꝝ.7 uiꞔꞔi.i.caꝝ.7 alia

poſſet fieri.Ibi.vi.uiꞔꞔi 7 vi.borđ p̄tū.iii.caꝝ.H̄ tra

cū æcc̄ta uaꞇ 7 ualuit.iiii.liꞇ.Wluui eꝑs ten.T.R.E.

Ⓜ *Loꞔꞇone* dn̄icū Ⓜ Regis p.xxx.hiđ ſe defđ.Tra.ē

ad q̄t x̄x̄ 7 ii.caꝝ.In dn̄io.iiii.caꝝ.Viꞔꞔi q̄t x̄x̄.caꝝ.

ii.miñ.Ibi.q̄t x̄x̄.uiꞔꞔi 7 xLvii.borđ.7 vi.molini

redđ.c.ſoꞇ.p̄tū.iiii.caꝝ.Silua.ii.miliū porc.7 de

c̄ſuetuđ.x.ſoꞇ 7 viii.deñ.De theloneo 7 mercato.c.ſoꞇ.

[In STANBRIDGE Hundred]

1a M. LEIGHTON (Buzzard), a household manor of the King's, now answers
for 47 hides; before 1066 there were only 30 hides. Of these 47
hides, 43 hides are in the King's hands. Land for 52 ploughs.
In lordship 6 ploughs. The villagers have 46 ploughs.
    82 villagers, 30 smallholders and 2 slaves.
    2 mills at 30s; meadow for 40 ploughs; woodland, 100 pigs;
        market tolls pay £7.
In total, it pays £22 by weight a year and half a day('s provisions)
to the King's revenue, in wheat, honey and other things which
belong to the revenue; for the Queen's work 2 ounces of gold;
for 1 pack-horse and for customary dog dues 70s, and 100s by
weight and 40s in white silver; Ivo Tallboys put this on from
the increase; 1 ounce of gold a year for the Sheriff's work.

b   Wynsi the Chamberlain held 10 hides of this manor's land from
King Edward. Ralph Tallboys placed them in Leighton, where
they were not attached before 1066; again, Ralph also placed
another 7 hides in this manor, which were not there before 1066.
Starker, a thane of King Edward's, held these 7 hides.

c   Bishop Remigius holds the church of this manor, with 4 hides
which belong to it. These 4 are accounted for in the 47 hides
of the manor. Land for 3 ploughs. In lordship 1 plough;
the villagers, 1 plough; another possible.
    6 villagers and 6 smallholders.
    Meadow for 3 ploughs.
The value of this land, with the church, is and was £4.
    Bishop Wulfwy held it before 1066.

[In MANSHEAD Hundred]

a M. LUTON, a household manor of the King's, answers for 30 hides.
Land for 82 ploughs. In lordship 4 ploughs. The villagers, 80
ploughs less 2.
    80 villagers and 47 smallholders.
    6 mills which pay 100s; meadow for 4 ploughs;
        woodland, 2000 pigs; customary dues, 10s 8d; from tolls
        and the market, 100s.

Int tot redd p annū . xxx . lib ad pensu . 7 dimid die ·
in frumto 7 melle 7 aliis csuetud ad firmā regis ptinent.
Reginæ . IIII . unc auri . 7 de sūmario 7 aliis csuetudinibz
minutis . LXX . sol . 7 de csuetud canū . VI . lib 7 x . sol.
7 de cremto qd misit Iuo tallebosc . VII . lib ad pensū.
7 XL . sol albi argenti . 7 unā unciā auri uicecomiti.
Æcclam huj ō ten Witts camerari de rege . cū . v.
hid træ quæ ad eā ptinent. Hæ . v . hid sux de xxx . hid ō.
Tra . ē . VI . car in dnio . I . car . 7 uitti hnt . v . car . Ibi XI.
uitti 7 IIII . bord . 7 III . serui . 7 I . molin . x . sol . Æccta . xx . sol
p annū redd . Silua . L . porc . Int totū uat 7 ualuit
LX . sol . Hanc æcctam cū tra tenuit Morcar ptr . T.R.E.

ō HEVSTONE dnicū ō Regis . p x . hid se defd . Tra . ē
.xxii car . In dnio . II . car . 7 uitti . xxii . car . Ibi xxx
7 VIII . uitti 7 XII . bord . l'tū . xII . car . Silua . c . porc.
Int totū redd p ann . x . lib ad pensū . 7 dimid die
de frumto 7 melle 7 aliis rebz ad firmā regis ptinentib.
De minutis csuetudinib 7 de . I . sūmario . LXV . sol.
De csuetud canū . LXV . sol . 7 Reginæ . II . unc auri.
De cremto qd misit Iuo tallebosc . III . lib ad pensū . 7 xx·
sot de albo argento . 7 I . unc auri uicecomiti.
Æcctam huj ō ten Witts camerari cū dim hida.
quæ ad eā ptin . 7 de . x . hid Manerij . ē . Tra . ē dim car.
7 ibi est . Valet . xII . sot . p annū.
SEWELLE p . III . hid se defd T.R.E . Tra . ē . II . car . Ibi est
.I . car 7 dim . 7 adhuc dim pot fieri . p'tū . IIII . boū.
Ibi . I . uitts 7 IIII . bord . H tra uat 7 ualuit . xx . sot . Hanc
tenuit Walraue hō Eddid reginæ . 7 potuit dare cui
uoluit . In Odecrost hund jacuit . T.R.E . Radulf u
taillebosc in ō houstone apposuit ccedente . W . rege
p cremtū qd ei dedit . Hoc dnt hōes ejd Rad . scdm

In total, it pays £30 a year by weight and half a day('s provisions) in wheat, honey and other customary dues which belong to the King's revenue; to the Queen 4 ounces of gold; for a pack-horse and other petty customary dues 70s; for customary dog dues, £6 10s; from the increase which Ivo Tallboys put on £7 by weight and 40s of white silver; 1 ounce of gold to the Sheriff.

2b William the King's Chamberlain holds the church of this manor, with 5 hides of land which belong to it. These 5 hides are of the 30 hides of the manor. Land for 6 ploughs. In lordship 1 plough. The villagers have 5 ploughs.

 11 villagers, 4 smallholders and 3 slaves.

 1 mill, 10s; the church pays 20s a year; woodland, 50 pigs.

In total, the value is and was 60s.

 Morcar the priest held this church with the land before 1066.

3 M. HOUGHTON (Regis), a household manor of the King's, answers 209 c for 10 hides. Land for 24 ploughs. In lordship 2 ploughs.

The villagers, 22 ploughs.

 38 villagers and 12 smallholders.

 Meadow for 12 ploughs; woodland, 100 pigs.

In total, it pays £10 a year by weight and half a day('s provisions) in wheat, honey and other things which belong to the King's revenue; from petty customary dues and from 1 pack-horse 65s; from customary dog dues 65s; to the Queen 2 ounces of gold; from the increase which Ivo Tallboys put on £3 by weight and 20s in white silver; 1 ounce of gold to the Sheriff.

 William the Chamberlain holds the church of this manor, with ½ hide which belongs to it. It is of the 10 hides of the manor. Land for ½ plough; it is there. Value 12s a year.

4 SEWELL answered for 3 hides before 1066. Land for 2 ploughs. 1½ there; a further ½ possible.

 Meadow for 4 oxen.

 1 villager and 4 smallholders.

The value of this land is and was 20s.

 Walraven, Queen Edith's man, held it; he could grant to whom he would. It lay in 'Woodcroft' Hundred before 1066, but Ralph Tallboys placed it in the manor of Houghton with King William's assent through the increase it gave him. This is what Ralph's men

BISSOPESCOTE . p v . hiđ ſe defđ . T.R.E . Tra . ē . v . cař.

Ibi . ıı . cař in dñio . 7 x . uiłłi hñt . ııı . cař . Ibi . ııı . ſerui.

7 p̃tū . ııı . cař . In totis ualent ual xl . ſoł . Q̱do Radulf^{tailleboſc 9}

tenebat: ſimił . T.R.E . lx . ſoł . Hoc m̃ tenuit Eduuin^9

hō Aſgari ſtalri . 7 potuit inde facere qđ uoluit . Hanc

appoſuit Radulf^9 tallieboſc . ~~appoſuit~~ in Loitone m̃

regis . p cremt̄u qđ ei dedit . 7 foris miſit de hund ubi ſe

defendeb . T.R.E . Econt sūpſit alias . v . hiđ de alio hund.

7 poſuit in Flictham hund.

.ıı. TERRA EP̃I BAIOCENSIS.

E ̃ PS BAIOCENSIS In dimidio hund de *STANBVRGE*

ten *EITONE* . p xıı . hiđ 7 ı . uirg ſe defđ . Tra . ē xx.

cař . In dñio . ıı . hidæ . 7 ibi ſunt . ıııı . cař . 7 ıı . adhuc

poſſunt fieri . Viłłi hñt . vııı . cař . 7 adhuc . vı . poſſ . eē.

Ibi xx uiłłi . 7 xııı . borđ . 7 ıı . ſerui . p̃tū . vı . cař . Silua

ccc . porč . 7 xıı . deñ inde . In totis ualent ual . xvı . liɓ.

Q̱do recep̃: xx . liɓ . T.R.E: ſimilit̃ . Hoc m̃ tenuit Alſi

hō regine Eddiđ . 7 dare 7 uende potuit.

In *HVND* de Maneſheue ten Anſgot de Roueceſtre

ıı . hiđ in Eureſhot . de fedo ep̃i Baioc . Tra . ē . ıı . cař . Ibi

eſt una 7 alia poteſt fieri . Ibi ſunt . ıııı . uiłłi . 7 ı . borđ.

P̃tū . ı . cař . Silua . l . porč . Int t̃otū ual . xx . ſoł . Q̱do

recep̃: xxx . ſoł . T.R.E: xl . ſoł . Hanc trā T.R.E . ıııı . teini

tenueř . 7 dare 7 uendẽ potueř.

Iſdem Anſgot ten^9 de eođ ep̃o in Mildentone . ıııı . hiđ.

Tra . ıııı . cař . In dñio . ı . cař . 7 altera pot fieri . Viłłi . ıı.

cař . Ibi . ıııı . uiłłi . 7 ııı . borđ . 7 vııı . ſerui . p̃tū . ıııı . cař.

Silua . xxx . porč . Int tot̃u ual 7 ualuit qdo recep̃.

ıııı . liɓ . T.R.E . xl . ſoł . Hanc tram tenueř . vıı . ſochi.

7 dare 7 uende potueř T.R.E.

state, according to what they heard him say.

5   BISCOT answered for 5 hides before 1066. Land for 5 ploughs.
In lordship 2 ploughs.
        10 villagers have 3 ploughs.
        3 slaves; meadow for 3 ploughs.
Total value 40s; when Ralph Tallboys held it, the same;
before 1066, 60s.
        Edwin, Asgar the Constable's man, held this manor; he could
do what he would with it. Ralph Tallboys placed it in the King's
manor of Luton through the increase it gave him, and put it
outside the Hundred where it answered before 1066; against it
he took another 5 hides from another Hundred and placed
them in Flitt Hundred.

2   **LAND OF THE BISHOP OF BAYEUX**

In the Half-Hundred of STANBRIDGE

1   M. The Bishop of Bayeux holds EATON (Bray). It answers for 12
hides and 1 virgate. Land for 20 ploughs. In lordship 2 hides;
4 ploughs; a further 2 possible. The villagers have 8 ploughs;
a further 6 possible.
        20 villagers, 13 smallholders and 2 slaves.
        Meadow for 6 ploughs; woodland, 300 pigs and 12d therefrom.
Total value £16; when acquired £20; before 1066 the same.
        Alfsi, Queen Edith's man, held this manor; he could grant
and sell.

In the Hundred of MANSHEAD

2   Ansgot of Rochester holds 2 hides in EVERSHOLT from the
Bishop of Bayeux's Holding. Land for 2 ploughs; 1 there;
another possible.
        4 villagers and 1 smallholder.
        Meadow for 1 plough; woodland, 50 pigs.
In total, value 20s; when acquired 30s; before 1066, 40s.
        4 thanes held this land before 1066; they could grant and sell.

3   Ansgot also holds 4 hides in MILTON (Bryan) from the Bishop.
Land for 4 ploughs. In lordship 1 plough; a second possible.
The villagers, 2 ploughs.
        4 villagers, 3 smallholders and 8 slaves.
        Meadow for 4 ploughs; woodland, 30 pigs.
In total, the value is, and was when acquired, £4; before 1066, 40s.
        Before 1066, 7 Freemen held this land; they could grant and sell. 209 d

In Hund de Stodene . teñ Toui p̄br dim̄ hid de ēpo
in Boleheſtre . Tra̅ . ē . I . car̄ . 7 ibi eſt . 7 I . uitⱡs 7 I . bord̄
P̄tū dim̄ car̄ . Silua . xxx . porc̄ . Int totū ual̄ x . fot.
7 tantd̄ qd̄o recep̄ . T.R.E. xii . fot . Hanc tr̄a tenuit Azor
hō Bored . 7 uend̄e potuit cui uellet.

I ᴮɪᴅ tenent . II . ſoc̄hi de ēpo dim̄ hid . Tra̅ . ē . I . car̄.
7 ibi . ē . cū . II . bord̄ . Silua . IIII . porc̄ . Int totū ual̄ . x . fot
7 tntd̄ qd̄o recep̄ . T.R. xii . fot . Idem ipſi q̄ tenent
tenuer̄ T.R.E. 7 uend̄e 7 dare potuer̄.

In dimid hund de Boch . . ai . teñ Herb̄t fili Iuonis de ēpo
III . hid 7 III . uirg in Stach . . . e . Tra̅ . ē . IIII . car̄ . Ibi ſuɴ
nc̄ . III . car̄ 7 dim̄ . 7 dim̄ p . . fieri . Ibi xii . uitⱡi 7 vi
bord̄ . p̄tū . I . car̄ . Silua . xl . porc̄ . Int tot̄ ual̄
vii . lib̄ . Qd̄o recep̄ . ix . lib̄ . T.R.E. xii . lib̄ . Hanc tr̄a
xii . ſoc̄hi tenuer̄ hōes regis . E . fuer̄ . 7 uend̄e potuer̄

In Hund de Wilga teñ . II . ſoc̄hi in Carlentone
I . hid 7 I . uirg . de Herb̄to filio iuonis . 7 ipſe de ēpo
Tra̅ . ē . I . car̄ 7 dim̄ . 7 ibi ſunt . P̄tū . I . car̄ . Int totū ual̄
xxvi . fot 7 viii . den̄ . Qd̄o recep̄ . 7 T.R.E. xxx . fot . Hanc
tr̄a id̄e ipſi qui nc̄ teneɴ tenuer̄ 7 dare 7 uend̄e potuer̄

In Torueie teñ Wimund de Herb̄to . 7 ipſe de ēpo
I . hid . Tra̅ . I . car̄ . 7 ibi . ē . p̄tū dim̄ car̄ . Int totū
ual̄ . xx . fot . Qd̄o recep̄ . 7 T.R.E. xl . fot . Hanc tr̄a
tenuit uñ hō Aluuoldi de Stiuetone . 7 uend̄e potuit.

M̄ In Hund de Bereforde . Herb̄t de ēpo 7 hugo nepos ej
de eo teñ v . hid̄ in Wildene . Tra̅ . ē xvi . car̄ In dñio
nulla . ē m̂ . 7 III . poſſunt fieri Vitⱡi hn̄t . x . car̄ . 7 adhuc
III . poſ̄ſ fieri . Ibi xx . ſoc̄hi . 7 xii . bord̄ . 7 I . ſeruus.
p̄tū . vi . car̄ . Silua . vi . porc̄ . Int totū ual̄ . ix . lib̄.
Qd̄o recep̄ . xii . lib̄ . T.R.E. xx . lib̄ . Hoc M̄ tenuer̄
xxiiii . ſoc̄hi . 7 potuer̄ dare 7 uend̄e tr̄a ſua cui uoluer̄

In the Hundred of STODDEN

4   Tovi the priest holds ½ hide in BOLNHURST from the Bishop.
Land for 1 plough; it is there.
> 1 villager and 1 smallholder.
> Meadow for ½ plough; woodland, 30 pigs.
In total, value 10s; when acquired as much; before 1066, 12s.
> Azor, Burgred's man, held this land; he could sell to whom
he would.

5   There 2 Freemen also hold ½ hide from the Bishop.
Land for 1 plough; it is there, with
> 2 smallholders.
> Woodland, 4 pigs.
In total, value 10s; when acquired as much; before 1066, 12s.
> The present holders held it before 1066; they could sell and grant.

In the Half-Hundred of BUCKLOW

6   Herbert son of Ivo holds 3 hides and 3 virgates in STAGSDEN from
the Bishop. Land for 4 ploughs; 3½ ploughs there now; ½ possible.
> 12 villagers and 7 smallholders.
> Meadow for 1 plough; woodland, 40 pigs.
In total, value £7; when acquired £9; before 1066 £12.
> 12 Freemen held this land; they were King Edward's men;
they could sell.

In the Hundred of WILLEY

7   2 Freemen hold 1 hide and 1 virgate in CARLTON from Herbert son of
Ivo; he holds from the Bishop. Land for 1½ ploughs; they are there.
> Meadow for 1 plough.
In total, value 26s 8d; when acquired and before 1066, 30s.
> The present holders held this land; they could grant and sell.

8   Wimund holds 1 hide in TURVEY from Herbert; he holds from
the Bishop. Land for 1 plough; it is there.
> Meadow for ½ plough.
In total, value 20s; when acquired and before 1066, 40s.
> A man of Alfwold of Stevington's held this land; he could sell.

In the Hundred of BARFORD

9   M. Herbert holds 5 hides in WILDEN from the Bishop and his nephew
Hugh from him. Land for 16 ploughs. In lordship now none; 3
possible. The villagers have 10 ploughs; a further 3 possible.
> 20 Freemen, 12 smallholders and 1 slave.
> Meadow for 6 ploughs; woodland, 6 pigs.
In total, value £9; when acquired £12; before 1066 £20.
> 24 Freemen held this manor; they could grant and sell their
land to whom they would.

Eps constantiensis ten CHENOTINGA

p v.hid se defd.Tra.e.v.car.In dnio.iii.hid

7 ii.car sunt ibi.Villi hnt.iii.car.Ibi.viii.uilli

7 v.bord.7 iiii.serui.Ptu.ii.car.Silua.cccc.porc.

Valet.iiii.lib.Qdo recep.iii.lib.7 tntd T.R.E.Hoc m̄

tenuit Burret.T.R.E.

Ipse eps ten MELCEBVRNE.p x.hid se defd.Tra

e.x.car.In dnio.iii.hidæ 7 iii.car.Villi hnt.vii.car.

Ibi.xiii.uilli 7 xv.bord.7 iii.serui.Ptu   car.

Silua.c.porc.Valet.viii.lib.Qdo recep.c.sol.T.R.E.

vi.lib.Hoc m̄ tenuit Burret.7 ibi fuer.vi.sochi.

7 potuer dare 7 uende tra sua absq lictia

★ Ipse eps ten in DENA.iiii.hid.Tra.e   7 ibi suN.

Ibi.vi.sochi.7 vi.bord.7 ii.serui.Valet.lx.sol.Qdo

recep.simil.T.R.E.xl.sol.Hoc m̄ tenuer.vi.sochi.

210 a

hōes Borret fuer.De soca regis.iii.hid 7 dim potuer

dare 7 uende 7 ad alteru dnm recede sine lictia Borred.

Dim u hid sine ej licentia ej dare t uende n potuer.

GOISFRID de Traillgi ten de epo cstantiensi GIVELDENE.

p x.hid se defd.Tra.e.xv.car.In dnio sunt.iiii.car.7

uilli hnt.xi.car.Ibi xvii.uilli.7 un miles.7 xii.bord.

7 i.seruus.Ptu.iiii.car.Silua.xx.porc.In totis ualent

ual.ix.lib.Qdo recep.c.sol...R.E.viii.lib.Hoc m̄

★ tenuit Borred.7 in eo fuer.v...chi q tenuer de hac tra

v.hid.7 cui uoluer dare t uende potuer.

De ipso epo ten Wills d...fer ej ESELTONE.p.v.hid

se defd.Tra.e.vi.car.In dnio.ii.car.7 uilli hnt.iiii.

In STODDEN Hundred

1   M. The Bishop of Coutances holds KNOTTING. It answers for 5 hides.
Land for 5 ploughs. In lordship 3 hides; 2 ploughs.
The villagers have 3 ploughs.
    8 villagers, 5 smallholders and 4 slaves.
    Meadow for 2 ploughs; woodland, 400 pigs.
Value £4, when acquired £3; the same before 1066.
Burgred held this manor before 1066.

2   M. The Bishop also holds MELCHBOURNE. It answers for 10 hides.
Land for 10 ploughs. In lordship 3 hides; 3 ploughs.
The villagers have 7 ploughs.
    13 villagers, 15 smallholders and 3 slaves.
    Meadow for ... ploughs; woodland, 100 pigs.
Value £8; when acquired 100s; before 1066 £6.
    Burgred held this manor. There were 6 Freemen there; they
could grant and sell their land without permission.

3   M. The Bishop also holds 4 hides in DEAN. Land for [5? ploughs] ;
they are there.
    6 Freemen, 6 smallholders and 2 slaves.
Value 60s; when acquired the same; before 1066, 40s.
    6 Freemen held this manor; they were Burgred's men.
They could grant or sell 3½ hides, of the King's jurisdiction,   210 a
or withdraw to another lord without Burgred's permission. But
½ hide they could not grant or sell without his permission.

4   M. Geoffrey of Trelly holds YELDEN   from the Bishop of Coutances.
It answers for 10 hides. Land for 15 ploughs. In lordship 4
ploughs. The villagers have 11 ploughs.
    17 villagers, 1 man-at-arms, 12 smallholders and 1 slave.
    Meadow for 4 ploughs; woodland, 20 pigs.
In total, value £9; when acquired 100s; before 1066 £8.
    Burgred held this manor. In it were 5 Freemen who held 5
hides of land; they could grant or sell to whom they would.

5   M. William, his Steward, holds SHELTON from the Bishop.
It answers for 5 hides. Land for 6 ploughs. In lordship 2 ploughs.
The villagers have 4.

Ibi . xiiii . 7 v . borđ . 7 iii . serui . 7 i . moliñ . iii . solid . Ptu.
. i . car . Silua . iiii . porc . Valet . c . sol . Qdo recep . lx . sol.
T.R.E. iiii . liƀ . Hoc ῶ tenuit Vlueua . sub Borret.
ñ potuit dare nec uende sine ej licentia.

In Estone teneꝧ . iiii . sochi de epo c̄stant . iii . uirg træ.
Tra . i . car . 7 ibi . ē . H tra ual 7 ualuit x . sol . T.R.E. v . sol.
Idē ipsi q̃ teneꝧ tenuer . hoēs Burred fuer . 7 cui uoluer
dare potuer . In his . iii . uirg reclamat eps sup Sigard
de cioches . xx . ac̃s siluæ . quæ ibi iacuer T.R.E. 7 hoc
hoēs de Hund attestant.

ῶ In Riselai tenent de epo . ii . francig . 7 vi . angli . vi . hid.
Tra . ē . vii . car . 7 ibi sunt . Ibi . vi . uilli 7 vii . borđ.
7 un seruus . Ptu . iii . car . Silua . cc . porc . Valet
lxxii . sol . Qdo recep . similit . T.R.E. c . sol . De hac
tra tenuit Burred . ii . hid in dñio . 7 vi . sochi hoēs ej
tenuer . iiii . hid . quas ubi uoluer dare 7 uende potuer.

In Bulehestre ten isdē eps . iii . uirg tre . p excābio
de Bledone . Tra . ē . i . car 7 dim . 7 ibi sunt . Vn uilℓs
7 iiii . borđ . Ptu . i . car . Silua . xx . porc . Val . xv . sol.
Qdo recep . similit . T.R.E. xx . sol . Hanc tra tenuit
Gudmunt hō regis . E . uende potuit cui uoluit.

In Neuuentone ten de epo Wilℓs dapifer ej . i . uirg.
Val 7 ualuit . xii . den . T.R.E. xvi . den . Hanc tra
tenuit Aluuin hō Borred . ñ potuit dare ł uende sine ej
ῶ In Hund de Wilga ten Goisfrid de tralgi ⌐ licentia.
iiii . hid de epo . Tra . ē . v . car . In dñio sunt . ii . car.
7 uilℓi hñt . iii . car . Ibi . xiiii . uilℓi . 7 v . borđ . 7 iiii . serui.
ptu . iiii . car . Val 7 ualuit . c . sol . Hoc ῶ tenuit
Turbt hō regis . E . 7 uende potuit . Hanc tra ten eps
p Excābio de Bledone . ut hoēs ej dicunt.

14 [villagers] , 5 smallholders and 3 slaves.
1 mill, 3s; meadow for 1 plough; woodland, 4 pigs.
Value 100s; when acquired 60s; before 1066 £4.
   Wulfeva held this manor under Burgred; she could not grant
or sell without his permission.

6   In EASTON 4 Freemen hold 3 virgates of land from the Bishop
     of Coutances. Land for 1 plough; it is there.
     The value of this land is and was 10s; before 1066, 5s.
        The present holders held it; they were Burgred's men; they
     could grant to whom they would.
        In these 3 virgates the Bishop claims against Sigar of
     Chocques 20 acres of woodland which lay there before 1066;
     this the men of the Hundred confirm.

7 M. In RISELEY 2 Frenchmen and 6 Englishmen hold 6 hides from
     the Bishop. Land for 7 ploughs; they are there.
        6 villagers, 7 smallholders and 1 slave.
        Meadow for 3 ploughs; woodland, 200 pigs.
     Value 72s; when acquired the same; before 1066, 100s.
        Burgred held 2 hides of this land in lordship. 6 Freemen, his
     men, held 4 hides which they could grant and sell where they would.

8   In BOLNHURST the Bishop also holds 3 virgates of land in
     exchange for Bleadon. Land for 1½ ploughs; they are there.
        1 villager and 4 smallholders.
        Meadow for 1 plough; woodland, 20 pigs.
     Value 15s; when acquired the same; before 1066, 20s.
        Godmund, King Edward's man, held this land; he could
     sell to whom he would.

9   In NEWTON (Bromshold) William, his Steward, holds 1 virgate
     from the Bishop.
     The value is and was 12d; before 1066, 16d.
        Alwin, Burgred's man, held this land; he could not grant
     or sell without his permission.

   In the Hundred of WILLEY
10 M. Geoffrey of Trelly holds 4 hides from the Bishop. Land for 5
     ploughs. In lordship 2 ploughs. The villagers have 3 ploughs.
        14 villagers, 5 smallholders and 4 slaves.
        Meadow for 4 ploughs.
     The value is and was 100s.
        Thorbert, King Edward's man, held this manor; he could
     sell. The Bishop holds this land in exchange for Bleadon, as
     his men state.

ⵎ In *TORNAI* ten iſd eṕs.ɪɪɪɪ.hiđ.Tra.ē.vɪ.caŕ.In dñio
ſunt.ɪɪ.hidæ.7 ɪɪɪ.caŕ.Ibi.ɪɪɪ.uilti hñt.ɪɪɪ.caŕ.7 vɪɪɪ·
borđ.7 ɪ.ſeruus.7 ɪ.moliñ.xx.ſol.Ṕtū.ɪɪ.caŕ.Silua
.xʟ.porc.Valet.vɪ.liƀ.Q̨do recep̄:xʟ.ſol.T.R.E:
vɪ.liƀ.Hoc ⵎ tenueŕ.ɪɪɪ.ſochi hões regis.E.7 uende
7 dare potueŕ.Hanc trā ht̄ eṕs ꝑ Excābio de Bledone.
ut hões ej dicunt.

In Hencuuic ten Turſtiñ de eṕo.ɪ.hiđ 7 dim.Tra.ē
ɪɪ.caŕ.In dñio eſt una.7 ɪɪɪ.uilti hñt.ɪ.caŕ.7 ɪ.borđ.
Val.xx.ſol.

210 b

In Sernebroc ten q̄dā Anglic Turgiſus de eṕo dim
hiđ.Tra.ē.ɪ.caŕ.7 ibi eſt.7 uñ uilts.Ṕtū.ɪ.caŕ.
Val.vɪ.ſol.Q̨do recep̄:ɪɪɪ.ſol.T.R.E:xv.ſol.Hanc
trā tenuit Aluuin hō Borret.7 potuit dare cui uoluit.
In eađ uilla teneN.vɪɪ.ſochi de eṕo.ɪɪɪ.hiđ.Tra.ɪɪɪ.
caŕ.7 ibi ſunt.Silua.xxɪɪɪɪ.porc.Val.xxɪɪɪɪ.ſol.
Q̨do recep̄:ſimit.T.R.E:ʟx.ſol.Idē ipſi tenueŕ.T.R.E.
hões Borred fueŕ.7 dare 7 uende ſine ej lictia potueŕ.
In ead ten Hunfrid de eṕo dim hiđ.Tra.ē.ɪ.caŕ.
7 ibi eſt.7 ɪɪ.borđ.Silua.xxx.porc.Val.vɪ.ſol.Q̨do
recep̄:x.ſol.T.R.E:xx.ſol.Hanc trā tenuit Aluric
hō Borred.7 potuit dare 7 uende cui uoluit.
In ead ten eṕs dim hiđ.Tra.ē.vɪ.boƀȝ.Ibi ſuN.ɪɪɪɪ.
borđ.Val.ɪɪɪ.ſol.7 tntđ q̄do recep̄.T.R.E:v.ſolid.
Hanc trā tenuit Borred teigñ regis.E.7 pot face qđ uol.
In Riſedene ten Aluuold de eṕo dim hiđ.Tra.vɪ.
boƀ.Ibi.ē dim caŕ.Ṕtū.vɪ.boū.Val.v.ſol.7 tntđ
q̄do recep̄.T.R.E:x.ſol.Hanc trā tenuit Aluric
hō Borred fuit.7 uende potuit cui uoluit.

11 M. In TURVEY the Bishop also holds 4 hides. Land for 6 ploughs.
In lordship 2 hides; 3 ploughs there.
 3 villagers have 3 ploughs; 8 smallholders and 1 slave.
 1 mill, 20s; meadow for 2 ploughs; woodland, 40 pigs.
Value £6; when acquired 40s; before 1066 £6.
 3 Freemen, King Edward's men, held this manor; they could
sell and grant. The Bishop has this land in exchange for
Bleadon, as his men state.

12 In HINWICK Thurstan holds 1½ hides from the Bishop.
Land for 2 ploughs. In lordship 1.
 3 villagers have 1 plough; 1 smallholder.
Value 20s.

13 In SHARNBROOK an Englishman, Thorgils, holds ½ hide from   210 b
the Bishop. Land for 1 plough; it is there.
 1 villager.
Meadow for 1 plough.
Value 6s; when acquired 3s; before 1066, 15s.
 Alwin, Burgred's man, held this land; he could grant to whom
he would.

14 In the same village 7 Freemen hold 3 hides from the Bishop.
Land for 3 ploughs; they are there.
 Woodland, 24 pigs.
Value 24s, when acquired the same; before 1066, 60s.
 The present holders held it before 1066; they were Burgred's
men; they could grant and sell without his permission.

15 In the same [village] Humphrey holds ½ hide from the Bishop.
Land for 1 plough; it is there.
 2 smallholders.
 Woodland, 30 pigs.
Value 6s; when acquired 10s; before 1066, 20s.
 Aelfric, Burgred's man, held this land; he could grant and sell
to whom he would.

16 In the same [village] the Bishop holds ½ hide. Land for 6 oxen.
 4 smallholders.
Value 3s; when acquired the same; before 1066, 5s.
 Burgred, a thane of King Edward's, held this land; he could
do what he would (with it).

17 In RUSHDEN Alfwold holds ½ hide from the Bishop.
Land for 6 oxen; ½ plough there.
 Meadow for 6 oxen.
Value 5s; as much when acquired; before 1066, 10s.
 Aelfric, Burgred's man, held this land; he could sell to
whom he would.

R TERRA EPI LINCOLIENS. *IN STODENE HVND.*

ᴿEMIGIVS eps ten in *DENE* . II . hid 7 dim uirg.

7 Godefrid de eo. Tra . ē . III . car 7 dim. In dnio fuÿ

II . car. 7 uilli hnt. I . car 7 dim. Ibi . VIII . bord. 7 II.

ſerui . ptū . I . car . Valet . XL . ſol . Qdo receþ.́ xxx . ſol.

7 tntđ . T.R.E . Hanc trā tenuit Godric teign . R.E.

7 qđ uoluit de tra ſua facere potuit.

In Eſtone ten Wills de caron dim hid 7 dim uirg de

epo. Tra . ē . I . car. 7 ibi eſt. 7 un bord 7 III . ſerui. ptū . I . car.

Silua . c . porc . Valet. xv . ſol. Qdo receþ.́ x . ſol. 7 tntđ

T.R.E. Hanc trā tenuit Aluuin̄ hō epi Lincolienſis.

7 q̃ uoluit de ea facere potuit. Soca tam̄ ſēp epi fuit.

In hac tra epifcopat reclamat Wills de caron . LX . acr

int planū 7 filuam fuþ Hugonē de Belcāp . unde

Radulf taillebofc defaifiuit patrē ejđ Willi . q̃ ipsā

trā tenebat. T.R.E. ut hōes de hund dñt.

In Rifelai ten Godefrid . I . hiđ de epo . Tra . ē . I . car.

7 ibi . ē . Ibi . I . uill. 7 I . bord . ptū dim car . Silua porc

xx . porc . Val 7 ualuit . x . ſol . T.R.E.́ xx . ſol . Hanc trā

tenuit Godric teign. R.E. 7 qđ uoluit facere potuit.

In dimiđ hund de Buchelai . Ernuin̄ þbr ten de epo

Remigio . I . hiđ 7 I . uirg in Bidehā. Tra . ē . I . car . 7 ibi ē.

Ibi . I . uills 7 I . mol redđ þ annū xxv . ſol. ptū . I . car.

Valet 7 ualuit . XL . ſol. Hanc trā tenuit Leuric hō

epi Lincolienſis . ſed ñ potuit dare nec uende fine licₜia ej.

In Hund de Bereforde ten Iuo tallebofc de epo dim

hiđ in ·Goldentone. Tra . ē dim car. 7 ibi eſt . cū . II . uillis.

ptū dim car . Valet 7 ualuit . v . ſol . Aluuin̄ tenuit

★

210 b

LAND OF THE BISHOP OF LINCOLN

In STODDEN Hundred

1   Bishop Remigius holds 2 hides and ½ virgate in DEAN and
Godfrey from him. Land for 3½ ploughs. In lordship 2 ploughs.
The villagers have 1½ ploughs.
    8 smallholders and 2 slaves.
    Meadow for 1 plough.
Value 40s; when acquired 30s; as much before 1066.
    Godric, a thane of King Edward's, held this land; he could
do what he would with his land.

2   In EASTON William of Cairon holds ½ hide and ½ virgate
from the Bishop. Land for 1 plough; it is there.
    1 smallholder and 3 slaves.
    Meadow for 1 plough; woodland, 100 pigs.
Value 15s; when acquired 10s; as much before 1066.
    Alwin Devil, the Bishop of Lincoln's man, held this land; he
could do what he would with it. However, the jurisdiction was
always the Bishop's.
    In this land of the Bishopric, William of Cairon claims 60 acres
of open land and woodland from Hugh of Beauchamp, of which
Ralph Tallboys dispossessed this William's father, who held the
land before 1066, as the men of the Hundred state.

3   In RISELY Godfrey holds 1 hide from the Bishop.
Land for 1 plough; it is there.
    1 villager and 1 smallholder.
    Meadow for ½ plough; woodland, 20 pigs.
The value is and was 10s; before 1066, 20s.
    Godric, a thane of King Edward's, held this land; he could
do what he would (with it).

In the Half-Hundred of BUCKLOW

4   Ernwin the priest holds 1 hide and 1 virgate in BIDDENHAM from
Bishop Remigius. Land for 1 plough; it is there.
    1 villager.
    1 mill which pays 25s a year; meadow for 1 plough.
The value was and is 40s.
    Leofric, the Bishop of Lincoln's man, held this land; he
could not grant or sell without his permission.

In the Hundred of BARFORD

5   Ivo Tallboys holds ½ hide from the Bishop in GOLDINGTON.
Land for ½ plough; it is there, with
    2 villagers.
    Meadow for ½ plough.
The value is and was 6s.

hō epī Lincol.7 potuit inde facé qđ uoluit.

In hunđ de Bichelefuuorde Wiłłs de caron teñ de epó.R

in Tamifeforde.1.hiđ.7 1.uirg 7 111.part uni uirg.Tra.ē

11.caŕ.7 ibi.ē un uiłłs.P̃tū.1.caŕ.7 11.molini de xl.foł.

7 cxx.Anguiłł.Vał.lx.foł.Q̃do recep̃:́xl.foł.T.R.E:́c.foł.

Aluuin tenui:.hō regis fuit.7 qđ uoluit de ea facé potuit.

210 c

In HVNĐ de Cliftone.Wiłłs de caron de epó.R.111.

hiđ 7 dim uirg in Cliftone.Tra.ē.11.caŕ.Ibi.ē una

caŕ.7 alia poteft fieri.Ibi.111.uiłłi.7 11.ferui.p̃tū

11.caŕ.Vał.xx.foł.7 tntđ qđo recep̃:́T.R.E.1111.liƀ.

Hanc trā tenuit Aĺuuin hō.R.E.7 potuit dare q̃ uoł.

In Chichefane teñ ifđē Wiłłs de eođ epó dim hiđ.

Tra.ē dim caŕ.Vał 7 ualuit.x11.den.T.R.E:́11.foł.

Aluuin tenuit.7 cui uoluit dare potuit.

Eccła de Bedeford cū adjacentiƀꝫ fibi ualet.c.foł.

Æccła de Leftone uał.1111.liƀ.Has teñ Remigi eps.

.V. TERRA EP̃I DVNELMSIS. *BICHELESWADE HVNĐ.*

EPS DVNELMENSIS.teñ de rege in Melehou

1111.hiđ 7 dim.Tra.ē.1111.caŕ.In dñio.111.hiđ

7 dim.7 ibi.ē.1.caŕ.7 alia pot fieri.Viłłi hñt.11.

caŕ.Ibi.1111.uiłłi.7 un feru.Vał.xl.foł.7 tntđ

qđo recep̃.T.R.E:́lx.foł.Hanc trā dedit rex Edw

æcclæ S crvcis de Walthā.ut hōēs de hunđ teftant.

In Hunđ de Cliftone.teñ ifđ eps.v111.hiđ in Alricefei.

7 11.part.1.uirg.Tra.ē v111.caŕ.In dñio.̇funt|111.caŕ.

7 v111.uiłłi hñt.1111.caŕ.7 v.pot fieri.Ibi.v.borđ.

7 11.ferui.7 11.molini.xxv1.foliđ.7 v111.den.p̃tū.111.caŕ.

Valet 7 ualuit.v11.liƀ.T.R.E:́v111.liƀ.Hoc M̃ tenueŕ

canonici S crucis de Wathā in elemofina.T.R.E.

Alwin Sack, the Bishop of Lincoln's man, held it;
he could do what he would with it.

In the Hundred of BIGGLESWADE

6 William of Cairon holds 1 hide and 1 virgate and 3 parts of 1
virgate in TEMPSFORD from Bishop Remigius.
Land for 2 ploughs.
1 villager.
Meadow for 1 plough; 2 mills at 40s and 120 eels.
Value 60s; when acquired 40s; before 1066, 100s.
Alwin Devil held it; he was the King's man; he could do
what he would with it.

In the Hundred of CLIFTON   210 c

7 William of Cairon holds 3 hides and ½ virgate in CLIFTON from Bishop
Remigius. Land for 2 ploughs; 1 plough there; another possible.
3 villagers and 2 slaves.
Meadow for 2 ploughs.
Value 20s; as much when acquired; before 1066 £4.
Alwin Devil, King Edward's man, held this land;
he could grant where he would.

8 In CHICKSANDS William also holds ½ hide from the Bishop.
Land for ½ plough.
The value is and was 12d; before 1066, 2s.
Alwin Devil held it; he could grant to whom he would.

9 Bedford church, with what is attached to it, value 100s.
Leighton (Buzzard) church, value £4; Bishop Remigius holds them.

5 LAND OF THE BISHOP OF DURHAM

BIGGLESWADE Hundred

1 In MILLOW the Bishop of Durham holds 4½ hides from the King.
Land for 4 ploughs. In lordship 3½ hides; 1 plough there;
another possible. The villagers have 2 ploughs.
4 villagers and 1 slave.
Value 40s; as much when acquired; before 1066, 60s.
King Edward gave this land to the Church of Holy
Cross of Waltham, as the men of the Hundred testify.

In the Hundred of CLIFTON

2 The Bishop also holds 8 hides and 2 parts of 1 virgate in ARLESEY.
Land for 8 ploughs. In lordship 3 ploughs.
8 villagers have 4 ploughs; a fifth possible. 5 smallholders; 2 slaves.
2 mills, 26s 8d; meadow for 3 ploughs.
The value was and is £7; before 1066 £8.
Before 1066 the Canons of Holy Cross of Waltham held this
manor in alms.

Abbas Balduin̉ S̃ Edmvndi h̄t in Bidenhā dim̉
hiđ.7 Ordui đe Bedeford ten̉ fub eo.Tra.ē dim̉ car̄.
7 ibi.ē.7 ii.ferui.p̃tū.dimiđ car̄.Val 7 ualuit.vi.fol.
Hanc tr̄a tenuit Vlmar p̃br regis.E.potuit dare
cui uoluit.fed Ordui cū ēet p̃pofit̉ burgi ei abftulit.
p̃ q̉đā forisfaċtura.7 m̄ dicit fe tenere de abb̄e S̃ Edm̄.
fed hōēs de hund̄ dn̄t q̄ā injufte eā occupauit.

In Hund̉ de Bichelefuuade.ten̉ ifđ abb̄ S̃ Edmundi
Chenemondewiche..p̃.iii.hiđ 7 iii.uirg̉ fe defđ.
Tr̄a.ē.iiii.car̄.In dn̄io.i.hiđ 7 iii.uirg̉.7 ibi funt
ii.car̄.7 vi.uiłłi hn̄t.ii.car̄.7 i.molin̄ de.xiii.fol.
7 iiii.den.p̃tū.i.car̄.Val.lx.fol.Q̉do recep̉.́xxx.
fol.T.R.Ẹ́iiii.lib.Hanc tr̄a tenuer̉.ii.foc̉hi.7 cui
uoluer̉ dare potuer̉.Hanc deđ S̃ Edmundo Wallef
7 uxor ej̉ in elemofina.T.R.Wiłłi.

In Hund̉ de Wich eftaneftou.ten̉ ifđ abb̄.iiii.hiđ
7 i.uirg̉ in Blunhā de rege.Tra.ē.iiii.car̄.In dn̄io
ii.hiđ 7 iii.uirg̉.7 ibi funt.ii.car̄.Ibi.viii.uiłłi
hn̄t.ii.car̄.7 v.borđ.7 i.feruus.7 i.molin̄.xx.fol.
p̃tū.iiii.car̄.Valet.iiii.lib.Q̉do recep̉.lxx.fol.
T.R.Ẹ́vi.lib.Hanc tr̄a tenuer̉.iiii.foc̉hi.7 cui
uoluer̉ dare ł uendere potuer̉. *IN STODENE HVND̄.*

Abb̄ de Bvrg ten̉ *STANEWIGA*..p̃ ii.hiđ 7 dim̉ fe
defđ.Tr̄a.ē.ii.car̄.7 dim̉.Ibi.ē.i.car̄.Alia.7 dim̉ pot
fieri.Ibi fuꝗ̃.ii.uiłłi 7 ii.borđ.P̃tū.ii.car̄.Val xxx.fol.
Q̉do recep̉.́l.fol.T.R.Ẹ́xl.fol.Hoc m̃ tenuit S̃ petr̉
Ꝼ de burg.T.R.E.

6   LAND OF ST. EDMUND'S

In the Half-Hundred of BUCKLOW

1   Abbot Baldwin of St Edmund's has ½ hide in BIDDENHAM. Ordwy
of Bedford holds it under him. Land for ½ plough; it is there.
2 slaves.
Meadow for ½ plough.
The value is and was 6s.
Wulfmer, a priest of King Edward's, held this land; he could
grant to whom he would. But Ordwy took it from him when he
was reeve of the borough, for a forfeiture; he now says that he
holds it from the Abbot of St Edmund's, but the men of the
Hundred state that he has appropriated it wrongfully.

In the Hundred of BIGGLESWADE

2   The Abbot of St Edmund's also holds 'KINWICK'.
It answers for 3 hides and 3 virgates. Land for 4 ploughs.
In lordship 1 hide and 3 virgates; 2 ploughs there.
6 villagers have 2 ploughs.
1 mill at 13s 4d; meadow for 1 plough.
Value 60s; when acquired 30s; before 1066 £4.
2 Freemen held this land; they could grant to whom they
would. After 1066 Earl Waltheof and his wife gave it to
St Edmund's in alms.

In the Hundred of WIXAMTREE

3   The Abbot also holds 4 hides and 1 virgate in BLUNHAM from
the King. Land for 4 ploughs. In lordship 2 hides and 3
virgates; 2 ploughs there.
8 villagers have 2 ploughs. 5 smallholders and 1 slave.
1 mill, 20s; meadow for 4 ploughs.
Value £4; when acquired 70s; before 1066 £6.
4 Freemen held this land; they could grant or sell to
whom they would.

7   LAND OF ST. PETER'S OF PETERBOROUGH

In STODDEN Hundred

1   The Abbot of Peterborough holds STANWICK. It answers for 2½
hides. Land for 2½ ploughs; 1 plough there; another 1½ possible.
2 villagers and 2 smallholders.
Meadow for 2 ploughs.
Value 30s; when acquired 50s; before 1066, 40s.
St Peter's of Peterborough held this manor before 1066.

.VIII. Terra ꝭ Beneꝺ De Ramesẏ. *In Radebvrnesoca* ᵀᴴᵛ́ᴺᴰ

Ⓜ Abbas Sͨı Benedicti de Ramesẏ ten̄ *Cran*
felle . ꝓ x . hiꝺ ſe defꝺ . Tra . ē . xıı . car . In dn̄io . ıı .
hidæ . 7 ıı . car ſunt ibi . Ibi xvııı . uitti hn̄t . x . car .
Ibi . ıı . borꝺ 7 v . ſerui . p̄tū . ıı . car . Silua mille porc̄ .
7 ferrū car . In̄t totū uat . ıx . liꝑ . Q̄do recep̄ . ſimilit .
T.R.E. xıı . liꝑ . Hoc Ⓜ iacuit 7 iacet in æccta ꝭ Beneꝺ .

Ⓜ Iſdē abꝑ ten̄ *Bertone* .   *In Flictha̅ Hvnd* .

ꝓ xı . hiꝺ ſe defꝺ . Tra . ē . xıı . car . In dn̄io . ııı . hidæ .
7 ibi ſunt . ıı . car . 7 tcia pot fieri . 7 xx . uitti hn̄t . ıx . car .
Ibi . vıı . borꝺ . 7 vı . ſerui . 7 ı . molin̄ . ıı . ſot . p̄tū . vı . car .
Silua . cc . porc . In̄t totū uat . x . liꝑ . 7 tn̄tꝺ qdo
recep̄ . T.R.E. xıı . liꝑ . Hoc Ⓜ iacuit ſēp in eccta Sͨı
Benedicti . Cū iſto Ⓜ reclam abꝑ . xıı . ac p̄ti . ſuꝑ
Nigellū albin 7 Walter̄ flāmen̄ . quæ ibi iacuer̄ . T.R.E .
ſed Joħs de roches eū iniuſte deſaiſiuit . 7 ħ hund teſtat .

Ⓜ Ipſe abꝑ ten̄ *Pechesdone* . ꝓ x . hiꝺ ſe defꝺ . Tra
ē . xıııı . car . In dn̄io . ıı . hidæ . 7 ibi ſuɴ̄ . ıı . car . 7 tcia
poteſt . ee . 7 xxxvıı . uitti hn̄t . xı . car . Ibi . vıı . borꝺ .
7 v . ſerui . 7 ıı . molini de xxvıı . ſot 7 vııı . den̄ . P̊tum
ııı . car . Silua . lx . porc . Valet x . liꝑ . 7 tn̄tꝺ qdo
recep̄ . T.R.E. xıı . liꝑ . Hoc Ⓜ iacuit 7 iacet in dn̄io æcctæ
ꝭ Benedicti .   *In Bereford Hvnd* .

In Wiboldeſtone ten̄ Eudo dapifer . ı . uirg 7 dim
ſub abꝑe de Ramesẏ . Vaſtata . ē . tam̄ . xvı . den uat .
Ħ terra fuit in æccta ꝭ Benedicti . T.R.E.

Ⓜ In Bereforde ten̄ Eudo dapif̄ *In Bicheleswade Hꝺ*
v . hiꝺ de feudo abꝑis . 7 Osꝑn de eo . Tra . ē . v . car . In
dn̄io . ı . car . 7 ıx . uitti hn̄t . ıııı . car . Ibi . ıııı . borꝺ .
7 ııı . ſerui . 7 ı . molin̄ . xıı . ſot . 7 cxxv . anguitt . p̄tū .

In REDBORNSTOKE Hundred

1 M. The Abbot of St Benedict's of Ramsey holds CRANFIELD. It
answers for 10 hides. Land for 12 ploughs. In lordship 2 hides;
2 ploughs there.
　　18 villagers have 10 ploughs. 2 smallholders and 5 slaves.
　　Meadow for 2 ploughs; woodland, 1000 pigs and plough iron.
In total, value £9; when acquired the same; before 1066 £12.
　　This manor lay and lies in (the lands of) St Benedict's church.

In FLITT Hundred

2 M. The Abbot also holds BARTON(-in-the-Clay). It answers for 11
hides. Land for 12 ploughs. In lordship 3 hides; 2 ploughs there;
a third possible.
　　20 villagers have 9 ploughs. 7 smallholders and 6 slaves.
　　1 mill, 2s; meadow for 6 ploughs; woodland, 200 pigs.
In total, value £10; the same when acquired; before 1066 £12.
　　This manor always lay in (the lands of) St Benedict's Church.
With this manor the Abbot claims against Nigel of Aubigny and
Walter the Fleming 12 acres of meadow which lay there before
1066, but John of Les Roches dispossessed him wrongfully, and
this the Hundred testifies.

3 M. The Abbot also holds PEGSDON. It answers for 10 hides. Land for 14
ploughs. In lordship 2 hides; 2 ploughs there; a third possible.
　　37 villagers have 11 ploughs. 7 smallholders and 5 slaves.
　　2 mills at 27s 8d; meadow for 3 ploughs; woodland, 60 pigs.
Value £10; as much when acquired; before 1066 £12.
　　This manor lay and lies in the lordship of St Benedict's Church.

In BARFORD Hundred

4 In WYBOSTON Eudo the Steward holds 1½ virgates under the
Abbot of Ramsey. It has been laid waste; value however 16d.
This land was in (the lands of) St. Benedict's Church before 1066.

In BIGGLESWADE Hundred

5 M. In (Little) BARFORD Eudo the Steward holds 5 hides from the
Abbot's Holding and Osbern from him. Land for 5 ploughs.
In lordship 1 plough.
　　9 villagers have 4 ploughs. 4 smallholders and 3 slaves.
　　1 mill, 12s and 125 eels; meadow for 2 ploughs.

ii.car̅.Val.iiii.lib.Qdo recep̅.iii.lib.T.R.E.iiii.lib.

Hoc M̅ ten̅ abb̅ S Benedicti.7 ibi in elemosina fuit.T.R.E.

In Cliftone ten̅ Leuuin̅.i.hid̅   IN CLISTONE HVND.

fub abb̅e.Tra.e̅ dim car̅.7 ibi.e̅.P̊tu̅ dim car̅.Val

7 ualuit.x.fol.T.R.E.xx.fol.Iftemet t̅c tenuit.fed

ab æccła feparare n̅ potuit.

M̅ Ipfe ide̅ abb̅ ten̅ *SETHLINDONE*.p x.hid̅ fe defd̅.

Tra.e̅.xiiii.car̅.In dn̅io.ii.hidæ.7 ibi funt.ii.car̅.

7 xxvii.uiłłi hn̅t.xii.car̅.Ibi.v.bord̅.7 iiii.ferui.

7 fract̅ molin̅ q̅ nichil redd̅.p̊tu̅.vi.car̅.Silua.c.

porc̅.Val.xii.lib̅.7 tntd̅ fe̅p ualuit.Hoc M̅ iacuit

in dn̅io æcclæ S Benedicti.T.R.E.

M̅ Ipfe abb̅ ten̅ *HOLEWELLE*.p.iii.hid̅ 7 dim.Tra.e̅.iiii.car̅.

In dn̅io.i.hid̅.7 ibi.e̅.i.car̅.7 viii.uiłłi hn̅t.iii.car̅.

7 i.bord̅.7 ii.ferui.P̊tu̅.i.car̅.Val.iiii.lib̅.7 tntd̅ fe̅p

ualuit.Hoc M̅ iacuit 7 iacet in dn̅io æcclæ S Benedicti.

In Standone ten̅ ifde̅ abb̅ dim hid̅.Tra.e̅ dim car̅.

7 ibi.e̅.H̅ tra iacet 7 iacuit in dn̅io æcclæ S Benedicti.

Val.xv.fol.

211 a

.IX. TERRA S PETRI WESTMON̅. *IN CLISTONE HVND.*

M̅ ABBAS de WESTmonaft.ten̅ vi.hid̅ 7 dim in *HO*

LEWELLA.Tra.e̅.vi.car̅.In dn̅io.iii.hidæ 7 dim uirg̅.

7 ibi funt.ii.car̅.7 xi.uiłłi hn̅t.iiii.car̅.Ibi.iiii.

bord̅.7 iii.ferui.7 ii.molini.xx.fol.P̊tu̅.i.car̅.

Valet 7 ualuit.c.fol.Hoc M̅ iacuit 7 iacet in dn̅io æcclæ

.X. TERRA SC̅Æ MARIÆ DE TORNYG.S pek̅i.

M̅ ABBAS de Torny ten̅.ii.hid̅ 7 i.uirg̅ træ in Boleheftre.

Tra.e̅.v.car̅.In dn̅io.e̅.i.carucata træ.7 ibi.e̅.i.car̅.
extra.ii.hidas.7 uirg.

Value £4; when acquired £3; before 1066, £4.
The Abbot of St. Benedict's holds this manor.
It was there, in alms, before 1066.

In CLIFTON Hundred

6   In CLIFTON Leofwin holds 1 hide under the Abbot. Land for ½
plough; it is there.
Meadow for ½ plough.
The value is and was 10s; before 1066, 20s.
He held it himself then, but could not separate it from the Church.

7   M. The Abbot also holds SHILLINGTON. It answers for 10 hides.
Land for 14 ploughs. In lordship 2 hides; 2 ploughs there.
27 villagers have 12 ploughs. 5 smallholders and 4 slaves.
1 broken mill which pays nothing; meadow for 6 ploughs;
woodland, 100 pigs.
The value is £12 and always was as much.
This manor lay in the lordship of St. Benedict's Church
before 1066.

8   M. The Abbot also holds HOLWELL, for 3½ hides.
Land for 4 ploughs. In lordship 1 hide; 1 plough there.
8 villagers have 3 ploughs. 1 smallholder and 2 slaves.
Meadow for 1 plough.
The value is £4 and always was as much.
This manor lay and lies in the lordship of St. Benedict's Church.

9   In STONDON the Abbot also holds ½ hide. Land for ½ plough;
it is there. This land lies and lay in the lordship of St Benedict's
Church.
Value 15s.

9   **LAND OF ST. PETER'S OF WESTMINSTER**   211 a

In CLIFTON Hundred

1   M. The Abbot of Westminster holds 6½ hides in HOLWELL.
Land for 6 ploughs. In lordship 3 hides and ½ virgate; 2
ploughs there.
11 villagers have 4 ploughs. 4 smallholders and 3 slaves.
2 mills, 20s; meadow for 1 plough.
The value is and was 100s.
This manor lay and lies in the lordship of St. Peter's Church.

10   **LAND OF ST. MARY'S OF THORNEY**

[In STODDEN Hundred]

1   M. The Abbot of Thorney holds 2 hides and 1 virgate of land in
BOLNHURST. Land for 5 ploughs. In lordship 1 carucate
of land, as well as the 2 hides and the virgate; 1 plough there.

7 ix.uilli hn̄t.v.car̄.Ibi.v.bord.p̄tū.ɪ.car̄.Silua

c 7 vɪ.porc.Val.ʟx.ſol.Q̇do recep̄:ˣxʟ.ſol.T.R.E:

.vɪ.liƀ.Hoc m̄ tenuit Ælfleda de rege.E.potuit dare

cui uoluit.In monaſterio de Torni iacuit.die quo rex

Edw uiuus 7 mortuus fuit.Hoc hōes de hund teſtan̄t.

.XI. TERRA ÆCCLÆ BERCHINGES. *IN RADBERNESTOCH HD*

Abbatissa de Berchinges ten̄ *LITINCLETONE*.

ꝑ x.hid ſe defd.Tra.ē.xɪ.car̄.In dn̄io.ɪɪ.hidæ.

7 ibi ſunt.ɪɪ.car̄.tcia pot fieri.7 xxɪɪɪ.uilli hn̄t

vɪɪɪ.car̄.Ibi.xvɪ.bord.7 vɪɪ.ſerui.p̄tū.vɪɪɪ.car̄.

Silua.cccc.porc.Val.vɪɪɪ.liƀ.7 tntd q̇do recep̄.

T.R.E:ˣxɪɪ.liƀ.Hoc m̄ iacuit 7 iacet in dn̄io æcclæ

S Marie de Berchinges.

.XII. TERRA SC̄I PAVLI LVNDON. *IN FLICTHÃ HVND.*

m̄ Canonici S pavli Lundon̄ ten̄ *CADENDONE*.

ꝑ v.hid ſe defd.Tra.ē.vɪ.car̄.In dn̄io.ɪɪ.hidæ.

7 ibi ſunt.ɪɪ.car̄.7 adhuc.ɪɪɪɪ.poſſ.ēē.Ibi.ɪ.uilli

7 ɪɪɪɪ.bord.7 ɪɪ.ſerui.Silua.cc.porc.Val.xʟ.ſol.

Q̇do recep̄:ˣx.ſol.T.R.E:ˣc.ſol.Hoc m̄ tenuit

Leuuin.T.R.E.Canonici hn̄t breuē regis.in quo

habet qd ipſe hoc m̄ dedit æcclæ S Pauli.

.XIII SC̄I PAVLI de BEDEFORD *IN DIMIDIO HVND*
DE BVCHELAI.

Canonicus oſmund S Pauli de Bedeford ten̄ in Bidehã

de rege.ɪɪɪ.uirg.Tra.ē.ɪ.car̄.7 ibi.ē.7 ɪ.uilli

7 ɪ.bord.P̄tū.ɪ.car̄.Val 7 ualuit.x.ſol.Hanc

trā tenuit Leuiet pƀr in elemoſina de rege.E.

7 poſtea de rege.W.Qui pƀr morieꝗ̄ c̄ceſſit æcclæ

S Pauli.ɪ.uirg de hac tra.Radulf ū tallgeboſc

alias duas uirg addidit eid æcclæ in elemoſina.

211 a

9 villagers have 5 ploughs. 5 smallholders.
Meadow for 1 plough; woodland, 106 pigs.
Value 60s; when acquired 40s; before 1066 £6.
 Aelfled held this manor from King Edward; she could grant to whom she would. It lay in (the lands of) the monastery of Thorney in 1066. This the men of the Hundred testify.

11   LAND OF BARKING CHURCH

In REDBORNSTOKE Hundred

1   The Abbess of Barking holds LIDLINGTON. It answers for 10 hides. Land for 11 ploughs. In lordship 2 hides; 2 ploughs there; a third possible.
 23 villagers have 8 ploughs. 16 smallholders and 7 slaves.
Meadow for 8 ploughs; woodland, 400 pigs.
Value £8; as much when acquired; before 1066 £12.
 This manor lay and lies in the lordship of St. Mary's Church of Barking.

12   LAND OF ST. PAUL'S OF LONDON

In FLITT Hundred

1 M. The Canons of St. Paul's of London hold CADDINGTON. It answers for 5 hides. Land for 6 ploughs. In lordship 2 hides; 2 ploughs there; a further 4 possible.
 1 villager, 4 smallholders and 2 slaves.
Woodland, 200 pigs.
Value 40s, when acquired 10s; before 1066, 100s.
 Young Leofwin held this manor before 1066. The Canons have the King's writ in which is recorded that he gave this manor himself to St. Paul's Church.

13   [LAND] OF ST PAUL'S OF BEDFORD

In the Half-Hundred of BUCKLOW

1   Canon Osmund of St. Paul's of Bedford holds 3 virgates from the King in BIDDENHAM. Land for 1 plough; it is there.
 1 villager and 1 smallholder.
Meadow for 1 plough.
The value is and was 10s.
 Leofgeat the priest held this land in alms from King Edward and later from King William. When he was dying this priest assigned 1 virgate of this land to St. Paul's Church, but Ralph Tallboys added the other 2 virgates to this Church, in alms.

In ead̄ ten̄ Ansfrid canonic̄.ı.uirḡ.T̄ra.ē.ıı.bob.

7 ibi ſunt.P̃tū.ıı.bob.Val̄ 7 ualuit.ııı.ſot.Hanc

trā tenuit Maruuen.cui uoluit uend̄e potuit.

Hanc appoſuit Rad̄ talleboſc in elem̄ æcclæ S̄ Pauli.

ERNVI PR̄BI TERRA IN WICHESTANESTOV HD̄.

RNVIN̄ pb̄r ten̄.ı.hid̄ in HERGHETONE.T̄ra.ē.ı.car̄.

7 ibi.ē dim̄ car̄.p̃tū dim̄ car̄.Silua.ıııı.porc̄.

Valet.x.ſot.Q̃do recep̄.v.ſot.T.R.E.x.ſot.

Hanc trā tenuit pat̄ huj p̄dicti hōis.hō regis.E.

fuit.De hac trā non h̄t iſte liberatorē.nec breuē.

ſed occupauit ſup̄ regē.ut hund̄ teſtatur.

XV. TERRA COMIT̄ EVSTACH̃ IN DIM̃ HD̄ DE BOCHELAI.

VSTACHIVS comes ten̄ in Brunehā.ı.hid̄ 7 dim̄.

Ernulf̄ de Arde ten̄ de eo.T̄ra.ē.ı.car̄ 7 dim̄.

Ibi.ē dimid̄ car̄.7 ı.car̄ poteſt fieri.P̃tū.ı.car̄.7 dim̄.

Val̄.x.ſot.Q̃do recep̄.xx.ſot.7 tntd̄.T.R.E.Hanc

trā tenuit Aluuold̄ 7 Leuric̄ hōes regis.E.7 cui uoluer̄

dare potuer̄.7 uendere.

M̃ In Stiuentone ten̄ iſdē Ernulf̄ de ipſo comite

ııı.hid̄.T̄ra.ē xxıııı.car̄.In dn̄io.ē.ı.car̄.7 ııı.car̄

poſſunt fieri.7 x.uiłłi hn̄t.v.car̄.7 adhuc xv.poſſ.ēe.

Ibi.xı.bord̄.7 ıı.ſerui.P̃tū.ıııı.car̄.Silua.xx.porc̄.

In totis ualent.ual̄ xıııı.lib̄.Q̃do recep̄.xx.lib̄.T.R.E.

xxx.lib̄.Hoc M̃ tenuit Adelold̄ teign̄.R.E.7 cui uoluit

uend̄e potuit.

In Stachedene ten̄ un̄ Anglic̄ Goduui.ı.uirḡ de comite

Euſt.T̄ra.ē dim̄ car̄.7 un̄ bos ibi arat.H̄ tra ual̄.ıı.ſot.

Q̃do recep̄.v.ſot.T.R.E.x.ſot.

2   In the same (village) Canon Ansfrid holds 1 virgate.
Land for 2 oxen; they are there.
    Meadow for 2 oxen.
The value is and was 3s.
    Merwen held this land; she could sell to whom she would.
Ralph Tallboys placed it in the alms (lands) of St. Paul's Church.

14]   ERNWIN THE PRIEST'S LAND

In WIXHAMTREE Hundred

1   Ernwin the priest holds 1 hide in HARROWDEN.
Land for 1 plough; ½ plough there.
    Meadow for ½ plough; woodland, 4 pigs.
Value 10s; when acquired 5s; before 1066, 10s.
    The said man's father held this land; he was King Edward's man.
He does not have a deliverer or a writ for this land, but has
appropriated it in the King's despite, as the Hundred testifies.

15   LAND OF COUNT EUSTACE   211 b

In the Half-Hundred of BUCKLOW

1   Count Eustace holds 1½ hides in BROMHAM. Arnulf of Ardres
holds from him. Land for 1½ ploughs; ½ plough there; 1
plough possible.
    Meadow for 1½ ploughs.
Value 10s; when acquired 20s; as much before 1066.
    Alfwold and Leofric, King Edward's men, held this land; they
could grant or sell to whom they would.

2 M. In STEVINGTON Arnulf holds 3 hides from the Count. Land
for 24 ploughs. In lordship 1 plough; 3 possible.
    10 villagers have 5 ploughs; a further 15 possible.
      11 smallholders and 2 slaves.
    Meadow for 4 ploughs; woodland, 20 pigs.
Total value £14; when acquired £20;
before 1066 £30.
    Alfwold, a thane of King Edward's, held this manor;
he could sell to whom he would.

3   In STAGSDEN an Englishman, Godwy, holds 1 virgate from
Count Eustace. Land for ½ plough; 1 ox ploughs there.
Value of this land 2s; when acquired 5s; before 1066, 10s.

Ꝏ In *PABENEHA* ten Ernulf⁹ de Arde. ıı. hid 7 dim.

Tra. ē. ııı. car. ſed n̄ ſunt ibi. jbi. ı. moliñ. xx. ſol. 7 ıı.
bord. p̄tū. ııı. car. Val. xxv. ſol. Q̇do recep̄. xl. ſol.
T.R.E. ıııı. lib. Hoc Ꝏ tenuit Aluuold teign regis. E.

In Wilge hund ten Ernulf⁹ de arde in Torueie
ıı. hid. de comite Euſtachio. Tra. ē. ıı. car. In dñio eſt
una car. 7 alia poteſt fieri. Ibi. ı. uilłs 7 ı. bord. p̄tū
. ı. car. Val. x. ſol. Q̇do recep̄. xx. ſol. 7 tntd T.R.E.
Hanc trā tenuit Aluuold teign. R.E. cui uoluit dare potuit.

In *WADELLE* ten Ernulf⁹ de Arde. ıııı. hid 7 dim.
7 tciā parte. ı. uirg ꝓ uno. Ꝏ. de comite euſtachio.
Ibi. ı. car in dñio. 7 altera pot fieri. 7 ııı. uiłłi hn̄t
ıı. car. 7 tcia pote fieri. Ibi. vıı. bord. 7 ıı. ſerui. p̄tū
. ııı. car. Silua. l. porc. Val. lx. ſol. Q̇do recep̄. c. ſol.
T.R.E. vııı. lib. Hanc trā tenuit Aluuold teign. R.E.
7 cui uoluit uende potuit.

In Serneburg ten Robt⁹ fili⁹ Rozelini de Euſt com
ıı. hid. Tra. ē. ıııı. car. In dñio. ıı. car. 7 ıııı. uiłłi
hn̄t. ıı. car. Ibi. ııı. bord. 7 ıııı. ſerui. P̄tū. ıı. car.
Silua. lx. porc. Val xl. ſol. 7 tntd qdo recep̄. T.R.E.
ıııı. lib. Hanc trā tenuit Aluuold hō. R.E. 7 uende pot.

.XVI. **TERRA WALTERII GIFARD** *IN MANESHEVE HVND.*
Ꝏ Walterivs Gifard ten *WOBVRNE*. ꝓ x. hid
ſe defd. Tra. ē. xxıııı. car. Hugo de Bolebec
ten de eo. Ibi in dñio. ıı. car. 7 aliæ duæ poſſunt. ee.
Ibi. vııı. uiłłi hn̄t. vı. car. 7 adhuc. xıııı. poſs fieri.
Ibi. vıı. bord 7 ıııı. ſerui. p̄tū. vı. car. Silua. c. porc.
Val. c. ſol. Q̇do recep̄. xıı. lib. T.R.E. xv. lib.
Hoc Ꝏ tenuit Alric teign. R.E. 7 in hoc Ꝏ fuer vı.
ſochi. ıı. hid de hac trā tenuer. 7 qd uoluer facere potuer.

4   M.   In PAVENHAM Arnulf of Ardres holds 2½ hides.
Land for 3 ploughs, but they are not there.
    1 mill, 20s; 2 smallholders; meadow for 3 ploughs.
Value 25s; when acquired 40s; before 1066 £4.
    Alfwold, a thane of King Edward's, held this manor.

In WILLEY Hundred

5   Arnulf of Ardres holds 1 hide in TURVEY from Count Eustace.
Land for 2 ploughs. In lordship 1 plough; another possible.
    1 villager and 1 smallholder.
    Meadow for 1 plough.
Value 10s; when acquired 20s; as much before 1066.
    Alfwold, a thane of King Edward's, held this land; he could
grant to whom he would.

6   In ODELL Arnulf of Ardres holds 4½ hides and the third part of 1
virgate as one manor from Count Eustace. 1 plough in lordship;
a second possible.
    3 villagers have 2 ploughs; a third possible. 7 smallholders
      and 2 slaves.
    Meadow for 3 ploughs; woodland, 50 pigs.
Value 60s; when acquired 100s; before 1066 £8.
    Alfwold, a thane of King Edward's, held this land;
he could sell to whom he would.

7   In SHARNBROOK Robert son of Rozelin holds 2 hides from
Count Eustace. Land for 4 ploughs. In lordship 2 ploughs.
    4 villagers have 2 ploughs. 3 smallholders and 4 slaves.
    Meadow for 2 ploughs; woodland, 60 pigs.
Value 40s; as much when acquired; before 1066 £4.
    Alfwold, King Edward's man, held this land; he could sell.

16   LAND OF WALTER GIFFARD

In MANSHEAD Hundred

1   M. Walter Giffard holds WOBURN. It answers for 10 hides.
Land for 24 ploughs. Hugh of Bolbec holds from him.
In lordship 2 ploughs; another 2 possible.
    8 villagers have 6 ploughs; a further 14 possible.
      7 smallholders and 4 slaves.
    Meadow for 6 ploughs; woodland, 100 pigs.
Value 100s; when acquired £12; before 1066 £15.
    Alric, a thane of King Edward's, held this manor. In this
manor were 6 Freemen; they held 2 hides of the land; they
could do what they would (with them).

Ⓜ In *BADELESDONE* .ten Ricard talebot . viiii . hid
de Walt Gifard . Tra . e̅ . viii . car . In d̅n̅io | sunt ii . carucæ.

7 tcia poteſt . e̅e̅ . Ibi . vii . uilli h̅n̅t . v . car . Ibi . x . bord
7 p̅t̅u̅ . viii . car . Val . c . ſol . 7 tntd̅ qd̅o recep̅ . T.R.E.
viii . lib̅ . Hoc Ⓜ tenuer̅ . vii . ſochi . T.R.E. 7 qd̅ uoluer̅
de tra ſua facere potuer̅ . *IN RADBORGESTOC HVND.*

In Mereſtone . ten Hugo de Bolebec de Walterio Gifard
ii . hid dim uirg min . Tra . e̅ . iii . car . In d̅n̅io . i . car .
7 vi . uilli h̅n̅t . ii . car . Ibi . v . bord . 7 p̅t̅u̅ . iii . car . Silua
ccc . porc . Val . l . ſol . Qdo recep̅ . xx . ſol . T.R.E. iiii . lib̅ .
Hanc tra̅ tenuer̅ . ii . taigni . T.R.E. 7 cui uoluer̅ dare potuer̅ .
Sup hanc tra̅ reclamat Erfaſt h̅o̅ Nigelli Albinienſis .
dimid̅ ſepe̅ . quæ jacebat ad Ⓜ Anteceſſoris Erfaſti . ut
h̅o̅e̅s de Hund teſtantur .

Ⓜ In Meldone ten Hugo de eod̅ Walterio . iii . hid . Tra
e̅ . iiii . car . In d̅n̅io ſunt . ii . car . 7 v . uilli h̅n̅t . ii . car .
P̅t̅u̅ . iiii . car . Silua . l . porc . Valet l . ſol . 7 tntd̅
qd̅o recep̅ . T.R.E. iiii . lib̅ . Hoc Ⓜ tenuit Aluuin fr
Wlui ep̅i . 7 cui uoluit dare potuit . *IN BICHELESWADE*
In Domtone ten Radulf de Langetot   *F HVND.*
i . hid 7 iii . uirg de Walterio Gifard . Tra . e̅ . ii . car .
7 ibi ſunt . 7 iiii . uilli 7 . ii . bord . Valet xxxiii . ſol .
7 iiii . den . 7 ſe̅p tntd̅ ualuit . Hanc tra̅ . iiii . ſochi te
nuer̅ . 7 tra̅ ſua̅ uende potuer̅ . H̅o̅e̅s Stigandi archiep̅i fuer̅ .

Ⓜ In Melehou ten ipſe Radulf de eod̅ Walterio . v .
hid . Tra . e̅ . v . car . 7 ibi ſunt . 7 viii . uilli 7 iiii . bord .
Val 7 ualuit ſe̅p . c . ſolid . Hoc Ⓜ . x . ſochi tenuer̅ .
7 tra̅ ſua cui uoluer̅ dare ł uende potuer̅ .

In Stratone ten Fulcher pariſiac de Walt Gifard
i . hid . 7 i . uirg 7 dim . Tra . e̅ . ii . car . In d̅n̅io . i . car .
7 un uills 7 v . bord cu̅ . i . car . P̅t̅u̅ . ii . car . Val . xxviii.

2 M. In BATTLESDEN Richard Talbot holds 9 hides from Walter Giffard.
Land for 8 ploughs. In lordship 2 ploughs; a third possible. 211 c
   7 villagers have 5 ploughs. 10 smallholders.
   Meadow for 8 ploughs.
Value 100s; as much when acquired; before 1066 £8.
   7 Freemen held this manor before 1066; they could do
what they would with their land.

In REDBORNSTOKE Hundred

3   In MARSTON (Moretaine) Hugh Bolbec holds 2 hides less ½ virgate
from Walter Giffard. Land for 3 ploughs. In lordship 1 plough.
   6 villagers have 2 ploughs. 5 smallholders.
   Meadow for 3 ploughs; woodland, 300 pigs.
Value 50s; when acquired 20s; before 1066 £4.
   2 thanes held this land before 1066; they could grant to
whom they would. Herfast, Nigel of Aubigny's man, claims
half an enclosure, which lay in the manor of Herfast's predecessor,
as the men of the Hundred testify.

4 M. In MAULDEN Hugh of Bolbec also holds 3 hides from Walter.
Land for 4 ploughs. In lordship 2 ploughs.
   5 villagers have 2 ploughs.
   Meadow for 4 ploughs; woodland, 50 pigs.
Value 50s; as much when acquired; before 1066 £4.
   Alwin, Bishop Wulfwy's brother, held this manor;
he could grant to whom he would.

In BIGGLESWADE Hundred

5   In DUNTON Ralph of Lanquetot holds 1 hide and 3 virgates from
Walter Giffard. Land for 2 ploughs; they are there.
   4 villagers and 2 smallholders.
The value is 33s 4d and always was as much.
   4 Freemen held this land; they could sell their land;
they were Archbishop Stigand's men.

6 M. In MILLOW Ralph holds 5 hides himself from Walter.
Land for 5 ploughs; they are there.
   8 villagers and 4 smallholders.
The value is and always was 100s.
   10 Freemen held this manor; they could grant or sell
their land to whom they would.

7   In STRATTON Fulchere of Paris holds 1 hide and 1½ virgates from
Walter Giffard. Land for 2 ploughs. In lordship 1 plough;
   1 villager and 5 smallholders with 1 plough.
   Meadow for 2 ploughs.

ſoł.7 tntđ qdo receþ.T.R.E.ꞌxxx.ſoł.Hanc t̄ra.ɪɪɪ.

ſochi tenueꞃ.7 cui uolueꞃ dare ł uendē potueꞃ.

Ⓜ In Cudeſſane ten̄ Germund de Radulfo Langetot
ɪɪɪ.hid 7 dim̄.p uno Ⓜ.Tra.ē.ɪɪɪ.caꞃ.In d̄nio.ē
una caꞃ.7 ɪ.uiłłs 7 ɪɪɪ.borđ cū.ɪɪ.caꞃ.7 un̄ ſeruus.
þtū.ɪɪɪ.caꞃ.Silua.xl.porc.Vał.xl.ſoł.Qdo
receþ.ꞌxx.ſoł.T.R.E.ꞌlx.ſoł.7 ɪ.molin̄ pot ibi fieri.
Hoc Ⓜ.ɪɪɪɪ.ſochi tenueꞃ.7 dare 7 uendē potueꞃ.

Ⓜ In Chābeltone ten̄ Rad de Langetot de Walt Gifard
ɪɪɪɪ.hid 7 dim̄ 7 ɪɪɪɪ.parte uni uirg.Tra.ē.ɪɪɪɪ.caꞃ.
Ibi.ɪ.caꞃ in d̄nio.7 ɪɪɪɪ.uiłłi hn̄t.ɪɪɪ.caꞃ.7 ɪ.molinū
.ɪɪɪ.ſolid.7 ɪɪɪ.den̄.þtū.ɪɪɪɪ.caꞃ.Silua.xl.porc.
Vał lx.ſoł.Qdo receþ.ꞌxx.ſoł.T.R.E.ꞌlxx.ſoł.
hanc t̄ra.vɪ.ſochi tenueꞃ.7 cui uolueꞃ dare potueꞃ.

.XVII. W̄TERRA WILLI DE WARENE. *IN STODENE HVND.*
ILLELM de Warenna ten̄ in *DENE*.ɪɪ.hid.
7 ɪɪɪ.ſochi de eo.Tra.ē.ɪɪɪ.caꞃ.7 ibi ſunt.Ibi.v.borđ.
7 ɪ.ſerū.Vał 7 ualuit ſēp.xxx.ſoł.Hanc t̄ra tenueꞃ
idē ipſi ſochi qui nc̄ tenent.Vn̄ eoꝛ n̄ potuit dare ł uen
dere t̄ra ſuā ſine licentia d̄ni ſui.Alij duo ū hoc faſe
potueꞃ.

De dim̄ hiđ 7 dim̄ uirga huꝰ t̄ræ fuit Wiłłs ſpec ſaiſit
p regē 7 ej libatorē.ſed W.de Warenna ſine breue
regis eū deſaiſiuit.7 ɪɪ.eꝗs ej hōibꝛ abſtulit.7 necdū
reddidit.Hoc hōes de hund atteſtant.

Ⓜ Ipſe Wiłłs de Waꞃ ten̄ Tilebroc.p.v.hid ſe defđ.
Tra.ē.vɪ.caꞃ.7 ibi ſunt.7 xx.ſochi.7 ɪɪɪɪ.borđ.þtū
v.caꞃ.Vał.c.ſoł.7 tntđ qdo receþ.T.R.E.ꞌɪɪɪɪ.lib.
Hoc Ⓜ idē ipſi ſochi qui teneᷠ tenueꞃ.7 ita de ſoca 7 ſaca
regis fueꞃ.qđ dare 7 uendē t̄ra ſuā cui uoluiſſeᷠ po

Value 28s; as much when acquired; before 1066, 30s.
3 Freemen held this land; they could grant or sell
to whom they would.

[In CLIFTON Hundred]

8 M. In *CUDESSANE* Germund holds 3½ hides from Ralph Lanquetot
as one manor. Land for 3 ploughs. In lordship 1 plough;
1 villager and 3 smallholders with 2 ploughs; 1 slave.
Meadow for 3 ploughs; woodland, 40 pigs.
Value 40s; when acquired 20s; before 1066, 60s; 1 mill possible.
4 Freemen held this manor; they could grant and sell.

9 M. In CAMPTON Ralph of Lanquetot holds 4½ hides and the
fourth part of 1 virgate from Walter Giffard.
Land for 4 ploughs. 1 plough in lordship.
4 villagers have 3 ploughs.
1 mill, 3s 3d; meadow for 4 ploughs; woodland 40 pigs.
Value 60s; when acquired 20s; before 1066, 70s.
6 Freemen held this land; they could grant to whom they would.

17   LAND OF WILLIAM OF WARENNE   211 d

In STODDEN Hundred

1 William of Warenne holds 2 hides in DEAN and 3 Freemen
from him. Land for 3 ploughs; they are there.
5 smallholders and 1 slave.
The value is and always was 30s.
The same Freemen who now hold this land held it;
one of them could not grant or sell his land without
his lord's permission; but the other two could do this.
William Speke was put in possession of ½ hide and ½
virgate of this land through the King and his deliverer, but
William of Warenne dispossessed him without the King's writ
and took away two horses from his men and has not
yet given them back. This the men of the Hundred confirm.

2 M. William of Warenne also holds TILBROOK. It answers for 5 hides.
Land for 6 ploughs; they are there.
20 Freemen and 4 smallholders.
Meadow for 5 ploughs.
Value 100s; as much when acquired; before 1066 £4.
The same Freemen who hold this manor held it. They were so
far of the King's full jurisdiction that they could grant and sell

tuer̃.7 recede ad aliũ dñm sine lictia ej sub quo fuer̃.

Hanc tr̃a de Tilebroc r̃eclamat Hugo belcãp . sup . W.

7 hões de hund portaɴ inde testim . qd Rad tallebosc

Antecessor ej de ea p rege saisit fuit.7 eã tenuit.

In Hanefelde ten̄ . W . de Warenna . iii . uirg tre . Tr̃a . ē

.i . car̃.7 ibi . ē . Val 7 sẽp ualuit . x . sol . H̃ tra jacuit

sẽp in Chenebaltone . ſʒ Warr̃a ded sẽp iuſte in Bede

In Eſtone ten̄ . W . de War̃ . i . uirg . Tr̃a . ē . ii . car̃ ⸗ fordſcira.

7 ibi ſunt.7 i . uilłs.7 ii . bord̃ . p̃tũ . i . car̃ . Silua . c . porc̃.

Val̃ . xx . sol . Qdo recep̃ꞏ xl . sol . T.R.E.ꞌ xx . sol . Hanc tr̃a

ten Auigi hõ Aſchil anteceſsoris Hugon̄ . potuit uende

cui uoluit . ſʒ socã ipſe Aſchil retinuit in Colmeborde m̃

ſuo . Hanc tr̃a reclamat Hugo ſup . W . de War̃ . unde õms

q̃ iurauer̃ de uicecomitatu portaɴ teſtim̃ . qd non p̃tiñ

ipſa tra ad Wiłłm.

In ead uilla ten̄ . W . de War̃ . i . hid 7 i . uirg̃ . Tr̃a . ē . i.

car̃.7 ibi . ē.7 ii . bord̃ . P̃tũ . i . car̃ . Val̃ . x . sol.7 tn̄td qdo

recep̃ . T.R.E.ꞌ xv . sol . Hanc tr̃a ten Avigi.7 potuit

dare cui uoluit . T.R.E . Hanc ei poſtea . W . rex c̃ceſsit.

7 p ſuũ breue Rad tallebosc c̃om̃dauit . ut eũ ſeruaret

qdiu uiueret . Hic die mortuus . ē dix̃ se . ēē . hõem

.W . de War̃.7 idõ . W . saisit . ē de hac terra.

In ead ten̄ iſd̃ . W . i . uirg træ . Tr̃a . ē . ii . bob̃.7 ibi ſuɴ

iiii . boues . Val̃ 7 ual̃ . ii . sol . T.R.E.ꞌ iii . sol . Hanc tr̃a

ten̄ Blach hõ Augi . pot dare cui uoluit.

In ead ten̄ Tedric̃ de Wiłło . i . uirg 7 iiii . part̃ . i . uirg̃

Tr̃a . ē . i . car̃.7 ibi . ē . P̃tũ . i . car̃ . Silua . xx . iiii . porc̃.

Val̃ 7 ualuit . x . sol . T.R.E.ꞌ vi . sol . Godric̃ tenuit hõ

uicecomitis .7 cui uoluit dare potuit.

their land to whom they might wish. They could withdraw to
another lord without the permission of the one they were under.
Hugh Beauchamp claims this land of Tilbrook against William.
The men of the Hundred bear witness thereto, that Ralph
Tallboys his predecessor was put in possession of it through
the King and held it.

3   In *HANEFELDE* William of Warenne holds 3 virgates of land.
Land for 1 plough; it is there.
The value is and always was 10s.
    This land always lay in Kimbolton (lands) but it always rightfully
gave its defence obligations in Bedfordshire.

4   In EASTON William of Warenne holds 1 virgate.
Land for 2 ploughs; they are there.
    1 villager and 2 smallholders.
    Meadow for 1 plough; woodland, 100 pigs.
Value 20s; when acquired 40s; before 1066, 20s.
    Augi, a man of Askell, Hugh Beauchamp's predecessor, held this
land; he could sell to whom he would, but Askell kept the jurisdiction
himself in his manor in Colmworth. Hugh of Beauchamp claims this
land against William of Warenne, whereto all the sworn men of the
Sheriffdom bear witness, that this land does not belong to William.

5   In the same village William of Warenne holds 1 hide and 1 virgate.
Land for 1 plough; it is there.
    2 smallholders.
    Meadow for 1 plough.
Value 10s; as much when acquired; before 1066, 15s.
    Augi held this land; he could grant to whom he would before 1066.
Later on, King William assigned it to him, and commended him
through his writ to Ralph Tallboys that he should protect him as
long as he lived. On the day he died, he said he was William of
Warenne's man, and William therefore took possession of this land.

6   In the same (village) William also holds 1 virgate of land.
Land for 2 oxen; 4 oxen there.
The value is and was 2s; before 1066, 3s.
    Black, Augi's man, held this land; he could grant to
whom he would.

7   In the same village Theodoric holds 1 virgate and the fourth
part of 1 virgate from William. Land for 1 plough; it is there.
    Meadow for 1 plough; woodland, 24 pigs.
The value is and was 10s; before 1066, 6s.
    Godric, the Sheriff's man, held it; he could grant
to whom he would.

WTERRA WILLI DE.OW. *IN FLICTHA HVND.*

ᚹ **W**ILLELM de Ow.tenet *SONEDONE* .p̄ x.ĥid ſe
deſđ.Tra.ē.xvi.car̄.In dn̄io.iiii.hidæ.7 ibi ſuꝗ.iīii.car̄.
Ibi.xx.uilli ĥn̄t xii.car̄.Ibi.xi.borđ.7 xii.ſerui.
Pᵗū.iiii.car̄.Silua.c.porc.In totis ualent ual.x.liɓ.
Q̄do recep̄.viii.liɓ.T.R.E.xx.liɓ.Hoc ᛗ tenuit Aleſtan
de Boſcube.teigñ.R.E.In eađ uilla ĥr̄.i.miles.i.car̄.

In Stradlei ten̄ Walter de Willo de ow.i.hid.Tra.ē
.ii.car̄.In dn̄io.i.car̄.7 ii.uilli.i.car̄.ĥn̄t.7 iii.borđ.
7 iii.ſerui.p̄tū.i.car̄.Silua.xx.porc.Val.xxx.ſol.
Q̄do recep̄.xx.ſol.T.R.E.xl.ſol.Hanc tenuit Goduin
ĥō Aleſtan teigni regis.E.uende potuit cui uoluit.

In Melehou ten̄ Wills de ow *IN BICHELESWADE HVND.*
dim̄ hid.Tra.ē dim̄ car̄.7 ibi.ē.cū.i.borđ.Val 7 ualuit
x.ſol.Hanc tr̄a tenuit Godmar ĥō Aleſtan.7 uende
potuit cui uoluit.

ᛗ **I**n Edeuuorde teneꝗ.ir.milites de Willo de ow.vii.hid
7 iii.uirg 7 dim̄.Tra.ē.viii.car̄.In dn̄io.iii.car̄.
7 viii.uilli ĥn̄t.v.car̄.Ibi.ii.borđ.7 v.ſerui.Pᵗū
ii.car̄.Val.viii.liɓ.Q̄do recep̄.x.liɓ.7 tn̄td T.R.E.
Hoc ᛗ ten̄ Aleſtan de Boſcume.7 ibi.ii.ſocĥi ĥōes ej
fuer̄.7 i.hiđ 7 dim̄ habuer̄.7 cui uoluer̄ uende potuer̄.
In Holme ten̄ Vluric de Willo de ow.iii.uirg træ
Tra.ē.i.car̄.7 ibi.ē.Val.xvi.ſol.Q̄do recep̄.xii.ſol.
T.R.E.xx.ſol.Hanc tr̄a tenuit Ælueua, ĥō Aſchil.
7 cui uoluit dare potuit. *IN CLISTONE HVND.*
In Alriceſeie ten̄ Burnard.v.hid 7 dim̄ 7 ii.part
uni hidæ.Tra.ē.vi.car̄.In dn̄io.i.car̄.7 xiii.uilli
ĥn̄t.v.car̄.7 x.borđ.7 i.molenđ.x.ſolid.p̄tū.vi.car̄.
Mercatū.ē ibi de.x.ſol.Val 7 ualuit ſēp.vii.liɓ.
Hoc ᛗ tenuit Aleſtan de Boſcume.7 ibi.i.ſocĥs ĥō
ej fuit.ii.partes.i.hidæ habuit.7 cui uoluit dare potuit.

LAND OF WILLIAM OF EU

In FLITT Hundred

1 M. William of Eu holds SUNDON. It answers for 10 hides.
Land for 16 ploughs. In lordship 4 hides; 4 ploughs there.
20 villagers have 12 ploughs. 11 smallholders; 12 slaves.
Meadow for 4 ploughs; woodland, 100 pigs.
Total value £10; when acquired £8; before 1066 £20.
Alstan of Boscombe, a thane of King Edward's, held this manor.
In the same village 1 man-at-arms has 1 plough.

2 In STREATLEY Walter holds 1 hide from William of Eu.   212 a
Land for 2 ploughs. In lordship 1 plough.
2 villagers have 1 plough; 3 smallholders and 3 slaves.
Meadow for 1 plough; woodland, 20 pigs.
Value 30s; when acquired 20s; before 1066, 40s.
Godwin, a man of Alstan, a thane of King Edward's, held this
land; he could sell to whom he would.

In BIGGLESWADE Hundred

3 In MILLOW William of Eu holds ½ hide. Land for ½ plough;
it is there, with
1 smallholder.
The value is and was 10s.
Godmer, Alstan's man, held this land; he could sell to whom
he would.

4 M. In EDWORTH 2 men-at-arms hold 7 hides and 3½ virgates from
William of Eu. Land for 8 ploughs. In lordship 3 ploughs.
8 villagers have 5 ploughs. 2 smallholders and 5 slaves.
Meadow for 2 ploughs.
Value £8; when acquired £10; before 1066 as much.
Alstan of Boscombe held this manor. 2 Freemen, his men, were
there; they had 1½ hides; they could sell to whom they would.

5 In HOLME Wulfric holds 3 virgates of land from William of Eu.
Land for 1 plough; it is there.
Value 16s; when acquired 12s; before 1066, 20s.
Aelfeva, Askell's man, held this land; she could grant to whom
she would.

In CLIFTON Hundred

6 In ARLESEY Bernard holds 5½ hides and 2 parts of 1 hide.
Land for 6 ploughs. In lordship 1 plough.
13 villagers have 5 ploughs; 10 smallholders.
1 mill, 10s; meadow for 6 ploughs. A market, at 10s.
The value is and always was £7.
Alstan of Boscombe held this manor. 1 Freeman, his man, was
there; he had 2 parts of 1 hide; he could grant to whom he would.

In Chābeltone teñ Fulbt dim̄ hiđ de.Wilto de ow.

Tra.ē dim̄ cař.7 ibi.ē.cū.ɪ.uilto.H̄ tra ual 7 ualuit

sēp.v.fol.Hanc trā tenuit Aluuin̄ hō Aleſtan.7 potuit

.XIX.   **TERRA MILONIS CRISPIN.** *dare cui uoluit.*

M̄ **M**ɪʟo criſpin teñ *CLOPEHA IN STODEN HVND.*

p v.hiđ.ſe defđ.Tra.ē.xxx.cař.P̄ter has.v.

hidas ſunt in dñio.x.carucate træ.7 ibi ſuꝗ.vɪɪɪ.

cař.7 adhuc.ɪɪ.poſſ.ēē.Ibi.xvɪɪɪ.uilti hn̄t.xx.cař.

7 xv.borđ.7 ɪɪɪɪ.ſerui.P̄tū.vɪ.cař.7 ɪ.molin̄.xʟ.

foliđ.Silua.cc.porc.7 vɪ.deñ.In totis ualent ual

xxɪɪɪɪ.libĕ.7 tntđ ꝗdo recep̄.T.R.E.xɪɪ.libĕ.Hoc m̄ tenuit

Bricxtric teign̄.R.E.de abbe de Rameſy.Abb 7 mona

chi reclamaꝗ hoc m̄.ꝗm eſt 7 fuit T.R.E.de uiĉtu eoꝛ.

7 totū hund portat de hoc teſtimoniū.

In Middeltone habuer.ɪɪ.ſochi.xvɪ.aĉs træ.7 ſuā

Warrā in eađ Middeltone deder.ſꝛ trā|cui uoluer

dare ł uende potuer.Hos ſochos Robt de Olgi in

Clopehā appoſuit injuſte ut hōes de hund dicuñt.

ꝗa nunꝗ ibi.T.R.E.jacuer. *IN WILGA HVND.*

In *LALEGA* teñ Leuric de Milone.ɪ.uirg træ.Tra.ē

.ɪ.cař.7 ibi.ē.Val 7 ualuit sēp.x.fol.Idē ipſe.T.R.E.

tenuit.hō Brixtrici fuit.7 uende 7 dare eā potuit.

.XX.   **TERRA ERNVLFI de HESDING** *IN MANESHEVE HVND.*

E **E**RNVʟFVs de Heſding teñ *DODINTONE* de rege.

p xv.hiđ 7 dim̄ ſe defđ.Tra.ē.xxx.cař.Ibi.x.

carucatæ træ in dñio.7 ibi ſunt.vɪɪ.cař.7 adhuc.ɪɪɪ.

poſſunt.ēē.p̄ter.xv.hiđ 7 dim̄.Ibi.xʟɪɪ.uilti hn̄t.xx.cař.

212 b

Ibi.xɪx.borđ.7 xɪx.ſerui.P̄tū.xxx.cař.Silua.ccɢ

porc.In totis ualent ual.xxv.libĕ.7 tntđ ꝗdo recep̄.

T.R.E.xxx.libĕ.Hoc m̄ tenuit Wluuarđ leuet.T.R.E.

7   In CAMPTON Fulbert holds ½ hide from William of Eu.
Land for ½ plough; it is there, with
   1 villager.
The value of this land is and always was 5s.
   Alwin, Alstan's man, held this land; he could grant to whom
he would.

19   LAND OF MILES CRISPIN

I n STODDEN Hundred

1   M. Miles Crispin holds CLAPHAM. It answers for 5 hides. Land for 30
ploughs. Besides these 5 hides there are 10 carucates of land in
lordship; 8 ploughs there; a further 2 possible.
   18 villagers have 20 ploughs; 15 smallholders and 4 slaves.
   Meadow for 6 ploughs; 1 mill, 40s; woodland, 200 pigs and 6d too.
Total value £24; as much when acquired; before 1066 £12.
   Brictric, a thane of King Edward's, held this manor from Ramsey
Abbey. The Abbot and the monks claim this manor, since it is, and
was before 1066, for their supplies; the whole Hundred bears
witness to this.

2   In MILTON (Ernest) 2 Freemen had 16 acres of land. They also gave
their defence obligations in Milton, but they could grant or sell
their land to whom they would. Robert d'Oilly placed these Freemen
in Clapham, wrongfully, as the men of the Hundred state,
because they never lay there before 1066.

In WILLEY Hundred

3   In THURLEIGH Leofric holds 1 virgate of land from Miles.
Land for 1 plough; it is there.
The value is and always was 10s.
   He also held it himself before 1066; he was Brictric's man; he
could sell and grant it.

20   LAND OF ARNULF OF HESDIN

In MANSHEAD Hundred

1   Arnulf of Hesdin holds TODDINGTON from the King. It answers for
15½ hides. Land for 30 ploughs. In lordship 10 carucates of land,
7 ploughs there; a further 3 possible; besides the 15½ hides.
   42 villagers have 20 ploughs. 19 smallholders and 19 slaves.   212 b
   Meadow for 30 ploughs; woodland, 300 pigs.
Total value £25; as much when acquired; before 1066 £30.
   Wulfward [son of?] Leofed held this manor before 1066.

In Celgraue ten̄ Ernulf tciã parte uni uirg træ.

Vał 7 ualuit sēp. ii. sol. Hanc trã tenuit Eduuard. T.R.E.

TERRA EVDONIS FILIJ HVBERTI.

ᵐ EVDO Dapifer ten̄ ETONE. p̄ xx. hid se defd. Tra. ē
xvi. car. In dn̄io. vii. hid 7 dim. 7 ibi sunt. iiii. car.

Ibi. xxxviii. uilti. hn̄t. xii. car. Ibi. vii. bord. 7 viii. serui.

7 ii. sochi. qui n̄ poteran̄ trã suã dare ł uende. Ibi. ii.

molini de xxxvi. sol. 7 vi. den. 7 c. anguilt. Ptū. xii.

car. Silua. cccc. porc. 7 ii. ac̄s uineæ. Int̄ totū uał. xv. lib.

Qdo recep. viii. lib. T.R.E. x. lib. Hoc ᵐ tenuit Vlmar
de Etone. teign. R.E. 7 in hoc ᵐ fuer. ii. sochi q̄ tram
suã uende potuer 7 dare. De hac tra reclamat Tedbald
hō juditæ comitissæ. i. hid. de qua eū Eudo desaisiuit
p̄quã ad hoc ᵐ uenit.

In WIBOLDESTONE ten̄ Eudo. vi. hid 7 iii. uirg. Tra. ē. v. car.
In dn̄io. iiii. hidæ 7 dim. 7 ibi sunt. ii. car. 7 viii. uilli hn̄t
iiii. car. Ibi. viii. bord 7 iii. serui. Ptū. ii. car. Int̄ totū
uał iii. lib. Qdo recep. xx. sol. T.R.E. x. lib. Hanc trã
.iiii. teigni R.E. tenuer. 7 cui uoluer uende potuer.

In Chauelestorne ten̄ Eudo. i. hid 7 i. uirg. Tra. ē. i. car.
7 ibi. ē. Ibi. iiii. uilli. 7 ptū. i. car. Vał 7 ualuit. x. sol.
T.R.E. xx. sol. Hanc trã. ii. hōes R.E. tenuer. 7 eã dare pot

In Tamiseforde ten̄ Eudo ten̄. i. hid. IN BICHELESWADA HD.
7 i. uirg træ. Tra. ē. ii. car. In dn̄io. i. hida. 7 ibi. ē. i. car.
7 i. uilts cū. i. car. 7 ii. bord 7 i. seru. 7 i. molin x. sol.
7 ptū. ii. car. Vał 7 ualuit. xl. sol. T.R.E. xlv. sol. Hanc
trã. ii. sochi tenuer. 7 cui uoluer dare potuer.

In ead uilla ten̄ Wilts de carun iiii. hid 7 i. uirg de Eudone
Tra. ē. iiii. car. In dn̄io. ii. car. 7 viii. uilli hn̄t. ii. car.
7 vi. serui. 7 i. molin. xii. sol. Ptū. iiii. car. Vał. lx. sol.
Qdo recep. xl. sol. T.R.E. lx. sol. Hanc trã tenuer

2   In CHALGRAVE Arnulf holds the third part of 1 virgate of land.
The value is and always was 2s.
   Edward White held this land before 1066.

21   **LAND OF EUDO SON OF HUBERT**

   [In BARFORD Hundred]
1 M. Eudo the Steward holds EATON (Socon). It answers for 20 hides.
Land for 16 ploughs. In lordship 7½ hides; 4 ploughs there.
   38 villagers have 12 ploughs. 7 smallholders and 8 slaves;
     2 Freemen who could not grant or sell their land.
   2 mills at 36s 6d and 100 eels; meadow for 12 ploughs;
     woodland, 400 pigs; vineyard, 2 acres.
In total, value £15; when acquired £8; before 1066 £10.
   Wulfmer of Eaton, a thane of King Edward's, held this manor.
In this manor were 2 Freemen who could sell and grant their land.
   Theodbald, Countess Judith's man, claims 1 hide of this land,
of which Eudo dispossessed him after he came to this manor.
2   In WYBOSTON Eudo holds 6 hides and 3 virgates. Land for 5
ploughs. In lordship 4½ hides; 2 ploughs there.
   8 villagers have 4 ploughs. 8 smallholders and 3 slaves.
   Meadow for 2 ploughs.
In total, value £3; when acquired 20s; before 1066 £10.
   4 thanes of King Edward's held this land; they could sell
to whom they would.
3   In CHAWSTON Eudo holds 1 hide and 1 virgate.
Land for 1 plough; it is there.
   4 villagers.
   Meadow for 1 plough.
The value is and was 10s; before 1066, 20s.
   2 of King Edward's men held this land; they could grant and sell.
   In BIGGLESWADE Hundred
4   In TEMPSFORD Eudo holds 1 hide and 1 virgate of land.
Land for 2 ploughs. In lordship 1 hide; 1 plough there.
   1 villager with 1 plough; 2 smallholders and 1 slave.
   1 mill, 10s; meadow for 2 ploughs.
The value is and was 40s; before 1066, 45s.
   2 Freemen held this land; they could grant to whom they would.
5   In the same village William of Cairon holds 4 hides and 1 virgate
from Eudo the Steward. Land for 4 ploughs. In lordship
2 ploughs.
   8 villagers have 2 ploughs; 6 slaves.
   1 mill, 12s; meadow for 4 ploughs.
Value 60s; when acquired 40s; before 1066, 60s.

.III. ſochi hões Vlmari de Etone. Vñ eoꝗ trã ſuã dare
ñ potuit ſine lictia dñi ſui. alij ; II. qd uolueꝛ facere potueꝛ.

ⓂSANDEIA teñ Eudo dapifer. *IN DIM HVND DE WENESLAI.*

p̾ XVI. hid ſe defd. 7 una uirg. Tra. ē. XVI. car. In dñio
VIII. hid 7 I. uirg. 7 ibi ſunt. III. car. 7 XXIIII. uilli hñt
VIII. car. 7 adhuc. V. poſſ fieri. Ibi. VI. bord. 7 II. ſerui.
7 II. molini. de. L. ſol. p̾tũ. XVI. car. Paſta ad pecuñ uillæ.
Int totũ ual. XII. lib. Q̾do recep̾. VIII. lib. T.R.E. x. lib.
Hoc Ⓜ tenuit Vlmar de Etone teigñ. R.E. Hic reclamat
Eudo. III. ac ſiluæ ſup̾ Hug̾ belcap̾. q̾s Vlmar tenuit.
ſꝝ Rad q̾do erat uicecom eũ deſaiſiuit. idõꝗ Eudo noluit
dare Warras de ead ſilua. Hoc idẽ hões de hund atteſtant.

In Suttone teñ Aluuin de Eudone. III. uirg træ. Tra. ē
VI. bobꝝ. 7 ibi ſunt. 7 I. uilli. p̾tũ bobꝝ. Val. VI. ſol. Q̾do
recep̾. III. ſol. T.R.E. x. ſol. Hanc trã. II. ſochi tenueꝛ.
7 potueꝛ uende cui uolueꝛ. *IN WICHESTAVESTOV HVND.*

In Sudgiuele teñ Willſ de caron dim uirg̾ de
Eudone. Tra. ē. II. bobꝝ. 7 ibi ſunt. P̾tũ. II. bobꝝ. Val. III. ſol.
T.R.E. IIII. ſol. Hanc trã tenuit Alric 7 cui uoluit dare potuit

212 c

In Stanford teñ Willſ de caron. IIII. hid de Eudone
Tra. ē. IIII. car. In dñio. II. car. 7 III. uilli hñt. II. car.
7 II. ſerui. 7 II. molini de. XXIX. ſol. 7 L. anguill. P̾tũ
IIII. car. Silua. LX. porc. 7 II. ſol. Int totũ ual. IIII.
lib. Q̾do recep̾. XL. ſol. T.R. IIII. lib. Hanc trã tenuit
Vlmar de Etone. teigñ. R.E. In hac tra fuit. I. ſochſ
hõ huj Vlmari. dim hid habuit. 7 uende potuit.

In ead ſunt VII. ſochi. tenentes VII. acras træ. hões
Vlmari fueꝛ. 7 trã ſuã dare potueꝛ. Modo Hugo
de belcap̾ tenet eã.

In Blunehã teñ Domnic̾. I. uirg̾ tre de Eudone.
Tra. ē. II. bob. 7 ibi ſunt. p̾tũ. II. bobꝝ. Val. II. ſol. Q̾do

3 Freemen, Wulfmer of Eaton's men, held this land. One
of them could not grant his land without his lord's permission;
the other two could do what they would.

In the Half-Hundred of WENSLOW

6 M. Eudo the Steward holds SANDY. It answers for 16 hides
and 1 virgate. Land for 16 ploughs. In lordship 8 hides
and 1 virgate; 3 ploughs there.
    24 villagers have 8 ploughs; a further 5 possible.
      6 smallholders and 2 slaves.
    2 mills at 50s; meadow for 16 ploughs; pasture for the
    village livestock.
In total, value £12; when acquired £8; before 1066 £10.
    Wulfmer of Eaton, a thane of King Edward's, held this manor.
Here Eudo claims 3 acres of woodland against Hugh Beauchamp,
which Wulfmer held; but Ralph dispossessed him when he was
Sheriff. Therefore Eudo refused to give the defence obligations
from this woodland. This the men of the Hundred also confirm.

7 In SUTTON Alwin holds 3 virgates of land from Eudo.
Land for 6 oxen; they are there.
    1 villager.
Meadow for the oxen.
Value 6s; when acquired 3s; before 1066, 10s.
    2 Freemen held this land; they could sell to whom they would.

In WIXAMTREE Hundred

8 In SOUTHILL William of Cairon holds ½ virgate from Eudo.
Land for 2 oxen; they are there.
Meadow for 2 oxen.
Value 3s; before 1066, 4s.
    Alric held this land; he could grant to whom he would.

9 In STANFORD William of Cairon holds 4 hides from Eudo.   212 c
Land for 4 ploughs. In lordship 2 ploughs.
    3 villagers have 2 ploughs. 2 slaves.
    2 mills at 29s and 50 eels; meadow for 4 ploughs;
    woodland, 60 pigs and 2s too.
In total, value £4; when acquired 40s; before 1066 £4.
    Wulfmer of Eaton, a thane of King Edward's, held this land.
    On this land was 1 Freeman, Wulfmer's man; he had ½
hide; he could sell.

10 In the same (village) are 7 Freemen who hold 7 acres of land;
they were Wulfmer's men; they could grant their land.
Now Hugh of Beauchamp holds it.

11 In BLUNHAM Domnic holds 1 virgate of land from Eudo.
Land for 2 oxen; they are there.
    Meadow, 2 oxen.

recep̃.́ɪɪɪ.ſoł.T.R.E.́v.ſoł.Hanc t̃ra.ɪɪɪɪ.ſocħi tenuer̃.

7 uend́e 7 dare potuer̃.

In BISTONE ten̄ Rolland́ de Eudone.ɪɪɪ.hid̃.T̃ra.e̅

ɪɪɪ.car̃.7 ibi ſunt.In dn̄io.ɪɪ.car̃.7 ɪɪɪɪ.uiłłi hn̄t.ɪ.

car̃.Ibi.ɪɪ.bord̃.7 ɪ.ſeru.̊P̊t̅u.ɪɪɪ.car̃.Vał xxx.ſoł.

Q̨do recep̃.́xx.ſoł.T.R.E.́xL.ſoł.

In ead̃ ten̄ Normann̊ de Eudone.ɪɪɪɪ.hid̃.T̃ra.e̅

ɪɪɪɪ.car̃.In dn̄io.ɪ.car̃.7 ɪɪɪɪ.uiłłi hn̄t.ɪɪɪ.car̃.

Ibi.ɪɪ.ſerui.7 ɪ.molin̄.xx.ſoł.P̊t̅u.ɪɪɪɪ.car̃.Valet

xL.ſoł.7 tn̄td̃ q̨do recep̃.T.R.E.́L.ſoł.Has.ɪɪɪɪ.hid̃

7 ɪɪɪ.ſupiores tenuit iſte Normann̊ T.R.E.7 T.R.Wiłłi.

N̄c ħt Eudo de rege ut h̊o̅es ej̊ dn̄t.ſ̨ n̄ eſt de feudo

In ead̃ ten̄ Pirot̊ de Eudone.ɪ.hid̃.   ⌐Liſois.

T̃ra.e̅.ɪ.car̃.7 ibi.e̅.cu̅.̊ɪ.bord̃.p̊t̅u.ɪ.car̃.Valet

x.ſoł.Q̨do recep̃.́v.ſoł.T.R.E.́xx.ſoł.Hanc t̃ra

tenuit Rauan h̊o Vlmari.7 cui uoluit dare potuit.

In Nortgiue ten̄ Pirot̊ de Eud̃.ɪ.hid̃ 7 dim̃.T̃ra.e̅.ɪ.car̃

7 dim̃.Ibi.e̅.ɪ.car̃.7 dim̃ pot̊ ſieri.7 ɪɪɪ.uiłłi ſuꝫ 7 ɪ.bord̃.

P̊t̅u.ɪ.car̃ 7 dim̃.7 ɪ.molin̄.xɪɪɪɪ.ſoł.Vał xx.ſoł.Q̨do

recep̃.́x.ſoł.T.R.E.́xxv.ſoł.Hanc t̃ra tenuit Rauan

h̊o Vlmari de Etone.7 uend́e potuit.

In ead̃ ten̄ Rad̃.ɪ.hid̃ 7 dim̃ de Eudone.T̃ra.e̅.ɪɪ.car̃.

7 ibi ſunt.7 v.bord̃ 7 ɪɪɪ.ſerui.P̊t̅u.ɪɪ.car̃.Silua.c.

porc̃.Vał.ɪɪɪ.lib̃.Q̨do recep̃.́xL.ſoł.T.R.E.́Lx.ſoł.

Hanc t̃ra tenuer̃.ɪɪ.ſocħi.7 dare 7 uend́e potuer̃.

⊂In CLISTONE ten̄ Wiłłs de caron IN CLISTON HVND̃.

de Eudone.vɪ.hid̃ 7 dim̃.T̃ra.e̅.ɪɪɪɪ.car̃ 7 dim̃.In dn̄io

.ɪɪ.car̃.7 ɪx.uiłłi hn̄t.ɪɪ.car̃ 7 dim̃.Ibi.ɪ.bord̃ 7 ɪɪɪ.ſerui.

7 ɪɪ.molini de.xL.ſoł.7 cL.anguiłł.P̊t̅u.ɪɪɪɪ.car̃ 7 dim̃.

Int totu̅ uał.c.ſoł.Q̨do recep̃.́ɪɪɪɪ.lib̃.T.R.E.́vɪ.lib̃.

Hoc ꝏ tenuit Vlmar̃ de Etone.7 ibi fuer̃.ɪɪɪ.ſocħi.

.ɪ.hid̃ 7 dim̃ uirg̃ habuer̃.7 cui uoluer̃ uend́e potuer̃.

Value 2s; when acquired 3s; before 1066, 5s.

4 Freemen held this land; they could sell and grant.

12 In BEESTON Roland holds 3 hides from Eudo. Land for 3 ploughs; they are there. In lordship 2 ploughs.

4 villagers have 1 plough. 2 smallholders and 1 slave.

Meadow for 3 ploughs.

Value 30s; when acquired 20s; before 1066, 40s.

13 In the same (village) Norman holds 4 hides from Eudo. Land for 4 ploughs. In lordship 1 plough.

4 villagers have 3 ploughs. 2 slaves.

1 mill, 20s; meadow for 4 ploughs.

Value 40s; as much when acquired; before 1066, 50s.

This Norman held these 4 hides and the 3 above before and after 1066. Now Eudo has it from the King, as his men state; but it is not of Lisois' Holding.

14 In the same (village) Pirot holds 1 hide from Eudo. Land for 1 plough; it is there, with

1 smallholder.

Meadow for 1 plough.

Value 10s; when acquired 5s; before 1066, 20s.

Raven, Wulfmer of Eaton's man, held this land; he could grant to whom he would.

15 In NORTHILL Pirot holds 1½ hides from Eudo. Land for 1½ ploughs. 1 plough there; ½ possible.

3 villagers and 1 smallholder.

Meadow for 1½ ploughs; 1 mill, 14s.

Value 20s; when acquired 10s; before 1066, 25s.

Raven, Wulfmer of Eaton's man, held this land; he could sell.

16 In the same (village) Ralph holds 1½ hides from Eudo. Land for 2 ploughs; they are there.

5 smallholders and 3 slaves.

Meadow for 2 ploughs; woodland, 100 pigs.

Value £3; when acquired 40s; before 1066, 60s.

2 Freemen held this land; they could grant and sell.

In CLIFTON Hundred

17 M. In CLIFTON William of Cairon holds 6½ hides from Eudo. Land for 4½ ploughs. In lordship 2 ploughs.

9 villagers have 2½ ploughs. 1 smallholder and 3 slaves.

2 mills at 40s and 150 eels; meadow for 4½ ploughs.

In total, value 100s; when acquired £4; before 1066 £6.

Wulfmer of Eaton held this manor. There were 3 Freemen there; they had 1 hide and ½ virgate; they could sell to whom they would.

Wᴛᴇʀʀᴀ Wɪʟʟɪ Pᴇᴠʀᴇʟ. *Iɴ Sᴛᴀɴʙᴠʀɢᴇ Hᴠɴᴅ.*

Witłs peurel ten de rege *PILEWORDE*.7 Ambrosi de eo.

.p x.hiđ se defđ.Tra.e̅.vɪɪɪ.car̅.In dn̅io.ɪ.car̅.7 alia

poteſt fieri.7 x.uiłti hn̅t.vɪ.car̅.Ibi.vɪ.borđ 7 ɪɪɪ.serui.

P̊tu̅.vɪ.car̅.Silua.c.porc̅.Hanc silua̅ Osuui abſtulit.

7 hunđ dicit q̇a in hoc ꝏ jacuit.T.R.E.Int totu̅

uał.vɪ.lib̅.Q̇do recep̅.́ɪɪɪɪ.lib̅.T.R.E.́x.lib̅.Hoc ꝏ

tenuit Leuric fili Osmundi teign regis.E. *Iɴ Wɪʟɢᴀ* ᴴᵛᴺᴰˑ

In Risedene ten Malet de Witło peurel.ɪ.uirg trǽ

212 d

Tra.e̅.ɪɪ.bob.7 ibi funt.Vał 7 ualuit.xvɪ.den.T.R.E.́

ɪɪ.soł.Hanc tra̅ tenuit Samar h̅o Godǽ comitiſſæ.7 cui

uoluit dare potuit.

Hᴛᴇʀʀᴀ Hᴠɢoɴ Dᴇ Bᴇʟᴄᴀᴍᴘ. *Iɴ Sᴛoᴅᴇɴᴇ ʜᴠɴᴅ.*

Hvɢo de belcāp ten *CHAISOT*.p.v.hiđ se defđ.

.ɪ.uirg min.Tra.e̅.v.car̅.7 ibi funt.7 ɪx.uiłti.7 vɪ.

borđ.7 un feruus.7 ɪ.molin̅.ɪɪ.soł.P̊tu̅.ɪɪɪɪ.car̅.

Silua.cc.porc̅.In totis ualeñt uał.c.soł.Q̇do recep̅.́

ɪɪɪɪ.lib̅.T.R.E.́c.soł.Hanc tra̅ tenuit Afchil teign

regis.E.7 ibi fuer̅.xɪɪ.fochi.q̇ habuer̅ ɪɪɪ.hiđ.7 dimiđ.

7 cui uoluer̅ uendè 7 dare potuer̅.

In Rifelai ten Hugo.ɪ.hiđ.7 e̅ Bereuuich de Caifot.

Tra.e̅.ɪɪ.car̅.7 ibi funt.Hanc tenuit Afchil anteceſſor ej.

ꝏ Ipfe Hugo ten *PVTENEHOV.́ Iɴ Bᴠᴄʜᴇʟᴀɪ ᴅɪᴍɪᴅ ʜᴠɴᴅ.*

.p ɪɪɪɪ.hiđ se defđ.Tra.e̅.v.car̅.In dn̅io.ɪɪ.hiđ.7 ibi

funt.ɪɪ.car̅.7 vɪ.uiłti hn̅t.ɪɪɪ.car̅.Ibi.ɪɪɪɪ.borđ.7 ɪɪ.

ferui.7 ɪ.molin̅.xxx.soł.7 c.anguiłł.Silua.c.porc̅.

Vał.ɪɪɪɪ.lib̅.Q̇do recep̅.́xʟ.soł.7 tn̅td T.R.E.Hoc ꝏ

tenuit Afchil teign regis.E.

LAND OF WILLIAM PEVEREL

In STANBRIDGE Hundred

1 M. William Peverel holds TILSWORTH from the King and Ambrose from him. It answers for 10 hides. Land for 8 ploughs. In lordship 1 plough; another possible.
    10 villagers have 6 ploughs. 6 smallholders and 3 slaves.
    Meadow for 6 ploughs; woodland, 100 pigs.
    Oswy took away this woodland; the Hundred states that
      it lay in this manor before 1066.
    In total, value £6; when acquired £4; before 1066 £10.
    Leofric son of Osmund, a thane of King Edward's, held
this manor.

In WILLEY Hundred

2   In RUSHDEN Malet holds 1 virgate of land from William Peverel.
Land for 2 oxen; they are there.   212 d
The value is and was 16d; before 1066, 2s.
    Saemer the priest, Countess Gytha's man, held this land;
he could grant to whom he would.

LAND OF HUGH OF BEAUCHAMP

In STODDEN Hundred

1 M. Hugh of Beauchamp holds KEYSOE. It answers for 5 hides.
less 1 virgate. Land for 5 ploughs; they are there.
    9 villagers, 6 smallholders and 1 slave.
    1 mill, 2s; meadow for 4 ploughs; woodland, 200 pigs.
Total value 100s; when acquired £4; before 1066, 100s.
    Askell, a thane of King Edward's, held this land. There
were 12 Freemen who had 3½ hides; they could sell and
grant to whom they would.

2   In RISELEY Hugh holds 1 hide. It is an outlier of Keysoe.
Land for 2 ploughs; they are there.
    Askell his predecessor held it.

In BUCKLOW Half-Hundred

3 M. Hugh holds PUTNOE himself. It answers for 4 hides.
    Land for 5 ploughs. In lordship 2 hides. 2 ploughs there.
    6 villagers have 3 ploughs. 4 smallholders and 2 slaves.
    1 mill, 30s and 100 eels; woodland, 100 pigs.
    Value £4; when acquired 40s; as much before 1066.
    Askell, a thane of King Edward's, held this manor.

丱 Ipſe Hugo ten STACHEDENE.p̄ v.hiđ ſe defđ.Tra.ē.v.
caŕ.In dn̄io.11.hidæ.7 ibi ſunt 11.caŕ.7 x11.uiłłi hn̄t
111 caŕ.Ibi.v111.borđ 7 11 ſerui.p̄tū.1.caŕ.Silua
.c.porc̄.⋇ Hoc 丱 tenueŕ.11.hōēs regis.E.7 un hō Heraldi꞉
7 un q́ſq̇ cui uoluit trā ſuā dare potuit.

丱 Ipſe Hugo ten CHAINHALLE.p̄.v.hiđ ſe defđ.Tra.ē
v.caŕ.In dn̄io.11.hidæ.7 ibi ſunt.11.caŕ.7 x11.uiłłi hn̄t
111.caŕ.Ibi.1x.borđ 7 v.ſerui.p̄tū.111.caŕ.7 1.moliñ
xL.ſoł.7 c.anguiłł.Silua.c.porc̄.In totis ualentijs
uał.v111.liƀ.Q̇do recep̄꞉c.ſoł.T.R.E꞉v11.liƀ.Hoc 丱
tenuit Aſchil teign regis.E.

In eađ ten Hugo dimiđ hiđ quæ jacet in putenehou
Tra.ē.1.caŕ.7 1111.boues ſuꞃ ibi.7 11.borđ.Vał 7 ualuit
11.ſoł.Hanc trā tenuit Anſchil teign regis.E.

In Goldentone ten Hugo.111.hiđ.7 1.uirg quæ jacet
in Putenehou.Tra.ē.111.caŕ.7 ibi ſunt.7 v11.uiłłi 7 1.
borđ.p̄tū.1.caŕ.7 1.moliñ.xxx.ſoliđ 7 c.anguiłł.Int
totū uał.Lx.ſoł.7 tn̄tđ q̇do recep̄.T.R.E꞉1111.liƀ.
De hac trā habuit Radulf tallgeboſc.11.hiđ 7 111.uirg.
p̄ excābio de Warres.Hanc trā tenueŕ.1x.ſochi. ⌈ HĐ.
7 cui uolueŕ dare ł uende potueŕ. IN WICHESTANESTOV
In Sudgible ten Hugo.11.hiđ 7 1.uirg.Tra.ē.111.
caŕ.7 ibi ſunt.P̄tū.111.caŕ.Silua.c.porc̄.Vał 7 ualuit
xL.ſoł.T.R.E꞉L.ſoł.Hanc trā.v111.ſochi tenueŕ.7 qđ
uolueŕ inde facere potueŕ.

In Stanford ten Hugo.1.hiđ 7 dim uirg træ.Tra.ē
.1.caŕ 7 dimiđ.7 ibi ſunt.7 1111.uiłłi 7 1.borđ.p̄tū.1.caŕ
7 dim.Vał 7 ualuit ſēp.xx.ſoł.Hanc trā tenueŕ.1111.
ſochi.quoꝫ.111.liberi fueŕ.1111.ů unā hiđ habuit.ſed
nec dare nec uende potuit.

4 M. Hugh holds STAGSDEN himself. It answers for 5 hides.
Land for 5 ploughs. In lordship 2 hides; 2 ploughs there.
12 villagers have 3 ploughs. 8 smallholders and 2 slaves.
Meadow for 1 plough; woodland, 100 pigs.

(Words omitted are entered at the foot of the column, in 23,10 below, with transposition signs).

2 of King Edward's men and a man of Earl Harold's held this manor; each could grant his land to whom he would.

5 M. Hugh holds *CHAINHALLE* himself. It answers for 5 hides.
Land for 5 ploughs. In lordship 2 hides; 2 ploughs there.
12 villagers have 3 ploughs. 9 smallholders and 5 slaves.
Meadow for 3 ploughs; 1 mill, 40s and 100 eels;
    woodland, 100 pigs.
Total value £8; when acquired 100s; before 1066 £7.
Askell, a thane of King Edward's, held this manor.

6 In the same (village) Hugh holds ½ hide which lies in Putnoe (lands). Land for 1 plough; 4 oxen there.
2 smallholders.
The value is and was 2s.
Askell, a thane of King Edward's, held this land.

7 In GOLDINGTON (Highfields) Hugh holds 3 hides and 1 virgate which lies in Putnoe (lands). Land for 3 ploughs; they are there.
7 villagers and 1 smallholder.
Meadow for 1 plough; 1 mill, 30s and 100 eels.
In total, value 60s; as much when acquired; before 1066 £4.
Ralph Tallboys had 2 hides and 3 virgates of this land in exchange for Ware.
9 Freemen held this land; they could grant or sell to whom they would.

In WIXAMTREE Hundred

8 In SOUTHILL Hugh holds 2 hides and 1 virgate. Land for 3 ploughs; they are there.
Meadow for 3 ploughs; woodland, 100 pigs.
The value is and was 40s; before 1066, 50s.
8 Freemen held this land; they could do what they would with it.

9 In STANFORD Hugh holds 1 hide and ½ virgate of land.
Land for 1½ ploughs; they are there.
4 villagers and 1 smallholder.
Meadow for 1½ ploughs.
The value is and always was 20s.
4 Freemen held this land; 3 of them were free; the fourth had 1 hide but could neither grant nor sell.

M̄ In Chernetone ten̄ Hugo . vi . hiđ 7 dim̄ 7 ii . part . i . uirg
Tra . ē . viii . car̄ . In dn̄io . ii . hiđ 7 dim̄ . 7 i . car̄ est ibi.
7 xii . uilli hn̄t . vii . car̄ . Ibi . vi . borđ . P̄tū . iii . car̄ . Silua ⌐ c . xx . porc.
✻ Ibi . ē parch̄ ferarū siluatic̄ . Int totū ual . c . sol.
Q̄do recep̄ . xl . sol . T.R.E. c . sol
213 a
7 i . molin̄ . xl . sol . 7 c . anguill . Int totū ual . vi . liƀ.
Q̄do recep̄ . c . sol . T.R.E. vi . liƀ . Hoc M̄ . xiii . sochi
tenuer̄ . 7 quó uoluer̄ cū tra sua recedere potuer̄.

M̄ Ipse Hugo ten̄ WELITONE . p̄ x . hiđ se defđ . Tra
est . ix . car̄ . In dn̄io . v . hide . 7 ibi sunt . iii . car̄.
7 iiii . potest fieri . 7 xiii . uilli hn̄t . v . car̄ . Ibi . viii.
serui . 7 i . molin̄ . xii . solid 7 c . anguill . P̄tū . v . car̄.
Silua . xl . porc . In totis ualent ual . vii . liƀ.
Q̄do recep̄ . xl . sol . T.R.E. vi . liƀ . Hoc M̄ tenuit
Aschil teign regis . E . 7 ibi fuer̄ . viii . sochi . q̄ cū tra
sua quo uoluer̄ recede potuer̄ . De hac tra . vii . hiđ.

M̄ Ipse Hugo ten̄ STOTFALT . IN GLIFTON HVND . ⌐ habuer̄.
p̄ xv . hiđ se defđ . Tra . ē . xv . car̄ . In dn̄io . v . hidæ.
7 ibi sunt . iii . car̄ . 7 xxi . uilli hn̄t . xii . car̄ . Ibi xiiii.
borđ 7 vi . serui . 7 iiii . molini de . iiii . liƀ . 7 cccc . anguill.
p̄tū . vii . car̄ . In totis ualent ual . xxv . liƀ . Q̄do re
cep̄ . xii . liƀ . T.R.E. xx . liƀ . Die quá Rad tallebosc
obijt . p̄ xxx . liƀ erat ad firmā . Hoc M̄ tenuit Aschil
teign regis . E . Ipse habuit . ix . hiđ 7 dim̄ . 7 vii . sochi
reliquā trā tenuer̄ . 7 cui uoluer̄ uendere potuer̄.
De hac tra p̄tin . i . hida ad æcclam S̄ Albani . 7 ut hōes
de hund dūt ibi jacuit . T.R.E. ⌐IN RATBORGESTOV HĐ.
In Meldone ten̄ Hugo dim̄ hiđ 7 dim̄ uirg . Tra . ē
. i . car̄ . 7 ibi est . 7 un uills 7 i . borđ . p̄tū . i . car̄ . Silua
xx . porc . Val x . sol . Q̄do recep̄ . v . sol . T.R.E. xii.
sol . Hanc trā tenuit Goduin hō Aschil . 7 dare 7 uende potuit.

10 M. In CARDINGTON Hugh holds 6½ hides and 2 parts of 1 virgate.
Land for 8 ploughs. In lordship 2½ hides; 1 plough there.
12 villagers have 7 ploughs. 6 smallholders.
Meadow for 3 ploughs; woodland. 120 pigs;

(23,4 Words omitted, directed to their proper place by transposition signs)

† A park for woodland beasts.
In total, value 100s; when acquired 40s; before 1066, 100s.

(23,10 continued)

1 mill, 40s and 100 eels. 213 a
In total, value £6; when acquired 100s; before 1066 £6.
13 Freemen held this manor; they could withdraw where
they would with their land.

11 M. Hugh holds WILLINGTON himself. It answers for 10 hides.
Land for 9 ploughs. In lordship 5 hides; 3 ploughs there.
a fourth possible.
13 villagers have 5 ploughs. 8 slaves.
1 mill, 12s and 100 eels; meadow for 5 ploughs;
woodland 40 pigs.
Total value £7; when acquired 40s; before 1066 £6.
Askell, a thane of King Edward's, held this manor.
8 Freemen were there; they could withdraw with their land
where they would; they had 7 hides of this land.

In CLIFTON Hundred
12 M. Hugh holds STOTFOLD himself. It answers for 15 hides.
Land for 15 ploughs. In lordship 5 hides; 3 ploughs there.
21 villagers have 12 ploughs. 14 smallholders and 6 slaves.
4 mills at £4 and 400 eels; meadow for 7 ploughs.
Total value £25; when acquired £12; before 1066 £20. On the
day that Ralph Tallboys died it was at a revenue for £30.
Askell, a thane of King Edward's, held this manor. He
had 9½ hides himself. 7 Freemen held the rest of the land;
they could sell to whom they would. 1 hide of this land
belongs to St. Alban's Church; as the men of the Hundred
state, it lay there before 1066.

In REDBORNSTOKE Hundred
13 In MAULDEN Hugh holds ½ hide and ½ virgate.
Land for 1 plough; it is there.
1 villager and 1 smallholder.
Meadow for 1 plough; woodland, 20 pigs.
Value 10s; when acquired 5s; before 1066, 12s.
Godwin, Askell's man, held this land; he could grant and sell.

Ⓜ In *Hovstone*. teñ Hugo. v. hiđ. Tra.ē.vi.caŕ. 7 ibi
ſunt. 7 viii. uilti 7 vi. borđ 7 ii. ſerui. Ptū.vi.caŕ.
Silua. cc. porc. Val 7 ualuit. c. ſol. T.R.E. vii. liƀ.
Hoc Ⓜ. vii. ſocħi tenueŕ. 7 cui uolueŕ dare potueŕ.

Ⓜ Ipſe Hugo teñ *Hagenes*. p. v. hiđ *In Flictha̅ Hvnđ*.
ſe defđ. Tra.ē.viii.car. In dñio. ii. hidæ 7 dimiđ. 7 ibi
ſunt. iii. caŕ. 7 xiiii. uilti h̅nt. v. car. Ibi. ix. borđ. 7 i.
ſeruus. p̊tū. i. caŕ. Silua q̅ngent porc. In totis ualent
ual. x. liƀ. Q̅do recep̅. vii. liƀ. 7 tñtđ. T.R.E. Hoc Ⓜ
tenuit Achi teigñ regis. E. *In Bereforde Hvnđ*.

Ⓜ Ipſe Hugo teñ *Salchov*. p v. hiđ ſe defđ. Tra.ē.viii.
caŕ. 7 ibi ſunt. Hanc tra̅ tenex̅ xi. ſocħi. 7 idem ipſi
tenueŕ. T.R.E. 7 cui uolueŕ dare 7 uendere potueŕ.
p̊tū. ii. caŕ. Silua. l. porc. Int totū ual. c. ſol. 7 tñtđ
q̅do recep̅. T.R.E. viii. liƀ. Hanc tra̅ habuit Rađ
tallgeboſc p excãbio de Wares ut d̅nt hões ej. 7 q̅do
recep̅. viii. liƀ ualebat. *In Manesheve Hvnđ*.

Ⓜ *Aspeleia* p x. hiđ ſe defđ. Acard de iuri teñ de
Hugone. Terra.ē. xii. car. In dñio. ii. caŕ. 7 tcia
poteſt fieri. 7 xvi. uilti h̅nt. viii. caŕ. 7 nona poteſt
fieri. Ibi. iiii. borđ 7 v. ſerui. 7 i. moliñ. x. ſolidoᵹ.
P̊tū. x. caŕ. Silua. l. porc. In totis ualent ual
viii. liƀ. Q̅do recep̅. c. ſol. T.R.E. x. liƀ. Hoc Ⓜ tenuit
Leueua co̅mdata Wallef comitis. 7 quo uoluit
cū terra ſua recedere potuit.

Ⓜ *Saleford* p. v. hiđ ſe defđ. Tra.ē. v. caŕ. In dñio
ē. i. caŕ. 7 xii. uilti h̅nt. iiii. caŕ. Ibi. i. borđ. 7 iiii. Ꝟ ſerui.

Ibi. i. moliñ. ix. ſol. 7 iiii. den. P̊tū. v. caŕ. Silua. cl.
porc. 7 de alia c̅ſuetudine. x. ſol. In totis ualent ual
iiii. liƀ. Q̅do recep̅. lx. ſol. T.R.E. c. ſol. Hoc Ⓜ
tenuit Turchil teigñ. R.E. 7 cui uoluit dare potuit.

4 M. In HOUGHTON (Conquest) Hugh holds 5 hides. Land for 6
     ploughs; they are there.
          8 villagers, 6 smallholders and 2 slaves.
          Meadow for 6 ploughs; woodland, 200 pigs.
     The value is and was 100s; before 1066 £7.
          7 Freemen held this manor; they could grant to whom they
     would.

   In FLITT Hundred
5 M. Hugh holds HAYNES himself. It answers for 5 hides.
     Land for 8 ploughs. In lordship 2½ hides; 3 ploughs there.
          14 villagers have 5 ploughs. 9 smallholders and 1 slave.
          Meadow for 1 plough; woodland, 500 pigs.
     Total value £10; when acquired £7; as much before 1066.
          Aki (Askell?), a thane of King Edward's, held this manor.

   In BARFORD Hundred
6 M. Hugh holds SALPH himself. It answers for 5 hides.
     Land for 8 ploughs; they are there.
          11 Freemen hold this land; they also held it before 1066;
     they could grant and sell to whom they would.
          Meadow for 2 ploughs; woodland, 50 pigs.
     In total value 100s; as much when acquired; before 1066 £8.
          Ralph Tallboys had this land in exchange for Ware, as his
     men state; when he acquired it the value was £8.

   In MANSHEAD Hundred
7 M. ASPLEY (Guise) answers for 10 hides. Acard of Ivry holds from
     Hugh. Land for 12 ploughs. In lordship 2 ploughs; a third possible.
          16 villagers have 8 ploughs; a ninth possible.
           4 smallholders and 5 slaves.
          1 mill, 10s; meadow for 10 ploughs; woodland, 50 pigs.
     Total value, £8; when acquired 100s; before 1066 £10.
          Leofeva, commended to Earl Waltheof, held this manor; she
     could withdraw where she would with her land.

8 M. SALFORD answers for 5 hides. Land for 5 ploughs.
     In lordship 1 plough.
          12 villagers have 4 ploughs. 1 smallholder and 4 slaves.
          1 mill, 9s 4d; meadow for 5 ploughs; woodland 150 pigs;   213 b
          from other customary dues 10s.
     Total value £4; when acquired 60s; before 1066, 100s.
          Thorkell, a thane of King Edward's, held this manor; he
     could grant to whom he would.

Ⓜ In Eureſhot ten Radulf⁹ vii . hid 7 dim de Hugone.
p̱ uno Ⓜ.Tra̅.e̅.viii.car̅.In dn̅io.ii.car̅.7 xv.uiłłi
hn̅t.vi.car̅.Ibi.iiii.ſerui.P̊tu̅.viii.car̅.Silua.c.
porc̓.Vał.c.ſoł.Q̸do recep̓.iii.lib̅.7 tn̅td T.R.E.
Hoc Ⓜ tenuit Turgis teign⁹.R.E.7 uende̓ potuit.

Ⓜ In Middeltone ten Wiłłs froiſſart de Hugone
vi.hid.p̱ uno Ⓜ.Tra̅.e̅.vi.car̅.In dn̅io.iii.car̅.
7 vi.uiłłi hn̅t.iii.car̅.Ibi.iii.bord.7 iiii.ſerui.P̊tu̅
vi.car̅.Silua.xl.porc̓.Vał.vi.lib̅.Q̸do recep̓
iiii.lib̅.T.R.E.̓viii.lib̅.Hoc Ⓜ tenuit Auti huſcarle
comitis Algari.7 qd uoluit inde facere potuit.

Ⓜ Idem Wiłłs ten de Hugone Crauenheſt.p̱.iii.hid
7 dim ſe defd.Tra̅.e̅.iiii.car̅.In dn̅io.ii.car̅.7 iiii.
uiłłi hn̅t.i.car̅.7 alia poteſt fieri.Ibi.iii.bord.
7 iiii.ſerui.P̊tu̅.iiii.car̅.Silua.c.porc̓.Vał.lx.ſoł.
7 tn̅td qdo recep̓.T.R.E.̓c.ſoł.Hoc Ⓜ tenuer̓
v.ſochi.7 cui uoluer̓ tr̅a ſu̅a dare 7 uende̓ potuer̓.

Ⓜ In Straillei ten Wiłłs de Locels.iiii.hid 7 i.uirg̓
de Hugone.p̱ uno Ⓜ.Tra̅.e̅.vi.car̅.In dn̅io.i.car̅.
7 alia poteſt fieri.7 vii.uiłłi hn̅t.iiii.car̅.Ibi.v.bord.
7 un⁹ ſeruus.Silua.xvi.porc̓.Vał.iiii.lib̅.Q̸do
recep̓.̓xl.ſoł.T.R.E.̓c.ſoł.Hoc Ⓜ tenuit Aſchil
teign⁹.R.E.7 ibi fuer̓.i.ſochs h̅o ej⁹.hn̅s.i.̊hid.7 cui
uoluit dare potuit.

Ⓜ Idem Wiłłs ten Ech̅a de Hugone.p̱.viiᵗᵒ.hid ſe defd.
Tra̅.e̅.xi.car̅.In dn̅io.iiii.car̅.7 xiiii.uiłłi hn̅t
vii.car̅.Ibi.ii.bord.7 v.ſerui.P̊tu̅.vi.car̅.Silua
.c.porc̓.Vał.viii.lib̅.7 tn̅td qdo recep̓.T.R.E.̓xii.lib̅.
Hoc Ⓜ tenuer̓.v.ſochi.7 cui uoluer̓ tr̅a ſu̅a dare potuer̓.

In Eſtone ten̓ Wimund⁹ de Hugone dim hid.Tra̅.e̅.iii. *IN STODDEN*
car̅.7 ibi ſunt.Ibi.ii.uiłłi 7 vi.bord.Silua.xl.porc̓. *HVND.*

19 M. In **EVERSHOLT** Ralph holds 7½ hides from Hugh as one manor.
Land for 8 ploughs. In lordship 2 ploughs.
  15 villagers have 6 ploughs. 4 slaves.
  Meadow for 8 ploughs; woodland, 100 pigs.
Value 100s; when acquired £3; as much before 1066.
  Thorgils, a thane of King Edward's, held this manor; he could sell.

20 M. In **MILTON** (Bryan) William Froissart holds 6 hides from Hugh as
one manor. Land for 6 ploughs. In lordship 3 ploughs.
  6 villagers have 3 ploughs. 3 smallholders and 4 slaves.
  Meadow for 6 ploughs; woodland, 40 pigs.
Value £6; when acquired £4; before 1066 £8.
  Auti, one of Earl Algar's Guards, held this manor; he could do
what he would with it.

[In FLITT Hundred]

21 M. William also holds **GRAVENHURST** from Hugh. It answers for 3½ hides.
Land for 4 ploughs. In lordship 2 ploughs.
  4 villagers have 1 plough; another possible.
    3 smallholders and 4 slaves.
  Meadow for 4 ploughs; woodland, 100 pigs.
Value 60s; as much when acquired; before 1066, 100s.
  5 Freemen held this manor; they could grant and sell their land
to whom they would.

22 M. In **STREATLEY** William of Loucelles holds 4 hides and 1 virgate from
Hugh as one manor. Land for 6 ploughs. In lordship 1 plough;
another possible.
  7 villagers have 4 ploughs. 5 smallholders and 1 slave.
  Woodland, 16 pigs.
Value £4; when acquired 40s; before 1066, 100s.
  Askell, a thane of King Edward's, held this manor; there was 1
Freeman, his man, who had 1 hide; he could grant to whom he would.

23 M. William also holds **HIGHAM** (Gobion) from Hugh. It answers for 8
hides. Land for 11 ploughs. In lordship 4 ploughs.
  14 villagers have 7 ploughs. 2 smallholders and 5 slaves.
  Meadow for 6 ploughs; woodland, 100 pigs.
Value £8; as much when acquired; before 1066 £12.
  5 Freemen held this manor; they could grant their land to whom
they would.

In STODDEN Hundred

24 In **EASTON** Wimund holds ½ hide from Hugh.
Land for 3 ploughs; they are there.
  2 villagers; 6 smallholders.
  Woodland, 40 pigs.

Val.xxx.fol.Qdo recep.7 T.R.E.´xx.fol.Hanc tram
tenuit Ouiet hõ Afchil.7 dare 7 uende potuit.fʒ foca
fẽp jacuit in Culmeuuorde M̃ Afchil.

In Rifelai teñ Aluric dim hid de Hugone.Tra.ẽ dim
car̃.7 ibi.ẽ.7 IIII.bord.Val.v.fol.Qdo recep.´fimil.
T.R.E.´VIII.fol.Hanc trã tenuit Vuenot hõ Godrici
uicec.7 potuit dare cui uoluit.

In Middeltone teñ Wilts baffet de Hugone.II.hid.
dim uirg min.Tra.ẽ.III.car̃.In dñio.II.car̃.7 uñ uilts
ht.I.car̃.Ibi.IIII.bord.7 II.ferui.ptũ.II.car̃.Silua
VI.porc̃.Val.xxx.fol.7 tntd qdo recep.T.R.E.´xL.fol.

M̃ In Blechefhou teñ Osbt IN DIMID HD DE BOCHELAI.
de broilg.II.hid 7 dim de Hugone.Tra.ẽ.IIII.car̃.
In dñio.I.car̃.7 VII.uilti hñt.III.car̃.Ibi.II.bord.
7 II.ferui.7 dim molin.x.folid.Ptũ.I.car̃.Silua.c.
porc̃.Val 7 ual fẽp.Lx.fol.Hoc M̃ tenuit Afchil.

213 c

7 III.fochi habuer̃ ibi.III.uirg.7 cui uoluer̃ uende pot.
In Bidehã teñ Serlo de ros.I.hid de hugone.Tra
ẽ.I.car̃.7 ibi eft.7 uñ bord 7 I.feru.ptũ.I.car̃.Val
7 ualuit fẽp.x.fol.Hanc trã tenuit Alfi de Brunehã.
hõ Eddid regine.7 cui uoluit dare potuit.

M̃ In BRVNELLA.teñ Serlo de ros.VI.hid de hugone.
Tra.ẽ.VI.car̃.In dñio.II.car̃.7 xVI.uilti hñt.IIII.car̃.
Ibi.v.bord 7 VI.ferui.7 I.molin.xx.folid.7 cxxv.an
guilt.Ptũ.VI.car̃.Silua.xL.porc̃.Int totũ ualet
VII.lib.Qdo recep.´c.fol.T.R.E.´IIII.lib.Hanc tram
tenuit Alfi hõ regine Eddid.7 uende potuit. IN WILGA
In Toruei teñ Warneri.I.hid de hugone. ⌈HVND.
Tra.ẽ.II.car̃.In dñio.I.car̃.7 uñ uilts.I.car̃.Ibi.IIII.
bord.Val.x.fol.7 tntd qdo recep.T.R.E.´xx.folid.
Hanc trã.II.fochi tenuer̃.7 cui uoluer̃ dare potuer̃.

213 b, c

Value 30s; when acquired and before 1066, 20s.

Wulfgeat, Askell's man, held this land; he could grant and sell; but the jurisdiction always lay in Colmworth, Askell's manor.

25   In RISELEY Alric the priest holds ½ hide from Hugh.

Land for ½ plough; it is there.

4 smallholders.

Value 5s; when acquired the same; before 1066, 8s.

Wulfnoth, Godric the Sheriff's man, held this land; he could grant to whom he would.

26   In MILTON (Ernest) William Basset holds 2 hides less ½ virgate from Hugh. Land for 3 ploughs. In lordship 2 ploughs.

1 villager has 1 plough. 4 smallholders and 2 slaves.

Meadow for 2 ploughs; woodland, 6 pigs.

Value 30s; as much when acquired; before 1066, 40s.

In the Half-Hundred of BUCKLOW

27   M.   In BLETSOE Osbert of Breuil holds 2½ hides from Hugh.

Land for 4 ploughs. In lordship 1 plough.

7 villagers have 3 ploughs. 2 smallholders and 2 slaves.

½ mill, 10s; meadow for 1 plough; woodland, 100 pigs.

The value is and always was 60s.

Askell held this manor.

3 Freemen had 3 virgates; they could sell to whom they would.   213 c

28   In BIDDENHAM Serlo of Rots holds 1 hide from Hugh.

Land for 1 plough; it is there.

1 smallholder and 1 slave.

Meadow for 1 plough.

The value is and always was 10s.

Alfsi of Bromham, Queen Edith's man, held this land; he could grant to whom he would.

29   M.   In BROMHAM Serlo of Rots holds 6 hides from Hugh. Land for 6 ploughs. In lordship 2 ploughs.

16 villagers have 4 ploughs. 5 smallholders and 6 slaves.

1 mill, 20s and 125 eels; meadow for 6 ploughs; woodland, 40 pigs.

In total, value £7; when acquired 100s; before 1066 £4.

Alfsi, Queen Edith's man, held this land; he could sell.

In WILLEY Hundred

30   In TURVEY Warner holds 1 hide from Hugh. Land for 2 ploughs.

In lordship 1 plough.

1 villager, 1 plough. 4 smallholders.

Value 10s; as much when acquired; before 1066, 20s.

2 Freemen held this land; they could grant to whom they would.

In Sernebroc ten̄ Osb̄n de Broilg . i . uirg 7 dim̄ de
hugone . Tra . ē . iii . bou̅ . Val 7 ualuit sēp . ii . sol . Hanc
tra̅ tenuer̄ . iii . sochi . 7 dare 7 uende potuer̄.

In Lalega ten̄ Leuiet dim̄ hid . Tra . ē . ii . car̄ . 7 ibi suṇ̄.
Ibi . iiii . bord̄ . 7 i . seru . Silua . xxx . porc̄ . Val . xxx . sol.
Q̧do recep̄ :́ xv . sol . T . R . E .́ xxx . sol . Hanc tra̅ tenuit
Moding . hō reginæ Eddid . 7 uende potuit . *IN BEREFORD*

In Wiboldestone ten̄ Wimund dim̄ uirḡ .   *Ϝ HVND.*
de Hugone . 7 ual 7 ualuit sēp . ii . sol . Hanc tra̅ tenuit
Aschil teign̄ . R . E.

In Calnestorne ten̄ Riuualo : iiii . uirḡ de hugone.
Tra . ē . ii°̄ . bou̅ . Ibi . ii . bord̄ . 7 p̄tu . ii . bou̅ . Silua . Lx ͘. porc̄.
Val . x . sol . Q̧do recep̄ :́ xv . sol . T . R . E .́ xx . sol . Hanc tra̅
ii . sochi tenuer̄ . 7 cui uoluer̄ dare potuer̄.

In Rochestone . ten̄ Rualon . i . hid̄ 7 i . virḡ . de hugone.
Tra . ē . i . car̄ . P̄tu . i . car̄ . Silua . iiii . porc̄ . Ibi . ii . bord̄.
7 i . seruus . Val x . sol . Q̧do recep̄ :́ 7 T . R . E .́ xx . sol.
Hanc tra̅ . iiii͡ or . sochi tenuer̄ . hōes . R . E . 7 uende potuer̄.

In Bereforde ten̄ Rualon de Hugone . iii . car̄ . Tra . ē
iiii . car̄ . In dn̄io . iii . car̄ . 7 iii . uilli hn̄t . i . car̄ . Ibi . v . bord̄.
7 iii . serui . 7 i . molin̄ . xxii . solid̄ . 7 q̄t xx . Anguill . P̄tu.
ii . car̄ . Val . iii . lib̄ . Q̧do recep̄ :́ xxx . sol . T . R . E .́ iii . lib̄.
Hanc tra̅ tenuer̄ . iii . sochi hōes regis . E . 7 uende potuer̄.

In ead̄ ten̄ Wimund de Taissel de Hugone . v . hidas
7 ii . part . uni hidæ . Tra . ē . xi . car̄ . In dn̄io . v . car̄ . 7 xvi.
uilli . hn̄t . vi . car̄ . Ibi . vi . bord̄ . 7 i . seruus . P̄tu . i . car̄.
Val . x . lib̄ . Q̧do recep̄ :́ xx . sol . T . R . E .́ Lx . sol . Hoc m̄
. iii . sochi tenuer̄ . 7 dare 7 uende potuer̄.

31 In SHARNBROOK Osbert of Breuil holds 1½ virgates from Hugh.
Land for 3 oxen.
The value is and always was 2s.
3 Freemen held this land; they could grant and sell.

32 In THURLEIGH Leofgeat holds ½ hide. Land for 2 ploughs; they are there.
4 smallholders and 1 slave.
Woodland, 30 pigs.
Value 30s; when acquired 15s; before 1066, 30s.
Moding, Queen Edith's man, held this land; he could sell.

In BARFORD Hundred
33 In WYBOSTON Wimund holds ½ virgate from Hugh.
The value is and always was 2s.
Askell, a thane of King Edward's, held this land.

34 In CHAWSTON Rhiwallon holds 4 virgates from Hugh. Land for 2 oxen.
2 smallholders.
Meadow for 2 oxen; woodland, 60 pigs.
Value 10s; when acquired 15s; before 1066, 20s.
2 Freemen held this land; they could grant to whom they would.

35 In ROXTON Rhiwallon holds 1 hide and 1 virgate from Hugh.
Land for 1 plough.
Meadow for 1 plough; woodland, 4 pigs.
2 smallholders and 1 slave.
Value 10s; when acquired and before 1066, 20s.
4 Freemen, King Edward's men, held this land; they could sell.

36 In (Great) BARFORD Rhiwallon holds 3 hides from Hugh. Land
for 4 ploughs. In lordship 3 ploughs.
3 villagers have 1 plough. 5 smallholders and 3 slaves.
1 mill, 22s and 80 eels; meadow for 2 ploughs.
Value £3; when acquired 30s; before 1066 £3.
3 Freemen, King Edward's men, held this land; they could sell.

37 In the same (village) Wimund of Tessel holds 5 hides and 2 parts
of 1 hide from Hugh. Land for 11 ploughs. In lordship 5 ploughs.
16 villagers have 6 ploughs. 6 smallholders and 1 slave.
Meadow for 1 plough.
Value £10; when acquired 20s; before 1066, 60s.
3 Freemen held this manor; they could grant and sell.

ⳍ Ipſe Wimund ten̄ COLMEWORDE. de hugone. ꝑ v. hiđ
ſe defđ. Tra. ē. x. car̄. In dn̄io. ii. car̄. 7 xii. uilli hn̄t. viii.
car̄. Ibi. xiii. borđ. 7 i. ſeruus. Silua. cc. porc̄. Val 7 ualuit
c. ſol. T.R.E. iiii. liƀ. Hoc ⳍ ten̄ Achi teign̄. R.E. 7 ibi. viii.
ſochi fuer̄. q̄ dare 7 uende tr̄a ſuā potuer̄ cui uoluer̄.

In Bereforde ten̄ Anſchetil pƀr. i. hiđ 7 dim de Hugone.
Tra. ē. ii. car̄. In dn̄io. i. car̄. 7 un uills. i. car̄. Ibi. vi. borđ
7 iii. ſerui. 7 i. mol. vii. ſol. p̄tū. i. car̄. Val 7 ualuit ſēp.
xl. ſol. Hanc tr̄a. ii. ſochi tenuer̄. 7 uende potuer̄.

In eađ ten̄ Tetbaud de Hugone. i. hiđ 7 iii. uirg 7 tcia
part uni uirg. Tra. ē. iii. car̄. In dn̄io. ii. 7 un uills h̄t. i.
car̄. Ibi. viii. borđ. 7 i. ſeruus. p̄tū. i. car̄. Val. xl. ſol.

213 d

Q̄do recep̄. xx. ſol. T.R.E. lx. ſol. Hoc ⳍ. iii. ſochi te
nuer̄. 7 dare 7 uende potuer̄.

In Goldentone ten̄ Roger fili Teodrici. ii. hiđ. de hugone.
Tra. ē. iii. car̄. In dn̄io. ii. car̄. 7 iii uilti hn̄t. i. car̄.
Ibi. ii. borđ. p̄tū. i. car̄. Val xxx. ſol. Q̄do recep̄.
xx. ſol. T.R.E. xl. ſol. Has. ii. hiđ tenuit Radulf talƀ
ꝑ excābio de Wares. Hanc tr̄a tenuer̄. iii. ſochi. q̄ dare
potuer̄ tr̄a ſua cui uoluer̄.

In eađ ten̄ Ricard. iii. hiđ de Hugone. ꝑ uno ⳍ. Tra. ē
iii. car̄. In dn̄io. ii. car̄. 7 v. uilti hn̄t. i. car̄. Ibi un ſeru
P̄tū. ii. car̄. Val xl. ſol. Q̄do recep̄. x. ſol. T.R.E. lx. ſol.
Has. iii. hiđ tenuit Rad tallgeboſc ꝑ excābio de Wares.
Hoc ⳍ tenuit Almær hō Aſchil. 7 uende potuit.

In eađ ten̄ Walter. i. hiđ de Hugone. Tra. ē. i. car̄.
7 ibi. ē. P̄tū dim car̄. 7 ibi. ii. ſerui. Val. xv. ſol. Q̄do
recep̄. x. ſol. T.R.E. xv. ſol. H̄ tra. ē eſcābiū de Wares.
Hanc tr̄a tenuer̄ hōes uillæ cōmunit. 7 uende potuer̄.

38 M. Wimund holds COLMWORTH himself from Hugh. It answers for
5 hides. Land for 10 ploughs. In lordship 2 ploughs.
12 villagers have 8 ploughs. 13 smallholders and 1 slave.
Woodland, 200 pigs.
The value is and was 100s; before 1066 £4.
Aki (Askell?), a thane of King Edward's, held this manor.
8 Freemen were there; they could grant and sell their land
to whom they would.

39 In (Great) BARFORD Ansketel the priest holds 1½ hides from Hugh.
Land for 2 ploughs. In lordship 1 plough.
1 villager (has) 1 plough. 6 smallholders and 3 slaves.
1 mill, 7s; meadow for 1 plough.
The value is and always was 40s.
2 Freemen held this land; they could sell.

40 In the same (village) Theodbald holds 1 hide, 3 virgates and the third
part of 1 virgate from Hugh. Land for 3 ploughs. In lordship 2.
1 villager has 1 plough. 8 smallholders and 1 slave.
Meadow for 1 plough.
Value 40s; when acquired 20s; before 1066, 60s.   213 d
3 Freemen held this manor; they could grant and sell

41 In GOLDINGTON Roger son of Theodoric holds 2 hides from Hugh.
Land for 3 ploughs. In lordship 2 ploughs.
3 villagers have 1 plough. 2 smallholders.
Meadow for 1 plough.
Value 30s; when acquired 20s; before 1066, 40s.
Ralph Tallboys held these 2 hides in exchange for Ware. 3
Freemen held this land; they could grant their land to whom they
would.

42 In the same (village) Richard holds 3 hides from Hugh as one manor.
Land for 3 ploughs. In lordship 2 ploughs.
5 villagers have 1 plough. 1 slave.
Meadow for 2 ploughs.
Value 40s; when acquired 10s; before 1066, 60s.
Ralph Tallboys held these 3 hides in exchange for Ware.
Aelmer, Askell's man, held this manor; he could sell.

43 In the same (village) Walter holds 1 hide from Hugh.
Land for 1 plough; it is there.
Meadow for ½ plough.
2 slaves.
Value 15s; when acquired 10s; before 1066, 15s.
This land is in exchange for Ware. The men of the village held
this land in common; they could sell.

In Holma teñ Mortuiñg *In Bicheleswade hvnd.*
de Hugone. i. uirg. Tra. iii. bob. 7 ibi funt. Val. iii. fol.
T.R.E. v. fol. Hanc trā tenuit. i. fochs fub Afchillo.
7 uende 7 dare potuit.

In Eftuuiche teñ Bernard de Hug. i. hid 7 i. uirg.
Tra. ē. ii. car 7 dim. In dñio. i. car. 7 ii. uitti hñt. ii.
car 7 dim. Ibi. iii. borđ. 7 ptū. iiii. boū. Val xx. fol.
Qdo recep. 7 T.R.E. x. fol. Hoc ᴍ tenueῗ. vi. fochi.
7 uende potueῗ.

In eađ teñ Wenelinc dim hid de Hugone. Tra. ē. i. car.
7 ibi. ē. Ibi. iii. borđ. Val. x. fol. Qdo recep. v. fol. T.R.E.
xx. fol. 7 uende potueῗ.

In eađ teñ Ledmar dim hid. Tra. ē dim car. 7 ibi eft.
Ibi. iii. borđ. 7 i. moliñ de. ix. fol. 7 iiii. deñ. Val 7 ualuit
fēp xx. fol. Ifdem q̇ teñ tenuit T.R.E. hō comitis Tofti.
7 cui uoluit uende potuit. *In Wichestanestov hvnd.*

In Stanforde teñ Roger de Hugone. i. hid. Tra. ē
. i. car. 7 dim. 7 ibi funt. 7 iiii. uitti 7 i. borđ. Ptū. i. car
7 dim. Silua. xvi. porc. 7 dim moliñ de. v. fol. Int
totū ual. xv. fol. Qdo recep. v. fol. T.R.E. x. fol. Hanc
trā tenuit Æilmar de Ouu. 7 potuit uende cui uoluit.

In Cochepol teñ Robt de Hug. iiii. hid. p uno. ᴍ.
Tra. ē. iiii. car. In dñio. ii. car. 7 vi. uitti hñt. ii. car.
Ibi uñ borđ 7 uñ feru. ptū. i. car. Silua. ē fup totā
Chochepol. c. porc. Val. lx. fol. Qdo recep. xx. fol. T.R.E.
lx. fol. Hanc trā. iii. fochi tenueῗ. 7 uende potueῗ.

In eađ teñ Raynald de Hug. i. hid 7 i. uirg. Tra. ē. i. car.
7 ibi. ē. 7 ii. borđ. 7 ptū. iiii. bob. Val. x. fol. Qdo recep.
v. fol. T.R.E. x. fol. Hanc trā. ii. fochi tenueῗ. 7 cui
uolueῗ uende potueῗ.

In BIGGLESWADE Hundred

44 In HOLME Mordwing holds 1 virgate from Hugh. Land for 3 oxen; they are there.
Value 3s; before 1066, 5s.
1 Freeman held this land under Askell; he could sell and grant.

45 In ASTWICK Bernard holds 1 hide and 1 virgate from Hugh.
Land for 2½ ploughs. In lordship 1 plough.
2 villagers have 2½ ploughs. 3 smallholders.
Meadow for 4 oxen.
Value 20s; when acquired and before 1066, 10s.
6 Freemen held this manor; they could sell.

46 In the same (village) Weneling holds ½ hide from Hugh.
Land for 1 plough; it is there.
3 smallholders.
Value 10s; when acquired 5s; before 1066, 20s.
[...and...held it;] they could sell.

47 In the same (village) Ledmer holds ½ hide. Land for ½ plough; it is there.
3 smallholders.
1 mill at 9s 4d.
The value is and always was 20s.
The same holder, Earl Tosti's man, held it before 1066; he could sell to whom he would.

In WIXAMTREE Hundred

48 In STANFORD Roger holds 1 hide from Hugh. Land for 1½ ploughs; they are there.
4 villagers and 1 smallholder.
Meadow for 1½ ploughs; woodland, 16 pigs; ½ mill at 5s.
In total, value 15s; when acquired 5s; before 1066, 10s.
Aelmer of Hoo held this land; he could sell to whom he would.

49 In COPLE Robert holds 4 hides from Hugh as one manor.
Land for 4 ploughs. In lordship 2 ploughs.
6 villagers have 2 ploughs. 1 smallholder and 1 slave.
Meadow for 1 plough; woodland in the whole of Cople, 100 pigs.
Value 60s; when acquired 20s; before 1066, 60s.
3 Freemen held this land; they could sell.

In the same (village)
50 Reginald holds 1 hide and 1 virgate from Hugh. Land for 1 plough; it is there.
2 smallholders.
Meadow for 4 oxen.
Value 10s; when acquired 5s; before 1066, 10s.
2 Freemen held this land; they could sell to whom they would.

In ead ten Gonfrid .ı. hid 7 dim uirg de Hugone.
Tra.ē.ı.car.7 ibi eſt. Ibi un uilłs 7 un ſeru.p̃tu̅.ıɪıɪ.
bou̅. Vał. x. ſoł. Q̃do receṕ.v. ſoł.T.R.E.x. ſoł. Hanc
trã. ıı. ſochi tenuer̃. Hōes regis fuer̃.7 uende potuer̃.
In ead ten Norman.ı. hid de Hug.Tra.ē.ı.car.7 ıı.
boues ibi ſunt.Ptu̅.ıɪɪɪ.bou̅. Vał.vı. ſoł. Q̃do receṕ.
ſimilit̃.T.R.E.vıɪɪ. ſoł.De hac tra. ıɪɪ. uirg ten Aſchil

214 a

quiæ jacuer̃ in Weltone m̃ ej.7 Aleſtan tenuit.ı. uirg
qua̅ potuit uende cui uoluit.
In ead tenuit Brahting.ı. hid. de Hugone.Tra.ē.ı.car.
7 ibi.ē.Ptu̅.ıɪɪ.bob₂. Vał 7 ualuit ſēp. x. ſoł. Hanc
trã. ıɪɪ. ſochi tenuer̃.7 cui uoluer̃ uende potuer̃.
In ead ten Robt.ıɪɪ. uirg de hugone.Tra.ē.ı.car.
7 ibi.ē.p̃tu̅.ıɪɪɪ.bob. Vał 7 ualuit ſēp.vıɪ. ſoł 7 dim̃.
Hanc trã. ıı. ſochi tenuer̃.7 uende potuer̃.
In ead ten Rogeri 7 Liboret dim̃ hid 7 dim̃ uirg.
Tra.ē.vı.bob.7 ibi ſunt.p̃tu̅.ıɪɪɪ.bob₂. Vał 7 uał ſēp
v. ſoł. Hanc trã. ıɪɪ. ſochi tenuer̃.7 cui uoluer̃ uende
potuer̃.De hoc m̃ Chochepol.habuit Rad tallgeb
ıx. hid p excābio de Wares ut dn̅t hōes ej.7 q̃do eas
receṕ.ıɪɪɪ. lib ualuer̃.
In Nortgible ten Walter dim̃ hid de Hugone.Tra
ē dim̃ car.7 ibi.ē.Ptu̅ dim̃ car. Vał.v. ſoł.Q̃do re
cepit.ſimił.T.R.E.x. ſoł.Hanc trã tenuit Oſiet hō
R.E.7 cui uoluit uende potuit. IN CLISTONE HVND.
In Cudeſſane ten.ıɪɪ. ſochi de Hugone. ıı. hid. Tra.ē
.ı.car 7 dim̃.7 ibi ſunt.7 ı.bord.p̃tu̅.ı.car 7 dim̃.
Silua.ıɪɪɪ.porc. Vał.xx. ſoł.7 tntd q̃do receṕ.T.R.E.
xxx. ſoł.Hanc trã.ıɪɪɪ. ſochi tenuer̃.7 cui uoluer̃
uende potuer̃.

51 Gunfrid holds 1 hide and ½ virgate from Hugh. Land for 1 plough;
it is there.
  1 villager and 1 slave.
  Meadow for 4 oxen.
Value 10s; when acquired 5s; before 1066, 10s.
  2 Freemen held this land; they were the King's men; they could sell.

52 Norman holds 1 hide from Hugh. Land for 1 plough; 2 oxen there.
  Meadow for 4 oxen.
Value 6s; when acquired the same; before 1066, 8s.
  Askell held 3 virgates of this land which lay in (the lands of)   214 a
his manor, Willington. Alstan held 1 virgate which he could sell
to whom he would.

53 Branting held 1 hide from Hugh. Land for 1 plough; it is there.
  Meadow for 4 oxen.
The value is and always was 10s.
  3 Freemen held this land; they could sell to whom they would.

54 Robert holds 3 virgates from Hugh. Land for 1 plough; it is there.
  Meadow for 4 oxen.
The value is and always was 7½s.
  2 Freemen held this land; they could sell.

55 Roger the priest and Liboret hold ½ hide and ½ virgate.
  Land for 6 oxen; they are there.
  Meadow for 4 oxen.
The value is and always was 5s.
  3 Freemen held this land; they could sell to whom they would. Ralph
Tallboys had 9 hides of this manor of Cople in exchange for Ware as
his men say; when he acquired them the value was £4.

56 In NORTHILL Walter holds ½ hide from Hugh. Land for ½ plough;
it is there.
  Meadow for ½ plough.
Value 5s; when acquired the same; before 1066, 10s.
  Osgeat, King Edward's man, held this land; he could sell to
whom he would.

  In CLIFTON Hundred
57 In CUDESSANE 3 Freemen hold 2 hides from Hugh. Land for 1½ ploughs;
they are there.
  1 smallholder.
  Meadow for 1½ ploughs; woodland, 4 pigs.
Value 20s; as much when acquired; before 1066, 30s.
  4 Freemen held this land; they could sell to whom they would.

TERRA NIGELLI DE ALBINGI. *IN MANESHEVE HVND.*

In CRAWELAI teñ Turgifus de Nigello Albinienfi.

v.hiđ.p.i.man.Tra.ē.v.car.Iñ dñio.ii.car.7 iii.
car uilloꝫ poſs fieri.Ibi uñ uilłs 7 vii.borđ.7 i.feru.
p̄tu.v.car.Int totū ual.xxx.fol.Qdo recep̄.xl.fol.
T.R.E.c.fol.Hoc m̄ tenuer.ix.teigni.7 cui uoluer
tra fuā dare 7 uende potuer.

In eođ Hund teñ Turgis de Nigello.i.hiđ.Tra.ē.i.
car.7 ibi.ē.car.7 ii.ferui.Silua.x.porc.H̄ tra
ual.xv.fol.Qdo recep̄.x.fol.T.R.E.xx.fol.
Hanc trā tenuit Suglo hō Alrici filij Godingi.
7 cui uoluit uende potuit.

Tingrei teñ Turgis de Nigello.p.ii.hiđ 7 i.uirg.
Tra.ē.iii.car.In dñio.i.car.7 iiii.uilłi hñt.ii.car.
Ibi.ii.borđ.p̄tu.iii.car.Silua.c.l.porc.Valet
xl.fol.Qdo recep̄.xxx.fol.T.R.E.c.fol.Hoc m̄
ii.teigni tenuer.7 cui uoluer uende potuer.

In Preftelai teñ Turgis de Nigello.i.hiđ 7 dim.Tra
ē.ii.car.7 ibi fuꝗ.p̄tu.ii.car.Silua.xl.porc.Ibi
uñ uilłs 7 iiii.borđ.Val.xx.fol.7 tntđ qdo recep̄.
T.R.E.lx.fol.Hanc trā.v.teigni tenuer.7 dare
7 uende potuer.

Nigellvs teñ HERLINGDONE.p.v.hiđ fe defđ.
Tra.ē.x.car.In dñio.iii.car 7 dim.7 ii.adhuc poſs
fieri.Ibi.xii.uilłi hñt.v.car.Ibi.vi.borđ 7 x.ferui.
p̄tu.iiii.car.Silua.cccc.porc.7 i.aries.7 i.sūmā auenæ
de filua.Val.vi.lib.Qdo recep̄.iiii.lib.T.R.E.ix.lib.
Hoc m̄.iiii.teigni tenuer.7 cui uoluer uende potuer.

In Effeltone tenet Erfaftus *IN RATBORGESTOCHE HĐ.*
de Nigello.i.hiđ.Tra.ē.i.car.7 ibi.ē car.p̄tu dim car.
Silua.xl.porc.Ibi uñ uilłs.7 ii.borđ.7 i.feruus.Val.xx.fol.

In MANSHEAD Hundred

1   M. In (Husborne) CRAWLEY Thorgils holds 5 hides from
Nigel of Aubigny as one manor. Land for 5 ploughs.
In lordship 2 ploughs. 3 villagers' ploughs possible.
 1 villager, 7 smallholders and 1 slave.
Meadow for 5 ploughs.
In total value 30s; when acquired 40s; before 1066, 100s.
 9 thanes held this manor; they could grant and sell their land
to whom they would.

2   In the same Hundred Thorgils holds 1 hide from Nigel.
Land for 1 plough; the plough is there.
 2 slaves.
Woodland, 10 pigs.
Value of this land 15s; when acquired 10s; before 1066, 20s.
 Fuglo, Alric son of Goding's man, held this land; he could sell
to whom he would.

3   M. Thorgils holds TINGRITH from Nigel. (It answers) for 2 hides and 1
virgate. Land for 3 ploughs. In lordship 1 plough.
 4 villagers have 2 ploughs. 2 smallholders.
Meadow for 3 ploughs; woodland, 150 pigs.
Value 40s; when acquired 30s; before 1066, 100s.
 2 thanes held this manor; they could sell to whom they would.

4   In PRIESTLEY Thorgils holds 1½ hides from Nigel. Land for 2
ploughs; they are there.
Meadow for 2 ploughs; woodland, 40 pigs.
 1 villager and 4 smallholders.
Value 20s; as much when acquired; before 1066, 60s.
 5 thanes held this land; they could grant and sell.

5   M. Nigel holds HARLINGTON. It answers for 5 hides. Land for 10
ploughs. In lordship 3½ ploughs; a further 2 possible.
 12 villagers have 5 ploughs. 6 smallholders and 10 slaves.
Meadow for 4 ploughs; woodland, 400 pigs; 1 ram;
 a pack-load of oats from the woodland.
Value £6; when acquired £4; before 1066 £9.
 4 thanes held this manor; they could sell to whom they would.

In REDBORNSTOKE Hundred

6   In SHELTON Herfast holds 1 hide from Nigel. Land for 1 plough;
the plough is there.
Meadow for ½ plough; woodland, 40 pigs.
 1 villager; 2 smallholders and 1 slave.

Q̇do recep̄.ꞌxv.foł.T.R.E.ꞌxx.foł.Hanc t̃ra tenuit
Aluuard hō Alrici filij Godingi.7 cui uoluit dare potuit.
In eađ ten̄ Stefan de Nigello dim̄ hiđ.Tra.ē dim̄ car̄.
7 ibi.ē.cū.ıı.borđ.p̄tū.ıı.bob.Silua.xıı.porc̄.
Vał.vı.foł.Q̇do recep̄.ꞌıııı.foł.T.R.E.ꞌx.foł.Hanc t̃ra
ten Fuglo hō Alrici filij Godingi.7 uende potuit.cui uoluit.
Ⓜ In Merftone ten̄ Erfaft de Nigello.vııı.hiđ 7 dim̄ uirḡ.
Tra.ē.x.car̄.In dn̄io.ııı.car̄.7 xıııı.uiłłi cū.vııı.car̄.
Ibi.ıı.borđ.7 ıııı.ferui.p̄tū.vııı.car̄.Silua.ccc.porc̄.
Vał.vıı.lib̄.Q̇do recep̄.ꞌc.foł.T.R.E.ꞌxıı.lib̄.Hoc Ⓜ
xxı.fochi tenuer̄.q̇ uende 7 dare potuer̄ tras fuas cui
Ⓜ Nigellus de Waft ten̄ de Nigello albinienfi ⌐uoluer̄.
Melebroc.ꝑ v.hiđ fe defđ.Tra.ē.vı.car̄.In dn̄io.ıı.car̄.
7 ıııı.uiłłi cū.ıııı.car̄.Ibi.ıı.borđ.7 ıı.molini de.vı.foł.
P̄tū.ıı.car̄.Silua.c.porc̄.Vał.ıııı.lib̄.Q̇do recep̄.ꞌ
xxx.foł.T.R.E.ꞌc.foł.Hoc Ⓜ ten̄ Goduin fili Leuuini.
qui om̄s potuer̄ dare ł uende t̃ra fuā cui uoleruꝴ.
Ⓜ Ipfe Nigellus ten̄ de Nigello albn AMMETELLE.ꝑ.v.hiđ
fe defđ.Tra.ē.vııı.car̄.In dn̄io.ıı.car̄.7 vı.uiłłi hn̄t
ıııı.car̄.7 adhuc.ıı.car pois fieri.Ibi.ıı.borđ.7 ı.feruus.
p̄tū.vı.car̄.Silua.ccc.porc̄.Vał.ıııı.lib̄.Q̇do recep̄.ꞌ
xl.foł.T.R.E.ꞌ ıııı.lib̄.Hoc Ⓜ tenuer̄.vıı.fochi.7 cui
uoluer̄ t̃ra fuā uende 7 dare potuer̄.

Id.Ni.ten de Ni.BRVME.
ꝑ.v.hiđ fe defđ.Tra.ē.v.car̄.
7 tot if ibi cū.ıx.uiłłis 7 v.borđ
Silua.xxx.porc.Vał.xl.fol
Septē fochi tenuer̄.7 dare
7 uende potuer̄.

Value 20s; when acquired 15s; before 1066, 20s.

Alfward, Alric son of Goding's man, held this land; he could grant to whom he would.

7 In the same village Stephen holds ½ hide from Nigel.
Land for ½ plough; it is there, with
2 smallholders.
Meadow for 2 oxen; woodland, 12 pigs.
Value 6s; when acquired 3s; before 1066, 10s.
Fuglo, Alric son of Goding's man, held this land; he could sell to whom he would.

8 M. In MARSTON (Moretaine) Herfast holds 8 hides and ½ virgate from Nigel. Land for 10 ploughs. In lordship 3 ploughs;
14 villagers with 8 ploughs. 2 smallholders and 4 slaves.
Meadow for 8 ploughs; woodland, 300 pigs.
Value £7; when acquired 100s; before 1066, £12.
21 Freemen held this manor; they could sell and grant their lands to whom they would.

9 M. Nigel of Le Vast holds MILLBROOK from Nigel of Aubigny. It answers for 5 hides. Land for 6 ploughs. In lordship 2 ploughs;
4 villagers with 4 ploughs. 2 smallholders.
2 mills at 6s; meadow for 2 ploughs; woodland, 100 pigs.
Value £3; when acquired 30s; before 1066, 100s.
Godwin son of Leofwin held this manor; . . . they could all grant or sell their land to whom they would.

10 M. Nigel of Le Vast holds AMPTHILL himself from Nigel of Aubigny.
It answers for 5 hides. Land for 8 ploughs. In lordship 2 ploughs.
6 villagers have 4 ploughs; a further 2 ploughs possible.
2 smallholders and 1 slave.
Meadow for 6 ploughs; woodland, 300 pigs.
Value £4; when acquired 40s; before 1066 £4.
7 Freemen held this manor; they could sell and grant their land to whom they would.

[In WIXAMTREE Hundred]
11 Nigel also holds BROOM from Nigel. It answers for 5 hides. Land for 5 ploughs; as many there, with
9 villagers and 5 smallholders.
Woodland, 30 pigs.
Value 40s.
7 Freeman held it; they could grant and sell.

In Meldone Johes de Roches occupauit injuſte xxv . acs.
ſup hoēs qui uillā teneɳ . ut hoēs de hund atteſtant.

7 m̄ hȳ Nigellus de albinic

⊕ Nɪɢᴇʟʟ Albinienſis ten Weſcote . ꝑ . ɪɪɪ . hid una uirga min
ſe defd . Tra . ē . ᴠɪ . car . Ibi ſunt . ᴠ . 7 ᴠɪ . poteſt fieri . Ibi
v . uilli 7 xɪ . bord . P̃tū . ɪɪ . car . Silua . c . porc . 7 ferrū
car . Val . ʟx . ſol . Q̇do recep̃ xʟ . ſol . T.R. ᴠɪ . lib . Hoc ⊕
tenuer . ᴠɪɪ . ſochi . 7 cui uoluer trā ſuā dare 7 uende potuer.

⊕ Ipſe Nigell ten Clopelle . ꝑ . v . hid ɪɴ Fʟɪᴄᴛʜᴀ̄ ʜᴠɴᴅ.
ſe defd . Tra . ē . ᴠɪɪɪ . car . In dñio . ɪɪɪ . hidæ . 7 ibi ſuɳ . ɪɪ . car.
7 v . uilli hn̄t . ᴠɪ . car . Ibi . v . bord . 7 un ſeruus . p̃tū.
ɪɪɪɪ . car . Silua . cc . porc . 7 xɪɪ . den . Val . ʟx . ſol . Q̇do
recep̃ xxx . ſol . T.R.E. ᴠɪɪɪ . lib . Hoc ⊕ . ɪɪ . teigni tenuer.
Hoēs Toſti comitis . De his . v . hid clam Nigell ipſe . ɪ . uirg
q̇ tenuit Anteceſſor ej T.R.E . Ipſe Nigell inde ſaiſit fuit
poſtq̇ ad honorē uenit . ſed Radulf tallgeboſc eū deſaiſiuit.

⊕ Ipſe Nigell ten Chainehou . ꝑ ɪɪɪɪ . hid ſe defd . Tra . ē . ᴠɪ . car.
Ibi . ɪɪ . hidæ 7 ɪɪɪ . uirg in dñio . 7 ɪɪ . car . 7 aliæ . ɪɪ . poſ fieri.
Ibi . ɪɪɪ . uilli hn̄t . ɪɪ . car . 7 ɪ . molin de . ᴠɪ . ſol . p̃tū . ᴠɪɪɪ . car.
Silua . c . porc . 7 ɪɪ . ſol . Ibi . ɪɪɪ . bord . 7 v . ſerui . Val . ʟx . ſol.
Q̇do recep̃ xxx . ſol . T.R.E. c . ſol . Hoc ⊕ tenuit Aluric
teign . R.E . 7 potuit dare 7 uende abſq̇ licentia ejus.

⊕ In Siuuileſſou . ten quædā c̄cubinā Nigelli . ɪɪ . hid . Tra . ē
ɪɪɪɪ . car . In dñio . ɪ . car . 7 ɪɪ . uilli hn̄t . ɪɪ . car . 7 tcia poteſt fieri.
Ibi . ɪɪɪ . bord . 7 ɪ . ſeruus . p̃tū . ɪɪɪ . car . Silua . ʟ . porc . Valet
xxx . ſol . 7 tntd q̇do recep̃ . 7 tntd T.R.E . Hanc trā tenuit
Aluric paruus teign regis . E.

⊕ Roger 7 Ruallon ten Nigell de albin ten ᴘᴏʟᴏᴄʜᴇꜱꜱᴇʟᴇ.
ꝑ . x . hid ſe defd . Tra . ē . xɪɪɪ . car . In dñio . ɪɪ . car . 7 aliæ . ɪɪ.

[In REDBORNSTOKE Hundred]

2   In MAULDEN John of Les Roches appropriated 25 acres wrongfully
from the men who hold the village, as the men of the Hundred
testify. Now Nigel of Aubigny has them.

3   M. Nigel of Aubigny holds 'WESTCOTTS'. It answers for 3 hides
less 1 virgate. Land for 6 ploughs. 5 there; a sixth possible.
    5 villagers and 11 smallholders.
    Meadow for 2 ploughs; woodland, 100 pigs and plough iron.
    Value 60s; when acquired 40s; before 1066 £6.
    7 Freemen held this manor; they could grant and sell their land
to whom they would.

In FLITT Hundred

4   M. Nigel holds CLOPHILL himself. It answers for 5 hides. Land for 8
ploughs. In lordship 3 hides. 2 ploughs there.
    5 villagers have 6 ploughs. 5 smallholders and 1 slave.
    Meadow for 4 ploughs; woodland, 200 pigs and 12d.
    Value 60s; when acquired 30s; before 1066 £8.
    2 thanes held this manor; they were Earl Tosti's men.
Of these 5 hides, Nigel claims 1 virgate himself which his predecessor
held before 1066. Nigel was put in possession himself after he
came to the Honour, but Ralph Tallboys dispossessed him.

5   M. Nigel holds CAINHOE himself. It answers for 4 hides. Land for 6 ploughs.
    In lordship 2 hides and 3 virgates; 2 ploughs there; another 2 possible.
    3 villagers have 2 ploughs.
    1 mill at 6s; meadow for 8 ploughs; woodland, 100 pigs and 2s too.
    3 smallholders and 5 slaves.
    Value 60s; when acquired 30s; before 1066, 100s.
    Aelfric, a thane of King Edward's, held this manor; he could grant
and sell without his permission.

6   M. In SILSOE a concubine of Nigel's holds 2 hides.
    Land for 4 ploughs. In lordship 1 plough.
    2 villagers have 2 ploughs; a third possible. 3 smallholders
      and 1 slave.
    Meadow for 3 ploughs; woodland, 50 pigs.
    Value 30s; as much when acquired; as much before 1066.
    Aelfric Small, a thane of King Edward's, held this land.

7   M. Roger and Rhiwallon hold PULLOXHILL from Nigel of Aubigny.
    It answers for 10 hides. Land for 13 ploughs. In lordship 2 ploughs;
    another 2 possible.

poſſ fieri.7 xi . uiłłi hńt . ix . car . Ibi . xiii . borđ.7 ii .ſerui.
p̃tũ . vi . car . Silua . c . porc . Vał . x . liɓ . Q̃do recep̃:́ viii . liɓ.

T.R.E.́ xiii . liɓ . Hoc m̄ tenuer̄ . viii . ſocħi.7 potuer̄
dare 7 uendĕ trā ſuī cui uoluer̄.

m̄ In Stradli . teń Pirot de Nigello . iiii . hiđ.7 tciā
parte uniꝰ hidæ .ꝑ uno m̄.Tra . e̅ . vi . car . In dñio
.ii . car.7 iiii . uiłłi hńt . i . car.7 adhuc . iii . poſſ fieri.
Ibi. iiii . borđ 7 uń ſeruus.P̃tũ . iii . car . Silua . xx .
porc . Ibi q̇đā . i . car h̄t . Vał . iiii . liɓ . Q̃do recep̃:́
xl . ſoł . T.R.E.́ vi . liɓ . Hoc m̄ tenuit Leuuin.7 alij
tres teigni regis . E.7 cui uoluer̄ trā ſuā uendĕ potuer̄.
De iſta tra teń Pirot . iii . hiđ de maritagio ſuæ femi
næ.7 unā hiđ 7 tciā parte uniꝰ hiđ teń in feuđũ de
Nigello albinienſi.

In Mildentone teń Turgiſus de Nigello . iii . hiđ . una
uirg miń . Tra . e̅ . iiii . car . In dñio . i . car.7 iiii . uiłłi
ii . car 7 dim.7 dim car uiłł.7 iii . borđ . p̃tũ . iii . car .
Vał xxx . ſoł.7 tntđ q̇đo recep̃ . T.R.E.́ xl . ſoł .
Hanc trā tenuer̄ . vi . ſocħi.7 potuer̄ dare ł uendĕ
trā ſuā cui uoluer̄.   In WILGE HVNĐ.
In Carlentone teń Chetel de Nigello . i . hidā
7 tciā parte uniꝰ hiđ . Tra . e̅ . i . car 7 dim.7 ibi ſuꝶ.
7 iii . uiłłi.7 ii . borđ . P̃tũ . i . car 7 dim . Vał xx .
ſoł . Q̃do recep̃:́ x . ſoł . T.R.E.́ xv . ſoł . Hanc trā
tenuit Golderon h̄o Leuenot.7 pot dare cui uoluit.
In eađ teń Bernard de Nigello . i . hiđ 7 dim uirg.
Tra . e̅ . i . car 7 dim.7 ibi ſunt:7 v . borđ . P̃tũ . i . car.
7 uń moliñ xiii . ſoliđ.7 iiii . den . Vał . xl . ſoł . Q̃do
recep̃:́ xx . ſoł . T.R.E.́ xxx . ſoł . Hanc trā tenuer̄. iii .
ſocħi.7 cui uoluer̄ dare potuer̄.

11 villagers have 9 ploughs. 13 smallholders and 2 slaves.
Meadow for 6 ploughs; woodland, 100 pigs.
Value £10; when acquired £8; before 1066 £13.   214 c
8 Freemen held this manor; they could grant and sell their land
to whom they would.

18   M. In STREATLEY Pirot holds 4 hides and the third part of 1 hide from
Nigel of Aubigny, as one manor. Land for 6 ploughs. In lordship 2
ploughs.
4 villagers have 1 plough; a further 3 possible. 4 smallholders
and 1 slave.
Meadow for 3 ploughs; woodland, 20 pigs.
Someone has 1 plough there.
Value £4; when acquired 40s; before 1066 £6.
Young Leofwin and 3 other thanes of King Edward's held this
manor; they could sell their land to whom they would.
Pirot holds 3 hides of this land from his wife's marriage portion and
1 hide and the third part of 1 hide as a Holding from Nigel of Aubigny.

[In STODDEN Hundred]
19   In MILTON (Ernest) Thorgils holds 3 hides less 1 virgate from Nigel.
Land for 4 ploughs. In lordship 1 plough;
4 villagers, 2½ ploughs; ½ villagers' plough [possible];
3 smallholders.
Meadow for 3 ploughs.
Value 30s; as much when acquired; before 1066, 40s.
6 Freemen held this land; they could grant or sell their land to
whom they would.

In WILLEY Hundred
20   In CARLTON Ketel holds 1 hide and the third part of 1 hide from Nigel.
Land for 1½ ploughs; they are there.
3 villagers and 2 smallholders.
Meadow for 1½ ploughs.
Value 20s; when acquired 10s; before 1066, 15s.
Golderon, Leofnoth's man, held this land; he could grant to whom
he would.

21   In the same (village) Bernard holds 1 hide and ½ virgate from Nigel.
Land for 1½ ploughs; they are there.
5 smallholders.
Meadow for 1 plough; 1 mill, 13s 4d.
Value 40s; when acquired 20s; before 1066, 30s.
3 Freemen held this land; they could grant to whom they would.

In Radeuuelle ten Nigell de Nigello. VII. hiđ. 7 unã
uirg 7 dim. Tra. ē. v. car. In dñio. I. 7 VI. uitti hñt
IIII. car. Ibi. VI. borđ. 7 III. ferui. 7 I. molin de. x. fol.
Ptu. v. car. Val. IIII. lib. 7 tñtđ qdo receP. T. R. E.
VIII. lib. Hoc Ϻ tenuer. x. fochi. 7 cui uoluer trã
fuã dare potuer.

In Torneia ten Nigell de Nigello. I. hiđ 7 dim uirg.
Tra. ē. I. car 7 dim. 7 ibi funt. 7 v. borđ. Ptu. I. car. Silua
xx. porc. Val. XIII. fol. 7 tñtđ qdo receP. T. R. E. xxx. fol.
Hanc trã tenuit Aluuard hõ Wluui epi. 7 cui uoluit
dare potuit.   IN BEREFORDE HVND.

In Wiboldeftune ten Pirot. IX. hiđ 7 una uirg de rege.
de feudo Nigelli. Tra. ē. IX. car. In dñio. IIII. car. 7 XII.
uitti hñt. v. car. Ibi. VI. borđ. ptu. II. car. Val. VI.
lib. Qdo receP. IIII. lib. T. R. E. x. lib. Hoc Ϻ. XII.
fochi tenuer. 7 cui uoluer uende potuer.

Fulcherus parifiacenfis IN BICHELESWADE HVND.
ten dim hiđ de Nigello. Tra. ē. I. car. 7 ibi. ē. Ptu. I. car.
7 un feru. Val. LII. fol. Qdo receP. x. fol. T. R. E.
xxx. fol. Hanc trã ten Samar hõ Leuuini. 7 uende
In Holme ten ipfe Fulcher de Nigello ſ potuit.
unã hiđ 7 dim uirg. Tra. ē. II. car. 7 ibi funt. 7 III.
uitti. Ptu. I. car. Val. xx. fol. Qdo receP. x. fol. T. R. E.
xxx. fol. Hanc trã. VII. fochi tenuer. 7 uende 7 dare potr.

In Herghetone ten Nigell IN WICHESTANESTOV HVND.
VI. hiđ. Tra. ē. VIII. car. In dñio. I. hiđ 7 dim. 7 dim
uirg. 7 ibi. ē. I. car. 7 XIIII. uitti hñt. VII. car. Ibi. x. borđ.
214 d
7 II. ferui. Ptu. II. car. Silua. L. porc. Int tot ual. c. fol.
Qdo receP. IIII. lib. T. R. E. c. fol. Hoc Ϻ. XIIII. fochi
tenuer. 7 cui uoluer trã fuã dare 7 uende potuer.

22 In RADWELL Nigel of Le Vast holds 7 hides and 1½ virgates from Nigel of Aubigny. Land for 5 ploughs. In lordship 1.
　　6 villagers have 4 ploughs. 6 smallholders and 3 slaves.
　　1 mill at 10s; meadow for 5 ploughs.
　　Value £4; as much when acquired; before 1066 £8.
　　10 Freemen held this manor; they could grant their land to whom they would.

23 In TURVEY Nigel of Le Vast holds 1 hide and ½ virgate from Nigel of Aubigny. Land for 1½ ploughs; they are there.
　　5 smallholders.
　　Meadow for 1 plough; woodland, 20 pigs.
　　Value 13s; as much when acquired; before 1066, 30s.
　　Alfward, Bishop Wulfwy's man, held this land; he could grant to to whom he would.

　In BARFORD Hundred
24 In WYBOSTON Pirot holds 9 hides and 1 virgate from the King, from Nigel's Holding. Land for 9 ploughs. In lordship 4 ploughs.
　　12 villagers have 5 ploughs. 6 smallholders.
　　Meadow for 2 ploughs.
　　Value £6; when acquired £4; before 1066 £10.
　　12 Freemen held this manor; they could sell to whom they would.

　In BIGGLESWADE Hundred
25 Fulchere of Paris holds ½ hide from Nigel. Land for 1 plough; it is there.
　　Meadow for 1 plough. 1 slave.
　　Value 52s; when acquired 10s; before 1066, 30s.
　　Saemer, Leofwin's man, held this land; he could sell.

26 In HOLME Fulchere holds 1 hide and ½ virgate himself from Nigel. Land for 2 ploughs; they are there.
　　3 villagers.
　　Meadow for 1 plough.
　　Value 20s; when acquired 10s; before 1066, 30s.
　　7 Freemen held this land; they could sell and grant.

　In WIXAMTREE Hundred
27 In HARROWDEN Nigel holds 6 hides. Land for 8 ploughs. In lordship 1½ hides and ½ virgate; 1 plough there.
　　14 villagers have 7 ploughs. 10 smallholders and 2 slaves.　　214 d
　　Meadow for 2 ploughs; woodland, 50 pigs.
　　In total, value 100s; when acquired £4; before 1066, 100s.
　　14 Freemen held this manor; they could grant and sell their land to whom they would.

In Cliftone ten Witts de caron *In Cliston Hvnd.*

ii . hid de Nigello. Tra . e . i . car 7 dim . Ibi . e una car.

7 dim poteft fieri. Ptu . i . car . Val . xv . fot . Qdo recep:

x . fot. T.R.E. xx . fot. Hanc tra . iiii . fochi tenuer.

7 dare 7 uende potuer.

In Haneflau ten Erfaft de Nigello . v . hid 7 dim.

Tra . e . v . car 7 dim . In dnio . ii . car . 7 x . uitti hnt

iii . car 7 dim . Ibi . iii . ferui . 7 i . molin de . v . fot . ptu

v . car . De paftura . x . den. Int tot ual . c|.x . fot.

Qdo recep: iiii . lib . T.R.E. vii . lib . Hanc tra . ix . fochi

tenuer. 7 cui uoluer dare 7 uende potuer.

De his . v . hid 7 dimida: tene℣ m̊ S Nicolai Ande

gauenfis. iii . uirg de Nigello in elemofina.

In Alricefeia . ten Erfaft de Nigello . iii . uirg 7 tcia

parte uni uirg . Tra . e . i . car . 7 ibi . e . Ptu . i . car.

Val . xvii . fot . 7 tntd qdo recep . T.R.E. xx . fot . Hanc

tra . ii . fochi tenuer. 7 cui uoluer uende potuer.

.XXV.   TERRA WILLI SPECH. *In Manesheve Hvnd.*

ⳉ Witts SPECH ten in holecote . iiii . hid p uno ⳉ.

7 Radulf paffaq de eo . Tra . e . iii . car . In dnio . i.

car . 7 v . uitti hnt . ii . car . Ibi . viii . bord 7 un feru . 7 un

molin . v . folid 7 iiii . den . Silua . l . porc . Int tot ual

lx . fot . Qdo recep: xx . fot . T.R.E. xl . fot . Hoc ⳉ tenuit

Aluuard belrap ho Alrici . 7 cui uoluit uende potuit.

H tra e de excabio de Totingedone q excabiauit.

Witts fili Rainaldi tenet   *In Ratbernestoche Hvnd.*

de Witto fpech Stepigelai . p . v . hid fe defd . Tra . e

vii . car . In dnio . i . car 7 dim . 7 xiiii . uitti hnt . v . car

7 dim . 7 ii . ferui . Ptu . vii . car . Silua . c . porc . Int totu

214 d

In CLIFTON Hundred

28 In CLIFTON William of Cairon holds 2 hides from Nigel.
Land for 1½ ploughs. 1 plough there; ½ possible.
    Meadow for 1 plough.
Value 15s; when acquired 10s; before 1066, 20s.
    4 Freemen held this land; they could grant and sell.

29 In HENLOW Herfast holds 5½ hides from Nigel. Land for 5½ ploughs.
In lordship 2 ploughs.
    10 villagers have 3½ ploughs. 3 slaves;
    1 mill at 5s; meadow for 5 ploughs; from pasture 10d.
In total, value 110s; when acquired £4; before 1066 £7.
    9 Freemen held this land; they could grant and sell to whom
they would.
    Of these 5½ hides [the monks of] St. Nicholas of Angers now
hold 3 virgates from Nigel in alms.

30 In ARLESEY Herfast holds 3 virgates and the third part of 1 virgate
from Nigel. Land for 1 plough; it is there.
    Meadow for 1 plough.
Value 17s; as much when acquired; before 1066, 20s.
    2 Freemen held this land; they could sell to whom they would.

25   **LAND OF WILLIAM SPEKE**

In MANSHEAD Hundred

1 M. William Speke holds 4 hides in HOLCOT as one manor and Ralph
Passwater from him. Land for 3 ploughs. In lordship 1 plough.
    5 villagers have 2 ploughs. 8 smallholders and 1 slave.
    A mill, 5s 4d; woodland, 50 pigs.
In total, value 60s; when acquired 20s; before 1066, 40s.
    Alfward Bellrope, Alric's man, held this manor; he could sell
to whom he would.
    This land is in exchange for Toddington which he gave in exchange.

In REDBORNSTOKE Hundred

2 William son of Reginald holds STEPPINGLEY from William Speke.
It answers for 5 hides. Land for 7 ploughs. In lordship 1½ ploughs.
    14 villagers have 5½ ploughs. 2 slaves.
    Meadow for 7 ploughs; woodland, 100 pigs.

ual . iiii . liƀ . Q̑do receƥ . xl . fol . T.R.E. viii . liƀ . Hoc ꝏ̃

tenuit Almar̄ hō Alurici de Fliƈteuuite . 7 ibi fuer̄

.ii . foċhi hōēs ej . qui potuer̄ tr̄a fuā uende cui uoluer̄.

Ín Stradlei teñ Hugo de Witto *IN FLICTHĀ HVND*.

ii . part̄ . i . uirg̃ . Tra . ē . ii . bob . Val 7 ualuit sēƥ . ii . fot.

Hanc tr̄a tenuit Aluric hō Alurici parui . 7 potuit

uende cui uoluit.

ꝏ̃ Ín Bidehā teñ Radulf̄ 7 Serlo de Ros de Witto

iiii . hiđ . una uirg̃ 7 dim̃ min . Tra . ē . iiii . car̄ . In dn̄io

.ii . car̄ . 7 vi . uitti hn̄t . ii . car̄ . Ibi . ii . borđ . 7 ii . ferui.

7 uñ molin̄ . x . fot . Ƥtū . iiii . car̄ . Val . xl . fot . Q̑do

receƥ . xx . fot . T.R.E. xl . fot . Hoc ꝏ̃ tenuer̄ . xi . foċhi.

7 cui uoluer̄ tr̄a fuā dare 7 uende potuer̄ . Hanc tr̄a

diċ Witts fe habe ꝓ excābio de Totingedone.

Ín Heneuuic . teñ Walter̄ de Witto *IN WILGE HVND*.

i . hiđ . Tra . ē . ii . car̄ . Ibi . ē dim̃ car̄ . 7 altera ċ 7 dim̃

poteſt fieri . Val . x . fot . 7 tntđ q̑do receƥ . T.R.E. xx . fot..

Hanc tr̄a tenuit Vlnod hō Vlfi filij Borgret . 7 cui

uoluit dare potuit.

Ín Wimentone teñ Walter̄ de Witto . iii . uirg̃.

215 a

Tra . ē dim̃ car̄ . Val . ii . fot . Q̑do receƥ . x . fot . T.R.E.

x . fot . Hanc tr̄a tenuit Leuric hō Borgred . 7 cui uoluit

dare potuit.   *IN BEREFORDE HVND*.

Ín Chaueleſtorne teñ Witts fili Raineuuardi . de Witto

vii . hiđ 7 i . uirg̃ . Tra . ē . vii . car̄ . In dn̄io . i . car̄ . 7 xvi.

uitti hn̄t . vi . car̄ . Ibi . ii . borđ . 7 i . feru . 7 i . molin̄

de . xiii . fot . 7 iiii . den̄ . ƥtū . vii . car̄ . Silua x . porc̄.

Int̄ tot̄ ual . vi . liƀ . Q̑do receƥ . iiii . liƀ . T.R.E. ix . liƀ.

Hanc tr̄a . xii . foċhi tenuer̄ . 7 uende potuer̄ cui uoluer̄.

In total, value £4; when acquired 40s; before 1066 £8.

Aelmer, Aelfric of Flitwick's man, held this manor.
There were 2 Freemen there, his men, who could sell their land
to whom they would.

In FLITT Hundred

3   In STREATLEY Hugh holds two parts of 1 virgate from William.
Land for 2 oxen.
The value is and always was 2s.

Aelfric, Aelfric Small's man, held this land; he could sell to
whom he would.

[In BUCKLOW Hundred]

4   M. In BIDDENHAM Ralph and Serlo of Rots hold 4 hides less 1½ virgates
from William. Land for 4 ploughs. In lordship 2 ploughs.
6 villagers have 2 ploughs. 2 smallholders and 2 slaves.
A mill, 10s; meadow for 4 ploughs.
Value 40s; when acquired 20s; before 1066, 40s.
11 Freemen held this manor; they could grant and sell their land
to whom they would.
William says that he has this land in exchange for Toddington.

In WILLEY Hundred

5   In HINWICK Walter holds 1 hide from William. Land for 2 ploughs;
½ plough there; another 1½ ploughs possible.
Value 10s; as much when acquired; before 1066, 20s.

Wulfnoth, Wulfsi son of Burgred's man, held this land;
he could grant to whom he would.

6   In WYMINGTON Walter holds 3 virgates from William.
Land for ½ plough.   215 a
Value 2s; when acquired 10s; before 1066, 10s.

Leofric, Burgred's man, held this land; he could grant to whom
he would.

In BARFORD Hundred

7   In CHAWSTON William son of Rainward holds 7 hides and 1 virgate
from William. Land for 7 ploughs. In lordship 1 plough.
16 villagers have 6 ploughs. 2 smallholders and 1 slave.
1 mill at 13s 4d; meadow for 7 ploughs; woodland, 10 pigs.
In total, value £6; when acquired £4; before 1066 £9.
12 Freemen held this land; they could sell to whom they would.

De his.vii.hid 7 una uirg.reclam hoes Witti fpec
.i.acra pti 7 dim.fup hoes Eudonis dapif.7 hund
teftat qd ej anteceffor habuit.T.R.E.7 alias.vii.
acs træ reclamat ifde Witts fup quenda hoem
Hugonis de belcap.unde ipfe defaifit.fz anteceffor
ej fuit faifitus.De pdicta tra reclamat Eudo dapif.
.i.acra.fup Ruallon hoem Hugonis de belcamp.
In ead ten Witts gros.dim hid de Witto fpec.Tra.e
dim car.7 ibi.e.ptu dim car.Ibi.ii ;uitti.Vat;v.fot.
Qdo recep.v.fot.T.R.E.x.fot.Hanc tra tenue.ii.
hoes regis.E.7 cui uolue uende potue.

In *ROCHESDONE* ten Witts fpec.viii.hid.7 iii.uirg.
Tra.e.viii.car.In dnio.iiii.hide 7 iii.uirg.7 ibi funt
ii.car.7 xii.uitti hnt.vi.car.Ibi.i.bord.7 i.feru.7 un
molin de xxxiii.fot 7 cclx.anguitt.Ptu.iii.car.Silua
xx.porc.Vat.vii.lib.Qdo recep.l.fot.T.R.E.x.lib.
Hoc M xii.fochi tenue.7 cui uolue tra fua uende potue.

In Aiffeuuorde tenet *IN BICHELESWADE HVND.*
Witts fpec.ix.hid p uno M.Tra.e.ix.car.In dnio.v.
hidæ 7 dimidia.7 ibi funt.iii.car.7 xiii.uitti hnt
vi.car.Ibi.ii.bord 7 vi.ferui.7 i.molin de.viii.fot.
ptu.ix.car.Vat vii lib.Qdo recep.fimilit.T.R.E.
viii.lib.Hoc M tenue.xx.fochi.7 tra fua cui uo
lue dare t uende potue.fine licentia dnoz fuoz.

In Sudgiuele tene *IN WICHENESTANESTOV HD.*
.ii.franc de Witto fpech.v.hid 7 dim uirg.Tra.e
vii.car.In dnio.iiii.car.7 viii.uitti hnt.iii.car.
Ibi.viii.bord.7 vi.ferui.ptu.vii.car.Silua.cc.
porc.Vat iiii.lib 7 x.fot.Qdo recep.iiii.lib.T.R.E.
iii.lib.Hoc M tenue.xvi.fochi.7 tra fua cui uo
lue dare 7 uende potue.

Of these 7 hides and 1 virgate William Speke's men claim 1½ acres of meadow from Eudo the Steward's men; the Hundred testifies that his predecessor had them before 1066. William also claims another 7 acres of land against a man of Hugh of Beauchamp by whom he was dispossessed; but his predecessor was put in possession. Eudo the Steward claims 1 acre of the said land against Rhiwallon, Hugh of Beauchamp's man.

In the same (village) William Gross holds ½ hide from William Speke. Land for ½ plough; it is there.
    Meadow for ½ plough.
    2 villagers.
Value 5s; when acquired 5s; before 1066, 10s.
    2 of King Edward's men held this land; they could sell to whom they would.

9   M. In ROXTON William Speke holds 8 hides and 3 virgates.
    Land for 8 ploughs. In lordship 4 hides and 3 virgates; 2 ploughs there.
    12 villagers have 6 ploughs. 1 smallholder and 1 slave.
    A mill at 33s and 260 eels; meadow for 3 ploughs;
      woodland, 20 pigs.
Value £7; when acquired 50s; before 1066 £10.
    12 Freemen held this manor; they could sell their land to whom they would.

In BIGGLESWADE Hundred
10   M. In EYEWORTH William Speke holds 9 hides as one manor. Land for 9 ploughs. In lordship 5½ hides. 3 ploughs there.
    13 villagers have 6 ploughs. 2 smallholders and 6 slaves.
    1 mill at 8s; meadow for 9 ploughs.
Value £7; when acquired the same; before 1066 £8.
    20 Freemen held this manor; they could grant or sell their land to whom they would without their lords' permission.

In WIXAMTREE Hundred
11   M. In SOUTHILL 2 Frenchmen hold 5 hides and ½ virgate from William Speke. Land for 7 ploughs. In lordship 4 ploughs.
    8 villagers have 3 ploughs. 8 smallholders and 6 slaves.
    Meadow for 7 ploughs; woodland, 200 pigs.
Value £4 10s; when acquired £4; before 1066 £3.
    16 Freemen held this manor; they could grant and sell their land to whom they would.

In Stanford. teñ Hugo de Wilto fpech . 1 . hiđ . Tra . ē

.1 . car . 7 ibi eſt . 7 dim moliñ . v . folid . Ibi . 11 . ſerui.

p̃tū . 1 . car . Silua . xx . porc . Val . xv . fot . Qđo recep̃.

xx . fot . 7 tñtđ . T.R.E. Hanc tr̄a tenuit Lemar teigñ

ⓂIn Wardone teñ Wilts fpec . ix . hiđ de rege . ⌐ R.E.

p uno Ⓜ . Tra . ē . ix . car . In dñio . 111 . hiđ 7 dimiđ . 7 ibi . ē

una car . 7 altera poteſt fieri . Ibi xv111 . uilti hñt

v11 . car . Ibi . 1111 . borđ . 7 1111 . ſerui . 7 1 . moliñ . x11 . fot.

P̃tū . v1 . car . Val . v1 . liƀ . 7 tñtđ qdo recep̃ . T.R.E.

v111 . liƀ . Hoc Ⓜ tenuer̄ . v111 . fochi . 7 tr̄a ſuā cui

uoluer̄ dare potuer̄.

In Biſtone teñ Wilts fpech . 111 . uirg 7 dim . Tra . ē . 1 . car.

Ibi . ē dim̄ car . 7 dim̄ poteſt fieri . p̃tū dim̄ car . Val

. x . fot . 7 tñtđ qdo recep̃ . T.R.E. xx . fot . Hanc tr̄a

215 b

tenuit Leuuiñ teigñ regis.

In Nortgiuele teñ Wilts fpec . v1 . hiđ 7 dim p uno Ⓜ .

Tra . ē . v11 . car . In dñio . 1111 . hiđ . 7 ibi funt . 111 . car . 7 x . uilti

hñt . 1111 . car . Ibi . 1111 . ſerui . 7 dim̄ moliñ de . x111 . folid.

p̃tū . v11 . car . Silua . cc . porc . Int totū ual . v1 . liƀ.

7 tñtđ qdo recep̃ . T.R.E. v111 . liƀ . Hoc Ⓜ tenuer̄ . v1 . fochi.

potuer̄ dare 7 uende cui uoluer̄ . T.R.E.

.XXVI. R TERRA ROBERTI DE TODENI. *IN STANBVRGE HĐ.*

Ⓜ Rotbert de Todeni de rege . teñ Eſtodhā . 7 Baldric

de Roƀto . p v1 . hiđ ſe defđ . Tra . ē . v1 . car . In dñio . 11 . car.

7 x . uilti hñt . 1111 . car . Ibi un borđ . 7 1111 . ſerui . Silua

c . porc . Val . 1111 . liƀ . Qđo recep̃. xl . fot . T.R.E. v111 . liƀ.

Hoc Ⓜ tenuit Oſulf fili Frane . teigñ regis . E.

In Achelei tenent . 11 . milites de Roƀto . 1111 . hiđ . Tra . ē

v111 . car . In dñio . 111 . car . 7 1111 . poteſt . ee . Ibi . v11 . uilti

12   In STANFORD Hugh holds 1 hide from William Speke. Land for 1 plough; it is there.

     ½ mill, 5s. 2 slaves; meadow for 1 plough; woodland, 20 pigs.

     Value 15s; when acquired 20s; as much before 1066.

     Leofmer, a thane of King Edward's, held this land.

13 M. In (Old) WARDEN William Speke holds 9 hides from the King as one manor. Land for 9 ploughs. In lordship 3½ hides; 1 plough there; a second possible.

     18 villagers have 7 ploughs. 4 smallholders and 4 slaves.

     1 mill, 12s; meadow for 6 ploughs.

     Value £6; as much when acquired; before 1066 £8.

     8 Freemen held this manor; they could grant their land to whom they would.

14   In BEESTON William Speke holds 3½ virgates. Land for 1 plough; ½ plough there; ½ possible.

     Meadow for ½ plough.

     Value 10s; as much when acquired; before 1066, 20s.   215 b

     Young Leofwin, a thane of the King's, held this land.

15   In NORTHILL William Speke holds 6½ hides as one manor.

     Land for 7 ploughs. In lordship 4 hides; 3 ploughs there.

     10 villagers have 4 ploughs.

     4 slaves; ½ mill at 13s; meadow for 7 ploughs; woodland, 200 pigs.

     In total, value £6; as much when acquired; before 1066 £8.

     6 Freemen held this manor; they could grant and sell to whom they would before 1066.

26   LAND OF ROBERT OF TOSNY

In STANBRIDGE Hundred

1 M. Robert of Tosny holds STUDHAM from the King and Baldric from Robert. It answers for 6 hides. Land for 6 ploughs. In lordship 2 ploughs.

     10 villagers have 4 ploughs. 1 smallholder and 4 slaves.

     Woodland, 100 pigs.

     Value £4; when acquired 40s; before 1066 £8.

     Oswulf son of Fran, a thane of King Edward's, held this manor.

[In STODDEN Hundred]

2   In OAKLEY 2 men-at-arms hold 4 hides from Robert. Land for 8 ploughs. In lordship 3 ploughs; a fourth possible.

hīt.IIII.car̄.7 III.borđ.7 v.ſerui.7 I.moliñ.xxvI.ſoliđ.

7 cc.Anguiłł.p̄tū.IIII.car̄.Vał.IIII.lib̄.Q̄do recep̄:ſimilit̄.

T.R.E.:IIII.lib̄ 7 x.ſoł.Hanc tr̄a tenuit Oſulf teign.R.E.

In Toruei tenent.II.milites de Rob̄to In WILGE HVNĐ.

II.hiđ.7 I.uirg.Tra.ē.iiii.car̄ 7 dim.In dñio.II.car̄.

7 III.uiłłi hñt.II.car̄.7 dim car̄ poteſt fieri.Ibi.vI.borđ.

7 II.ſerui.p̄tū.I.car̄.Silua.x.porc̄.Vał.xL.ſoł.Q̄do

recep̄:Lx.ſoł.T.R.E.:Lxx.ſoł.Hanc tr̄a tenuit Oſulf p̄dict̄.

.XXVII TERRA GISLEB̄TI DE GAND.IN DIMIĐ HVNĐ de STANBVRGE.

GISLEBERT de gand ten Edingeberge.p.x.hiđ

ſe defđ.Tra.ē.vII.car̄.In dñio.v.hidæ.7 ibi ſuɴ.IIII.

car̄.7 x.uiłłi hñt.IIII.car̄.In totis ualentijs uał.c.ſoł.7 x.

Q̄do recep̄:ſimilit̄.T.R.E.:x.lib̄.Hoc M̄ tenuit Vlf

teign.R.E.7 potuit inde facere qđ uoluit.

.XXVI. TERRA ROBERTI DE OILGI. IN WILGE HVNĐ.

ROTBERT de Olgi.ten jn Lalega.7 Ricard baſſet de eo

dim hiđ.Tra.ē.II.car̄.Vna m̄ ibi ē.7 alta poteſt fieri.

Ibi.I.uiłłs 7 III.borđ.7 II.ſerui.Silua.xxx.porc̄.Vał

7 ualuit ſēp.xL.ſoł.Hanc tr̄a tenuit Ouiet teign.R.E.

7 cui uoluit uendē potuit.Hanc clamant hōes Eudonis

p anteceſſorē dñi ſui.cuj tras oms W.rex ſibi donauit.

In eađ ten Salomon p̄br.I.uirg de Rob̄to de olgi.

Tra.ē.I.car̄.7 ibi eſt.cū uno borđ.Vał 7 ualuit ſēp.x.ſoł.

Hanc tr̄a Aluuin tenuit hō Wluui epi.7 uendē potuit.

7 villagers have 4 ploughs; 3 smallholders and 5 slaves.
1 mill, 26s and 200 eels; meadow for 4 ploughs.
Value £4; when acquired the same; before 1066 £4 10s.
Oswulf, a thane of King Edward's, held this land.

In WILLEY Hundred

3 In TURVEY 2 men-at-arms hold 2 hides and 1 virgate from Robert.
Land for 4½ ploughs. In lordship 2 ploughs.
   3 villagers have 2 ploughs; ½ plough possible. 6 smallholders
   and 2 slaves.
   Meadow for 1 plough; woodland, 10 pigs.
Value 40s; when acquired 60s; before 1066, 70s.
The said Oswulf held this land.

27   LAND OF GILBERT OF GHENT

In the Half-Hundred of STANBRIDGE

1 Gilbert of Ghent holds EDLESBOROUGH. It answers for 10 hides.
Land for 7 ploughs. In lordship 5 hides; 4 ploughs there.
   10 villagers have 4 ploughs.
Total value 100s 10[d]; when acquired the same; before 1066 £10.
   Ulf, a thane of King Edward's, held this manor; he could do
what he would with it.

28   LAND OF ROBERT D'OILLY

In WILLEY Hundred

1 Robert d'Oilly holds ½ hide in THURLEIGH and Richard Basset from him.
Land for 2 ploughs; 1 now there; a second possible.
   1 villager; 3 smallholders and 2 slaves.
   Woodland, 30 pigs.
The value is and always was 40s.
   Wulfgeat, a thane of King Edward's, held this land; he could sell to
whom he would.
   Eudo's men claim this land through their lord's predecessor, all of
whose lands King William bestowed upon him.

2 In the same (village) Solomon the priest holds 1 virgate from
Robert d'Oilly. Land for 1 plough; it is there, with
   1 smallholder.
The value is and always was 10s.
   Alwin, Bishop Wulfwy's man, held this land; he could sell.

.XXIX. TERRA RANÑ FR̄IS ILGERIJ. *IN DIM̄ HVND̄ DE BOCHELAI.*

Rᴀɴɴᴠʟꜰ fr̄ Ilgerij teñ. v. hid in Pabeneha.7 Rob̄t
filius Nigelli de eo. Tra. ē. vi. car̄. In dñio. i. car̄. 7 alia
potest fieri. 7 ix. uilti hñt. ii. car̄. 7 aliæ. ii. poſſuꝴ fieri.
Ibi. ii. bord̄. 7 iii. ſerui. P̊tū. vi. car̄. Val. iii. lib̄. Q̇do
recep̄. iiii. lib̄. T.R.E. vi. lib̄. Hoc ⟨M⟩ tenuit Goduiñ
teigñ. R.E. De ista tra reclamat Rannulf fr̄ Ilgerij
xii. aċs træ. ſup Gisleb̄tū filiū Salomonis. 7 iiii. aċs p̄ti
ſup Hug de Grentmaiſnil. unde Rannulf deſaiſit est
injuste. 7 hōēs de dimid hund̄ dn̄t qd̄ ista tra quā m̄
teneꝴ Hugo 7 Gisleb̄t. jacuit ad trā quā tenet Rannulf
fr̄ Ilgerij. T.R.E.

.XXX. Rᴏᴛʙᴇʀᴛᴠꜱ Fafiton teñ de rege *FLICTHA*. p̄ v. hid ſe defd̄.

TERRA ROBERTI FAFITON. *IN FLICTHĀ HVND̄.*

215 c
Tra. ē. vi. car̄. In dñio. ii. hidæ. 7 ibi ſuꝴ. ii. car̄. Ibi
iii. uilti hñt. ii. car̄. 7 aliæ. ii. poſſunt. ēē. Ibi. iiii.
bord̄ 7 iiii. ſerui. P̊tū. vi. car̄. Silua. l. porċ. Int̄
tot ual. lx. ſot. 7 tntd̄ qdo recep̄. T.R.E. c. ſot. Hoc
⟨M⟩ tenuit Aluuiñ horim teigñ regis. E.

.XXXI. Aʟᴠᴇʀᴇᴅ de Lincolia 7 Gleu de eo teñ in Wimen

TERRA ALVREDI DE LINCOLIA *IN WILGE HVND̄.*

tone. iii. hid̄. Tra. ē. iiii. car̄. In dñio. i. car̄. 7 alia
potest fieri. Ibi uñ uilts 7 vi. bord̄. 7 iii. ſerui. cū. ii. car̄.
p̄tū. ii. car̄. Val. xl. ſot. Q̇do recep̄. l. ſot. T.R.E.
lx. ſot. Hoc ⟨M⟩ tenuit Goduin Franpold. 7 uende
potuit. Cū his. iii. hidis reclamat Aluered ſup Walt
flandr̄ dim hid. de qua injuste deſaiſiuit eū. ut
hōēs de hund̄ inde portaꝴ teſtimon. q̄m Anteceſſor
ej. T.R.E. inde ſaiſit fuit. 7 iſde Aluered poſtea fuit

215 b, c

29 LAND OF RANULF BROTHER OF ILGER

1   Ranulf brother of Ilger holds 5 hides in PAVENHAM, and Robert son
of Nigel from him. Land for 6 ploughs. In lordship 1 plough;
another possible.
    9 villagers have 2 ploughs; another 2 possible. 2 smallholders
      and 3 slaves.
    Meadow for 6 ploughs.
Value £3; when acquired £4; before 1066 £6.
    Godwin, a thane of King Edward's, held this manor.
    Of this land Ranulf brother of Ilger claims 12 acres of land against
Gilbert son of Solomon and 4 acres of meadow against Hugh of
Grandmesnil, of which Ranulf was wrongfully dispossessed; the men
of the Half-Hundred state that before 1066 this land, which Hugh and
Gilbert now hold, lay with the land which Ranulf brother of Ilger holds.

30   LAND OF ROBERT [SON OF] FAFITON

In FLITT Hundred
1   Robert Fafiton holds FLITTON from the King. It answers for 5 hides.
Land for 6 ploughs. In lordship 2 hides; 2 ploughs there.   215 c
    3 villagers have 2 ploughs; another 2 possible. 3 smallholders
      and 4 slaves.
    Meadow for 6 ploughs; woodland, 50 pigs.
In total, value 60s; as much when acquired; before 1066, 100s.
    Alwin Horn, a thane of King Edward's, held this manor.

31   LAND OF ALFRED OF LINCOLN

In WILLEY Hundred
1 M. Alfred of Lincoln holds 3 hides in WYMINGTON, and Glew from him.
Land for 4 ploughs. In lordship 1 plough; another possible.
    1 villager, 6 smallholders and 3 slaves with 2 ploughs.
    Meadow for 2 ploughs.
Value 40s; when acquired 50s; before 1066, 60s.
    Godwin Frambold held this manor; he could sell.
    With these 3 hides Alfred claims ½ hide against Walter of Flanders,
of which he wrongfully dispossessed him, as the men of the Hundred
bear witness thereon, since his predecessor was possessed of it before
1066, and Alfred was possessed afterwards. Further, with this land

saifit. Cū hac t̃ra adhuc reclamat ifdē Aluered
fup epm conſtantienſē filuā. c. quā habuit ſuus ante
ceſſor. T.R.E. ſed eṗs defaiſiuit eū injuſte. ut hōes
de hund teſtant.

.XXXII. TERRA WALTERIJ FLANDRENS IN DIM HVND DE STAN

ⓂWALTERVS Flandrenſis 7 Osbt de eo teñ TOTENEHOV
ꝑ xv. hid ſe defd. T.R.E. Sed poſtq; rex.W. uenit
in Anglia. ñ ſe defd nifi ꝑ.x. hid.7 hōes qui. v. hid
tenuer 7 tenent. ōms ēfuetudines regis 7 gabl reti
nuer 7 retinent. Tra. ē. x. car. In dñio. ii. car. 7 xxii.
uilli hñt. iiii. car. 7 aliæ. iiii. poſs fieri. Ibi. ii. bord
7 iiii. ſerui. Ibi. iii. molini de.x. ſol 7 viii. den. Ptū
iiii. car. Silua. cl. porc. Int tot ual viii. lib. Qdo
receṗ. x. lib. T.R.E. xvi. lib. Hoc Ⓜ tenuit Leuenot
teign regis. E. 7 cui uoluit uende potuit. ſ HVND.

In Mildentone teñ Rainald de Waltero IN STODEN
ii. hid. Tra. ē. iii. car. In dñio. ē. i. car. 7 ii. uilli hñt
.i. car. 7 alia poteſt fieri. Ibi. i. bord. Ptū. ii. car.
Val. xx. ſol. 7 tñtd qdo receṗ. T. R. E. xxv. ſol. Hanc
t̃ra tenuer. ii. fochi hōes Brietric. 7 cui uoluer dare potr.

In Tornei teñ Hugo de Waltero IN WILGE HVND.
.i. hid. Tra. ē. ii. car. In dñio. una. ē. 7 viii. bord 7 uñ
ſeru cū.i. car. ṗtū. i. car. Silua. xl. porc. Val. xxx.
ſol. Qdo receṗ. x. ſol. T.R.E. xl. ſol. Hanc tram
tenuit Leuenot teign. R.E. 7 cui uoluit uende potuit.

Ⓜ In Wadehelle teñ Walter fland de rege. v. hid.
7 unā uirg. 7 ii. partes uni uirg. Tra. ē. v. car. In dñio
ii. hidæ. 7 ibi ſunt. ii. car. 7 xiii. uilli cū. iii. car. Ibi
v. bord. 7 v. ſerui. 7 i. molin de. xxxvi. ſol. 7 viii. den.
7 cc. Anguill. ṗtū. v. car. Silua. lx. porc. Val. c. ſol.

Alfred also claims from the Bishop of Coutances woodland for
100 pigs, which his predecessor previously had before 1066, but the
Bishop wrongfully dispossessed him, as the men of the Hundred testify.

32   **LAND OF WALTER OF FLANDERS**

In the Half-Hundred of STANBRIDGE

1 M. Walter of Flanders holds TOTTERNHOE and Osbert from him. It
answered for 15 hides before 1066, but after King William came to
England it did not answer, except for 10 hides. The men who
held and hold the 5 hides kept and keep all the King's customary
dues and tribute. Land for 10 ploughs. In lordship 2 ploughs.
        22 villagers have 4 ploughs; another 4 possible.
            2 smallholders and 4 slaves.
        3 mills at 10s 8d; meadow for 4 ploughs; woodland, 150 pigs.
In total, value £8; when acquired £10; before 1066 £16.
        Leofnoth, a thane of King Edward's, held this manor; he could
sell to whom he would.

In STODDEN Hundred

2 In MILTON (Ernest) Reginald holds 2 hides from Walter. Land for 3
ploughs. In lordship 1 plough.
        2 villagers have 1 plough; another possible. 1 smallholder.
        Meadow for 2 ploughs.
Value 20s; as much when acquired; before 1066, 25s.
        2 Freemen, Brictric's men, held this land; they could grant
to whom they would.

In WILLEY Hundred

3 In TURVEY Hugh holds 1 hide from Walter. Land for 2 ploughs.
In lordship 1;
        8 smallholders and 1 slave with 1 plough.
        Meadow for 1 plough; woodland, 40 pigs.
Value 30s; when acquired 10s; before 1066, 40s.
        Leofnoth, a thane of King Edward's, held this land; he could
sell to whom he would.

4 M. In ODELL Walter of Flanders holds 5 hides, 1 virgate and 2 parts
of 1 virgate from the King. Land for 5 ploughs. In lordship 2 hides;
2 ploughs there;
        13 villagers with 3 ploughs. 5 smallholders and 5 slaves.
        1 mill at 36s 8d and 200 eels; meadow for 5 ploughs;
            woodland, 60 pigs.

Q̃do recep̃. viii . lib. T.R.E. x . lib. Hoc M̃ Leuenot te

nuit. teign. R.E. 7 ibid un̄ foc̄s dim̄ hid̄ habuit. q̃ po

tuit dare cui uoluit.

M̃ In Podintone ten̄ Hugo de Waltero . i . hid̄ 7 iii . uirg.

Tra . ē . v . car̄ . 7 dim̄. In dn̄io fuⁿ . ii . car̄ . 7 iiii . uilli

hn̄t . iii . car̄ . 7 dim̄ . Ibi . ix . bord̄ 7 ii . ferui . p̃tu . i . car̄.

Silua. xx . porc̄. Val . iiii . lib 7 x . fol. Q̃do recep̃. l . fol.

7 tn̄td̄. T.R.E. Hoc M̃ tenuit Leuenot teign regis . E.

215 d

M̃ In Wimentone ten̄ Osb̄t de Walterio . iiii . hid̄ p̃ uno

M̃. Tra . ē . v . car̄ . In dn̄io . iii . car̄. 7 ibi un̄ uills 7 viii.

bord̄ 7 iiii . ferui . cū . i . car̄. p̃tu . ii . car̄ . Val . iii . lib.

7 tn̄td̄ qdo recep̃. T.R.E. iiii . lib . Hoc M̃ tenuit Lant

hō Leuenot teigni regis. 7 ibi un̄ foc̄s . i . hid̄a habuit.

7 cui uoluit dare potuit.

In ead̄ uilla ten̄ if d̄ Osb̄t de Walterio dim̄ hid̄. Tra . ē

dim̄ car̄. f ʒ non . ē ibi . Val . ii . fol. Q̃do recep̃. iiii . fol.

T.R.E. x . fol. Hanc tr̄a tenuit Goduin franpalt.

7 cui uoluit dare potuit. Hanc eand̄ reclamat Alured̄

Lincol fup Walteriū Flandrenfem.

In Lalega ten̄ Hugo de Walterio . iii . hid̄ p̃ uno M̃

Tra . ē . vii . car̄ . In dn̄io . ii . car̄. 7 viii . uilli hn̄t . v . car̄.

Ibi . xii . bord̄. 7 iii . ferui . Silua . cl . porc̄. Val . c . fol.

Q̃do recep̃. lx . fol . T.R.E. iiii . lib . Hoc M̃ tenuit

Leuenot teign regis. E.

In ead̄ ten̄ Raynald̄ de Walterio dim̄ hid̄. Tra . ē

ii . car̄ . In dn̄io . i . car̄. 7 iiii . bord̄ cū . i . car̄ . Val . xx . fol.

Q̃do recep̃. x . fol. T.R.E. v . fol. Hanc tr̄a tenuit

Ordric hō Leuenot. 7 uend̄ potuit. *In Bicheleswade*

In Stratone ten̄ . i . hid̄ 7 i . uirg. Tra . ē   *Hvnd.*

. i . car̄ 7 dim̄. 7 una car̄ 7 dim̄ poteft fieri . Ibi . iii . bord̄.

Value 100s; when acquired £8; before 1066 £10.

Leofnoth, a thane of King Edward's, held this manor; there also 1 Freeman had ½ hide which he could grant to whom he would.

5 M. In PODINGTON Hugh holds 1 hide and 3 virgates from Walter.
Land for 5½ ploughs. In lordship 2 ploughs.
    4 villagers have 3½ ploughs. 9 smallholders and 2 slaves.
    Meadow for 1 plough; woodland, 20 pigs.
Value £4 10s; when acquired 50s; as much before 1066.
Leofnoth, a thane of King Edward's, held this manor.

6 M. In WYMINGTON Osbert holds 4 hides from Walter as one manor.   215 d
Land for 5 ploughs. In lordship 3 ploughs;
    1 villager, 8 smallholders and 4 slaves with 1 plough.
    Meadow for 2 ploughs.
Value £3; as much when acquired; before 1066 £4.

Lank, a man of Leofnoth's, a thane of King Edward's, held this manor. 1 Freeman had 1 hide there; he could grant to whom he would.

7 In the same village Osbert also holds ½ hide from Walter.
Land for ½ plough; but it is not there.
Value 2s; when acquired 4s; before 1066, 10s.

Godwin Frambold held this land; he could grant to whom he would. Alfred of Lincoln claims this (land) from Walter of Flanders.

8 In THURLEIGH Hugh holds 3 hides from Walter as one manor.
Land for 7 ploughs. In lordship 2 ploughs.
    8 villagers have 5 ploughs. 12 smallholders and 3 slaves.
    Woodland, 150 pigs.
Value 100s; when acquired 60s; before 1066 £4.
Leofnoth, a thane of King Edward's, held this manor.

9 In the same (village) Reginald holds ½ hide from Walter.
Land for 2 ploughs. In lordship 1 plough;
    4 smallholders with 1 plough.
Value 20s; when acquired 10s; before 1066, 5s.
Ordric, Leofnoth's man, held this land; he could sell.

In BIGGLESWADE Hundred
10 In STRATTON [.....] holds 1 hide and 1 virgate. Land for 1½ ploughs; 1½ ploughs possible.
    3 smallholders.

P̃tũ . i . caŕ . Vaĺ . x . ſoĺ . 7 ſēp̄ ualuit . Hanc t̃rã tenuit
Leuuin Steign regis . E . 7 dare 7 uende potuit . H̄ jacet
7 jacuit in Langeford ₥ ejd Walterii.

In Holme ten Walteri . i . hid . T̃ra . ē . i . caŕ 7 dim̃ . Ibi
ē una caŕ . 7 dim̃ poteſt fieri . Ibi . iii . borđ . P̃tũ . i . caŕ
7 dim̃ . Vaĺ xx . ſoĺ . Qđo recep̃ꞏ xvi . ſoĺ . T.R.E.ꞏ xx . ſoĺ.
Hanc t̃rã tenueŕ . ii . ſocĥi . 7 potueŕ dare cui uolueŕ.

In Eſtuuiche ten Hugo . i . uirǵ de Walterio . T̃ra . ē . ii . boh.
7 ibi ſunt . Ibi . i . borđ . 7 i . moliñ de xiii . ſoĺ . Vaĺ 7 ualuit
ſēp̄ xvi . ſoĺ . Hanc t̃rã tenuit Leuuin teign regis . E.

₥ Ipſe Walteri ten *LANGEFORD* . p̄ x . hiđ ſe defđ . T̃ra . ē
xvi . caŕ . In dñio . iiii . hiđ 7 i . uirǵ . 7 ibi ſuɴ . iiii . caŕ . 7 v̊ꞇᵃ
poteſt fieri . Ibi . xii . uiɫɫi . vii . borđ . v . ſerui . cũ . ix . caŕ.
7 adhuc . ii . poſſ fieri . Ibi . ii . molini . de xxvi . ſoĺ . 7 viii . den.
p̃tũ xvi . caŕ . 7 ii . ſoĺ deſup̄ plus . De paſtura . vi . ſoliđ.
7 adhuc paſt . ē ad . ccc . oues . Silua . xvi . porc . Int tot
uaɫ xv . liƀ . 7 x . ſoĺ . Qđo recep̃ꞏ x . liƀ . T.R.E.ꞏ xv . liƀ.
Hoc ₥ tenuit Leuuin teign regis . E . 7 ibi un ſocĥs ha
buit . i . hiđ . 7 cui uoluit dare potuit . *IN WICHESTANESTOV*

In Sudgiuele ten Walteri dim̃ hiđ ſiluæ ⎾ *HVND*.
quã Anteceſſor ej tenuit . T.R.E.

In ead uilla ten Alric de Walterio . i . uirǵ . T̃ra . ē . iiii.
boh . 7 ibi ſunt . P̃tũ . iɪɪi . boh . Vaĺ . v . ſoĺ . Qđo recep̃ꞏ iii.
ſoliđ . T.R.E.ꞏ x . ſoĺ . Hanc t̃rã tenuit Leuuin teign regis
in uadimonio . T.R.E. Sꝗ poſtꝗ rex . W . uenit in angliã.
ille ipſe qui inuadiauit hanc t̃rã redemit . 7 Seiheŕ
eã occupauit ſup̄ regē . ut hões de hund teſtantur.

In Hanſlaue ten Hugo de Walto ⎾*IN CLISTON HVND*.
iii . hiđ 7 dim̃ . T̃ra . ē . iii . caŕ 7 dim̃ . In dñio . i . caŕ . 7 alia
poteſt fieri . Ibi . iiiɪ . uiɫɫi cũ . ii . caŕ . 7 iiii . borđ 7 ii . ſerui.

Meadow for 1 plough.

Value 10s; it always was.

Leofwin, a thane of King Edward's, held this land; he could grant and sell. It lies and lay in (the lands of) Langford, Walter's manor.

11 In HOLME Walter holds 1 hide. Land for 1½ ploughs; 1 plough there; ½ possible.

3 smallholders.

Meadow for 1½ ploughs.

Value 20s; when acquired 16s; before 1066, 20s.

2 Freemen held this land; they could grant to whom they would.

12 In ASTWICK Hugh holds 1 virgate from Walter. Land for 2 oxen; they are there.

1 smallholder.

1 mill at 13s.

The value is and always was 16s.

Leofwin, a thane of King Edward's, held this land.

13 M. Walter holds LANGFORD himself. It answers for 10 hides. Land for 16 ploughs. In lordship 4 hides and 1 virgate; 4 ploughs there; a fifth possible.

12 villagers, 7 smallholders and 5 slaves with 9 ploughs; a further 2 possible.

2 mills at 26s 8d; meadow for 16 ploughs and 2s over and above; from pasture 6s; in addition, pasturage for 300 sheep; woodland, 16 pigs.

In total, value £15 10s; when acquired £10; before 1066 £15.

Leofwin, a thane of King Edward's, held this manor. 1 Freeman had 1 hide; he could grant to whom he would.

In WIXAMTREE Hundred

14 In SOUTHILL Walter holds ½ hide of woodland which his predecessor held before 1066.

15 In the same village Alric holds 1 virgate from Walter. Land for 4 oxen; they are there.

Meadow for 4 oxen.

Value 5s; when acquired 3s; before 1066, 10s.

Leofwin, a thane of King Edward's, held this land in pledge before 1066; but after King William came to England, the man who pledged it redeemed this land, and Sihere appropriated it in the King's despite as the men of the Hundred testify.

In CLIFTON Hundred

16 In HENLOW Hugh holds 3½ hides from Walter. Land for 3½ ploughs. In lordship 1 plough; another possible.

4 villagers with 2 ploughs; 4 smallholders and 2 slaves.

Ptū . iii . car 7 dim . 7 i . moliñ de xxx.iiii . fot . Int totū uat
lx . fot . Q̃do recep̃ xl . fot . T . R . E . lxx . fot . Hanc tra
tenuer vi . fochi . 7 cui uoluer tra sua dare potuer.

216 a

.XXXIII. Ƿ TERRA WALTERIJ FRIS SEIER *In Ratborgestoc hvnd.*

Ƿ ALTERVS Fr Seiheri . ten Segenehov . p x . hid se
defd . Tra . e . x . car . In dñio . iiii . hidæ . 7 ibi . e una car . 7 ii .
car poss fieri . Ibi xxiiii . uitti hūt . vii . car . Ibi . iiii . bord .
7 iii . serui . p̃tū . viii . car . Silua . ccc . porc . 7 de csuetudine
siluæ . x . arietes p annū . Int totū uat . vi . lib . Q̃do recep̃
x . lib . T . R . E . xvi . lib . Hoc Ɯ tenuit Leuenot teign . R . E .
7 ibi un sochs habuit dim hid . 7 cui uoluit uende potuit.

Ɯ In Sewilessov . ten Hugo   *In Flictha hvnd.*
de Walterio . iiii . hid p uno Ɯ . Tra . e . x . car . In dñio
ii . car . 7 vi . uitti 7 viii . bord 7 iiii . serui . cū . vii . car . 7 viii .
potest fieri . Ibi . i . moliñ de . xxvi . den . Ptū . vi . car .
Silua . c . porc . 7 ii . sot . Int tot uat . viii . lib . Q̃do recep̃
. c . solid . T . R . E . xi . lib . Hoc Ɯ tenuit Leuenot teign
R . E . 7 ibi . iii . sochi dim hid tenuer . 7 cui uoluer dare
7 uende potuer . Hanc dim hid ten Hugo de rege . ut dñt

.IIII.
.XXX Ⱶ TERRA HVGON FLANDR *In Wilga hvnd.* E hoes ej.

Ⱶ VGO Flandrensis ten de rege in Podintone . ii . hidas
7 unā uirg . Tra . e . ii . car 7 dim . In dñio dimid hida .
7 una car . 7 iii . uitti hūt . i . car 7 dim . Ibi . vi . bord 7 un
seruus . Vat . xxx . fot . 7 tntd q̃do recep̃ . T . R . E . xl . fot .
Hanc tra . iiii . sochi tenuer . 7 cui uoluer uende potuer.

Ipse Hugo ten in Haneuuich . i . hid 7 dim de rege . Tra
e . iii . car . In dñio . ii . ear . 7 i . uitts 7 iiii . bord 7 iii . serui
cū . i . car . Vat xxx . fot . Q̃do recep̃ xx . fot . T . R . E . xl . fot.
Hanc tra tenuit Aluuold hō Wluui ep̃i . 7 uende potuit.

Meadow for 3½ ploughs; 1 mill at 34s.
In total, value 60s; when acquired 40s; before 1066, 70s.
6 Freemen held this land; they could grant their land to
whom they would.

LAND OF WALTER BROTHER OF SIHERE 216 a

In REDBORNSTOKE Hundred
1 M. Walter brother of Sihere holds SEGENHOE. It answers for 10 hides.
Land for 10 ploughs. In lordship 4 hides; 1 plough there;
2 ploughs possible.
24 villagers have 7 ploughs. 4 smallholders and 3 slaves.
Meadow for 8 ploughs; woodland, 300 pigs; from customary
woodland dues, 10 rams a year.
In total, value £6; when acquired £10; before 1066 £16.
Leofnoth, a thane of King Edward's, held this manor. 1 Freeman
had ½ hide; he could sell to whom he would.

In FLITT Hundred
2 M. In SILSOE Hugh holds 4 hides from William as one manor.
Land for 10 ploughs. In lordship 2 ploughs;
6 villagers, 8 smallholders and 4 slaves with 7 ploughs;
an eighth possible.
1 mill at 26d; meadow for 6 ploughs; woodland, 100 pigs
and 2s too.
In total, value £8; when acquired 100s; before 1066 £11.
Leofnoth, a thane of King Edward's, held this manor. 3 Freemen
held ½ hide; they could grant and sell to whom they would.
Hugh holds this ½ hide from the King, as his men state.

34 LAND OF HUGH OF FLANDERS

In WILLEY Hundred
1 Hugh of Flanders holds 2 hides and 1 virgate in PODINGTON from
the King. Land for 2½ ploughs. In lordship ½ hide; 1 plough.
3 villagers have 1½ ploughs. 6 smallholders and 1 slave.
Value 30s; as much when acquired; before 1066, 40s.
4 Freemen held this land; they could sell to whom they would.

2 Hugh holds 1½ hides in HINWICK himself from the King.
Land for 3 ploughs. In lordship 2 ploughs;
1 villager, 4 smallholders and 3 slaves with 1 plough.
Value 30s; when acquired 20s; before 1066, 40s.
Alfwold, Bishop Wulfwy's man, held this land; he could sell.

In Sernebroc ten Robt de Hugone dim̄ hid̄ 7 iiii.
parté uni uirg. Tra.ē.i.car.7 ibi eſt.7 un̄ bord 7 un̄
feruus.p̄tū.i.car.Val.x.ſol.Qdo recep̄.v.ſol.T.R.E.
xx.ſol.Hanc trā tenuit Leuric hō abbis de Ramefy.
7 cui uoluit dare potuit.

.XXXV. **H**TERRA HVGON PINCERNÆ *IN STODEN HVND.*

Hvgo pincerna ten̄ de rege. In Eſtone.ii.hidas
7 iii.uirg.Tra.ē.iiii.car.In dn̄io.i.hid.7 ibi.ii.car.
Ibi.iiii.uilli.7 un̄ bord 7 un̄ feruus eū.ii.car.p̄tū
.i.car.Silua.cc.porc.Val.xl.ſol.Qdo recep̄.lxx.
ſol.T.R.E.xl.ſol.Hoc M̄ tenuit Wig teign̄.R.E.
7 ibidé un̄ fochs dim̄ hid habuit.7 cui uol dare pot.
In Segreſdone ten̄ Hugo.i.uirg.7 ual̄ xii.den.
T.R.E.ii.ſol.Hanc trā tenuit Aluuin̄ hō Heialdi com.
7 cui uoluit dare potuit.   *IN STODEN HVND.*

.XXXVI. **S**TERRA SIGARI DE CIOCHES.

Sygarvs de Cioches ten̄ in Eſtone.ii.hid de rege.
Tra.ē.v.car.In dn̄io.ii.carucatæ træ.7 ibi fuŋ.ii.car.
7 vi.uilli hn̄t.iii.car.Ibi.xii.bord.7 ii.ſerui.p̄tū.
.i.car.Silua.lx.porc.Val.iiii.lib.Qdo recep̄.iii.lib.
T.R.E.iiii.lib.Hanc trā Wig teign̄.R.E.tenuit.
7 cui uoluit dare 7 uende potuit.

.XXXVII. **G**TERRA GVNFRIDI DE CIOCHES *IN WILGA HVND.*

Gvnfrid de cioches ten̄ jn Haneuuic.i.hid 7 iii.uirg.
Tetbald de eo.Tra.ē.iii.car.In dn̄io.i.car.7 ii.car
poſs fieri.Ibi.iii.uilli.Val.xx.ſol.Qdo recep̄.x.ſol.
T.R.E.xl.ſol.Hanc trā tenuer.ii.fochi.7 cui uoluer
dare 7 uendere potuer.

3 In SHARNBROOK Robert holds ½ hide and the fourth part of 1 virgate from Hugh. Land for 1 plough; it is there.
1 smallholder; 1 slave.
Meadow for 1 plough.
Value 10s; when acquired 5s; before 1066, 20s.
Leofric, the Abbot of Ramsey's man, held this land; he could grant to whom he would.

35   LAND OF HUGH BUTLER

In STODDEN Hundred

1 Hugh Butler holds 2 hides and 3 virgates in EASTON from the King. Land for 4 ploughs. In lordship 1 hide; 2 ploughs there.
4 villagers, 1 smallholder and 1 slave with 2 ploughs.
Meadow for 1 plough; woodland, 200 pigs.
Value 40s; when acquired 70s; before 1066, 40s.
Wig, a thane of King Edward's, held this manor. There also 1 Freeman had ½ hide; he could grant to whom he would.

2 In 'SHIRDON' Hugh holds 1 virgate.
Value 12d; before 1066, 2s.
Alwin, Earl Harold's man, held this land; he could grant to whom he would.

36   LAND OF SIGAR OF CHOCQUES

In STODDEN Hundred

1 Sigar of Chocques holds 2 hides in EASTON from the King.
Land for 5 ploughs. In lordship 2 carucates of land besides the 2 hides. 2 ploughs there.
6 villagers have 3 ploughs. 12 smallholders and 2 slaves.
Meadow for 1 plough; woodland, 60 pigs.
Value £4; when acquired £3; before 1066 £4.
Wig, a thane of King Edward's, held this land; he could grant and sell to whom he would.

37   LAND OF GUNFRID OF CHOCQUES

In WILLEY Hundred

1 Gunfrid of Chocques holds 1 hide and 3 virgates in HINWICK, and Theodbald from him. Land for 3 ploughs. In lordship 1 plough; 2 ploughs possible.
3 villagers.
Value 20s; when acquired 10s; before 1066, 40s.
2 Freemen held this land; they could grant and sell to whom they would.

TERRA RICARDI FILIJ GISLEBTI *In Bereford hvnd.*

.XXXVIII. RICARD fili Gislebti comitis ten in Subberie. 1. uirg
træ. quæ jacet in æccła S Neoti. 7 jacuit T.R.E.

In Wiboldeſtone tenent monachi S Neoti de Ricardo
p̄dicto. 11. hid 7 dim uirg. Tra. ē dim car. ſʒ n̄ eſt ibi.
Silua. c. porc. Val. xi. ſot. Q̣do recep̄. ſimił. T.R.E.
xxi. ſot. H tra jacuit in æccła S Neoti. T.R.E. in elem.

.XXXIX. TERRA RICARDI PVNGIANT. *In Bicheleswade hd.*

RICARDVS puniant ten de rege jn Daintone
.viii. hid 7 uirg p uno M. Tra. ē. viii. car.
In dn̄io. 1111. hid 7 1. uirg. 7 ibi ſunt. 111. car. Ibi. xii.
uiłłi hn̄t. v. car. 7 11. bord. 7 111. ſerui. Silua. lx.
porc. Int totu ual. viii. liƀ. Q̣do recep̄. vi. liƀ.
7 tāntd. T.R.E. Hoc M tenuit Stigand Archiep̄s.
In Tamiſeforde ten Roƀt de Ricardo pg. 11. hid de
feudo regis. Tra. ē. 11. car. In dn̄io. 1. car. 7 1111. uiłłi cū. 1.
car. p̄tū. 1. car. Val. xxx. ſot. Q̣do recep̄. xx. ſot. T.R.E.
xx. ſot. Hanc tra tenuer. 111. ſochi. 7 cui uoluer dare potuer.
In Sudgiuele ten Ricard pg dim hid ſiluæ *In Wichestanstov*
quā tenuit Stigand Archiep̄s T.R.E. *F hvnd.*

.XL. TERRA WILLI CAMERAR *In Manesheve hvnd.*

WILLELM camerarius ten in Poteſgraue. 1. hid de
rege. Tra. ē. 1. car. 7 ibi eſt. p̄tū. 1. car. Val. xv. ſot. Q̣do
recep̄. ſimilit. T.R.E. xl. ſot. Hanc tra tenuit Morcar pƀr
de Lintone. 7 uende potuit.

LAND OF RICHARD SON OF COUNT GILBERT

In BARFORD Hundred

1 Richard son of Count Gilbert holds 1 virgate of land in 'SUDBURY'
which lies in (the lands of) St Neot's Church and did so before 1066.

2 In WYBOSTON the monks of St Neot hold 2 hides and ½ virgate from
the said Richard. Land for ½ plough, but it is not there.
Woodland, 100 pigs.
Value 11s; when acquired the same; before 1066, 21s.
This land lay in (the lands of) St Neot's Church before 1066, in alms.

LAND OF RICHARD POYNANT

In BIGGLESWADE Hundred

1 M. Richard Poynant holds 8 hides and [a?] virgate in DUNTON from the
King as one manor. Land for 8 ploughs. In lordship 4 hides and 1
virgate. 3 ploughs there.
12 villagers have 5 ploughs. 2 smallholders and 3 slaves.
Woodland, 60 pigs.
In total, value £8; when acquired £6; as much before 1066.
Archbishop Stigand held this manor.

2 In TEMPSFORD Robert holds 2 hides, of the King's Holding, from
Richard Poynant. Land for 2 ploughs. In lordship 1 plough;
4 villagers with 1 plough.
Meadow for 1 plough.
Value 30s; when acquired 20s; before 1066, 20s.
3 Freemen held this land; they could grant to whom they would.

In WIXAMTREE Hundred
3 In SOUTHILL Richard Poynant holds ½ hide of woodland which
Archbishop Stigand held before 1066.

LAND OF WILLIAM THE CHAMBERLAIN

In MANSHEAD Hundred
1 William the Chamberlain holds 1 hide in POTSGROVE from the King.
Land for 1 plough; it is there.
Meadow for 1 plough.
Value 15s; when acquired the same; before 1066, 40s.
Morcar the priest of Luton held this land; he could sell.

In Badeleſtone ten Robt de Witto camer dim̃ hid. Tra . ē
dim̃ car̃ . Val . v . ſol . Q̃do recep̃. ſimilit. T.R.E. vii . lib. Hanc
tr̃a tenuit Morcar p̃br. 7 uende potuit. *IN DIM̃ HVND.*

(M) Ipſe Witts ten̄ Totenehou de rege   *┌ DE STANBVRGE.*
p̃ vii . hid una uirga min̄ ſe deſd . Tra . ē . vi . car̃ . In dñio
iii . hide 7 iii . uirg. 7 ibi . ē una car̃ . Ibi . iiii . uitti hñt
iii . car̃ . Ibi . iiii . bord̃. 7 iiii . ſerui. 7 uñ molin̄ . iii . ſolid̃.
P̊t̃u . iii . car̃ . Silua . xx . porc̃ . Val . l . ſol . Q̃do recep̃.
ſimit. T.R.E. viii . lib . Hoc (M) tenuit Leuuine hõ Wallef
comitis . Cũ hoc (M) reclamat . W . camerari . ii . hid.
q̃s ej anteceſſor tenuit T.R.E. ſ̃ic Hund̃ teſtat̃ . ſed eps
baiocenſis p̃ uim ei abſtulit. 7 Adelulfo ſuo cam̃ ded̃.

.XLI.   TERRA WILLI LOVET. *IN MANESHEVE HVND.*

(M) Witts Louet ten̄ in Crauelai de rege . v . hidas.
p̃ uno (M). Tra . ē . v . car̃ . In dñio . ii . hidæ. 7 ii . car̃.
7 v . uitti hñt . ii . car̃. 7 tcia poteſt fieri. Ibi . iii . bord̃.
7 ii . ſerui. 7 ii . molini . x . ſol . p̊t̃u . v . car̃ . Val xl . ſol.
Q̃do recep̃. xxx . ſol . T.R.E. c . ſol . Hoc (M) tenuit Grim
bald hõ regis . E. 7 cui uoluit dare potuit.   *┌ HVND.*

(M) Ipſe Witts ten̄ Flicteuuiche de rege. *IN RABORGESTOV*
p̃ v . hid ſe deſd . Tra . ē . vii . car̃ . In dñio . ii . hidæ. 7 ibi
. ii . car̃ . Ibi . iii . uitti hñt . iii . car̃. 7 ii . adhuc poſſuɲ fieri.
Ibi . vii . bord̃. 7 uñ molin̄ . iiii . ſolid̃ . p̊t̃u . v . car̃ . Silua
c . porc̃ . Val . l . ſol . Q̃do recep̃. lx . ſol . T.R.E. viii . lib.
Hoc (M) tenuit Aluuin teign regis. E.

.XLII. TERRA WILLI   *IN WILGE HVND.*
Witts ten̄ de rege in Fernadis . ii . hid. Tra . ē . ii . car̃
7 dim̃. In dñio ſunt . ii . car̃. 7 iii . uitti hñt dim̃ car̃ . Ibi . ii.
bord̃. 7 uñ ſeruus. p̊t̃u . i . car̃ . Val . xl . ſol . Q̃do recep̃.
xx . ſol . T.R.E. xl . ſol . Hanc tr̃a tenuer̃ . iii . ſochi. 7 cui
uoluer̃ dare 7 uendere potuer̃.

2   In BATTLESDEN Robert holds ½ hide from William the Chamberlain.
Land for ½ plough.
Value 5s; when acquired the same; before 1066 £7 (7s?).
Morcar the priest held this land; he could sell.

In the Half-Hundred of STANBRIDGE

3 M. William holds TOTTERNHOE himself from the King. It answers
for 7 hides less 1 virgate. Land for 6 ploughs. In lordship 3 hides
and 3 virgates. 1 plough there.
    4 villagers have 3 ploughs. 4 smallholders and 4 slaves.
    1 mill, 3s; meadow for 3 ploughs, woodland, 20 pigs.
Value 50s; when acquired the same; before 1066 £8.
    Leofwin, Earl Waltheof's man, held this manor. With this manor
William the Chamberlain claims 2 hides which his predecessor held
before 1066, as the Hundred testifies; but the Bishop of Bayeux
took them away from him by force and gave them to his chamberlain
Aethelwulf.

1   **LAND OF WILLIAM LOVETT**

In MANSHEAD Hundred

1 M. William Lovett holds 5 hides in (Husborne) CRAWLEY from the King, as
one manor. Land for 5 ploughs. In lordship 2 hides; 2 ploughs there.
    5 villagers have 2 ploughs; a third possible. 3 smallholders
    and 2 slaves.
    2 mills, 10s; meadow for 5 ploughs.
Value 40s; when acquired 30s; before 1066, 100s.
    Grimbald, King Edward's man, held this manor; he could grant
to whom he would.

In REDBORNSTOKE Hundred

2 M. William holds FLITWICK himself, from the King. It answers for 5 hides.
Land for 7 ploughs. In lordship 2 hides. 2 ploughs there.
    3 villagers have 3 ploughs; a further 2 possible. 7 smallholders.
    1 mill, 4s; meadow for 5 ploughs; woodland, 100 pigs.
Value 50s; when acquired 60s; before 1066 £8.
    Alwin, a thane of King Edward's, held this manor.

42   **LAND OF WILLIAM**

In WILLEY Hundred

1   William holds 2 hides in FARNDISH from the King. Land for 2½ ploughs.
In lordship 2 ploughs.
    3 villagers have ½ plough. 2 smallholders and 1 slave.
    Meadow for 1 plough.
Value 40s; when acquired 20s; before 1066, 40s.
    3 Freemen held this land; they could grant and sell to whom they
would.

.XLIII. TERRA HEN RICI FILII AZOR *IN WILGA HVND.*

HENRICVS filius Azor in Fernadis tẽ de rege
.ɪ.hiđ.Tra.ē.ɪ.caɼ.7 ibi eſt.7 ɪɪ.uiłłi ibi ſuɣ.p̃tum
dim caɼ.Vał 7 ualuit.x.ſoł.T.R.E.ʼxx.ſoł.Hanc
trã.ɪɪ.ſocħi tẽnucɼ.7 cui uolueɼ dare potueɼ.

.XLIÍ. TERRA OSBERNI FILII RICARDI *IN STODENE HVND.*

OSBERN filius Ricardi 7 Hugo hubald de eo tẽ in
Eſtone dim hiđ 7 dim uirg.Tra.ē.ɪ.caɼ.7 ibi eſt.
cũ uno ſeruo.P̃tũ.ɪ.caɼ.Silua.xx.porc.Vał.x.ſoł.
Q̇do recep̃.ſimił.T.R.E.ʼxɪɪ.ſoł.Hanc trã tenuit
Stori ħo Toſti comitis.7 ibi q̇đã ſocħs dim uirg ha
buit.q̇ dare 7 uende potuit.

In Riſelai tẽ Hugo hubald de Osbto Ricardi filio
dim hiđ.Tra.ē.dim caɼ.7 ibi.ē cũ uno borđ.p̃tũ dim
caɼ.Vał.v.ſoł.7 ualuit.T.R.E.ʼvɪɪɪ.ſoł.Hanc trã
tenuit Aluuin ħo Stori.7 potuit dare cui uoluit.
In Caiſſot tẽ Hugo hubald de Osbto.ɪ.uirg.Tra.ē.ɪɪ.
bob.Vał 7 ualuit.ɪɪ.ſoł.T.R.E.ʼɪɪɪɪ.ſoł.

Ipſe hugo tẽ de Osbno Eluendone.p̃ una hiđ 7 una
uirga ſe defđ.Tra.ɪ.caɼ 7 dim.7 ſunt ibi.p̃tũ.ɪ.caɼ.
Silua.xxx.porc.Vał 7 ualuit.x.ſoł.T.R.E.ʼxv.ſoł.
Hoc Ꝏ tenuit Aluuin ħo Stori.7 cui uoluit dare potuit.

.XLV. TERRA OSBNI FILIJ WALTERIJ. *IN BICHELESWADE HĐ.*

OSBERN filius Walterij tẽ de rege in Bereforde
ɪɪɪ.hiđ.p̃ uno Ꝏ.Tra.ē.ɪɪɪ.caɼ.In dñio.ɪɪ.caɼ.7 ɪɪɪɪ.
uiłłi hñt.ɪ.caɼ.Ibi.ɪɪ.borđ.7 v.ſerui.p̃tũ.ɪ.caɼ.
Vał.ʟx.ſoł.Q̇do recep̃.ʼxʟ.ſoł.T.R.E.ʼʟx.ſoł.Hoc
Ꝏ tenuit Vlmar de Etone teign regis.E.

LAND OF HENRY SON OF AZOR

In WILLEY Hundred

1 Henry son of Azor holds 1 hide in FARNDISH from the King. Land
for 1 plough; it is there.
2 villagers.
Meadow for ½ plough.
The value is and was 10s; before 1066, 20s.
2 Freemen held this land; they could grant to whom they would.

LAND OF OSBERN SON OF RICHARD

In STODDEN Hundred

1 Osbern son of Richard holds ½ hide and ½ virgate in EASTON
and Hugh Hubald from him. Land for 1 plough; it is
there, with 1 slave.
Meadow for 1 plough; woodland, 20 pigs.
Value 10s; when acquired the same; before 1066, 12s.
Stori, Earl Tosti's man, held this land. A Freeman had ½ virgate,
which he could grant and sell.

2 In RISELEY Hugh Hubald holds ½ hide from Osbern son of Richard.
Land for ½ plough; it is there, with
1 smallholder.
Meadow for ½ plough.
The value is and was 5s; before 1066, 8s.
Alwin, Stori's man, held this land; he could grant to whom he would.

3 In KEYSOE Hugh Hubald holds 1 virgate from Osbern. Land for 2 oxen.
The value is and was 2s; before 1066, 4s.

4 M.Hugh holds 'ELVEDON' himself from Osbern. It answers for 1 hide
and 1 virgate. Land for 1½ ploughs; they are there.
Meadow for 1 plough; woodland, 34 pigs.
The value is and was 10s; before 1066, 15s.
Alwin, Stori's man, held this manor; he could grant to whom he
would.

5

LAND OF OSBERN SON OF WALTER

In BIGGLESWADE Hundred

1 M. Osbern son of Walter holds 3 hides in (Little) BARFORD from the
King as one manor. Land for 3 ploughs. In lordship 2 ploughs.
4 villagers have 1 plough. 2 smallholders and 5 slaves.
Meadow for 1 plough.
Value 60s; when acquired 40s; before 1066, 60s.
Wulfmer of Eaton, a thane of King Edward's, held this manor.

O TERRA OSBERNI PISCATORIS. *IN WILGE HVND.*

Osbern piſcator ten̄ in Sernebroc de rege dim̄ hid̄.
Tra.ē.ı.car̄.7 ibi.ē.Vnū molin̄.xvı.den.p̄tū dim̄ car̄.
Silua.x.porc̄.7 unū uiuariū piſciū.Ibi un̄ uiłłs.7 ıı.
bord̄.Vał.xxvı.ſoł.Q̸do recep̄:´x.ſoł.T.R.E:´xl.ſoł.
Hanc tr̄a tenuit Toui Huſcarle regis.E.7 uend̄e potuit.
Cū iſta tra reclamat iſd̄ Osb̄n unā uirg 7 ıııı.parte᷃
uni uirg q̃ tenuit Anteceſſor ej.T.R.E:´Sed poſtquā
rex.W.in Angliā uenit.ille gablū de hac tra dare
noluit.7 Radulf tailgeboſc gablū dedit 7 p̃ forisfaɔ̄to
ipſam
|terrā sūpſit.7 cuidā ſuo militi tribuit.

In Carlentone ten̄ iſd̄ Osb̄n de rege.ı.hid̄ 7 unā uirg
7 dim̄.Tra.ē.ıı.car̄.In dn̄io.ı.car̄.7 ıı.uiłti.hn̄t.ı.car̄.
Ibi.ıııı.bord̄.p̄tū.ıı.car̄.Vał 7 ualuit.xx.ſoł.T.R.E.
T.R.E:´xl.ſoł.Hanc tr̄a tenuit Goduin̄ frambolt.
teign̄ regis.E.7 uend̄e potuit.

T TERRA TVRSTINI CAMERAR̄ *IN BVCHELAI HVND.*

Tvrstin̄ camerarius ten̄ de rege in Pabeneh̄a
ıı.hid̄ 7 dim̄.p̃ uno ꝏ.Tra.ē.ıııı.car̄.In dn̄io.ı.
hid̄a.7 una car̄.Ibi.vı.uiłti cū.ıı.car̄.7 ı.bord̄.
P̄tū.ııı.car̄.Vał.xl.ſoł.Q̸do recep̄:´ſimił.T.R.E:´
xl.v.ſoł.Hanc tr̄a tenuit Alſi hō Alli fr̄is ej.7 potuit

In Heneuuic ten̄ Turſtin̄ de rege.ı.hid̄.7 ıııı.uirg.
Tra.ē.ıı.car̄.In dn̄io.ı.hid̄ 7 ı.car̄.7 ıı.uiłti cū.ı.car̄.
7 ı.bord̄.p̄tū.ı.car̄.Vał xxx.ſoł.Q̸do recep̄:´x.ſoł.
T.R.E:´xxx.ſoł.Hanc tr̄a tenuit Goduin̄ fr̄abolt
teign̄ regis.E. *IN WICHESTANESTOV HVND.*

216 d

In Biſtone ten̄ Turſtin̄ p̄dict dim̄ hid̄ de rege.Tra.ē
dim̄ car̄:ſʒ n̄ ē ibi.P̄tū.ı.car̄.H̄ tra deuaſtata.ē

LAND OF OSBERN FISHER

In WILLEY Hundred

1 Osbern Fisher holds ½ hide in SHARNBROOK from the King.
Land for 1 plough; it is there.
A mill, 16d; meadow for ½ plough; woodland, 10 pigs; a fish-pond.
1 villager; 2 smallholders.
Value 26s; when acquired 10s; before 1066, 40s.
Tovi, one of King Edward's Guards, held this land; he could sell.
With this land Osbern also claims 1 virgate and the fourth part of
a virgate which his predecessor held before 1066; but after King
William came to England, he refused to give the tribute of this land,
and Ralph Tallboys gave the tribute, and took over this land as a
forfeiture, and gave it to one of his men-at-arms.

2 In CARLTON Osbern also holds 1 hide and 1½ virgates from the King.
Land for 2 ploughs. In lordship 1 plough.
2 villagers have 1 plough. 4 smallholders.
Meadow for 2 ploughs.
The value is and was 20s; before 1066, 40s.
Godwin Frambold, a thane of King Edward's, held this land; he could
sell.

47 LAND OF THURSTAN THE CHAMBERLAIN

In BUCKLOW Hundred

1 Thurstan the Chamberlain holds 2½ hides in PAVENHAM from the King,
as one manor. Land for 3 ploughs. In lordship 1 hide; 1 plough there;
6 villagers with 2 ploughs; 1 smallholder.
Meadow for 3 ploughs.
Value 40s; when acquired the same; before 1066, 45s.
Alfsi, his brother Alli's man, held this land; he could (sell).

[In WILLEY Hundred]

2 In HINWICK Thurstan holds 1 hide and 3 virgates from the King.
Land for 2 ploughs. In lordship 1 hide; 1 plough there;
2 villagers with 1 plough; 1 smallholder.
Meadow for 1 plough.
Value 30s; when acquired 10s; before 1066, 30s.
Godwin Frambold, a thane of King Edward's, held this land.

In WIXAMTREE Hundred

3 In BEESTON the said Thurstan holds ½ hide from the King.   216 d
Land for ½ plough, but it is not there.
Meadow for 1 plough.

ſ; q̇do Turſtiñ recep.̃ ualebat . x . ſoł . T.R.E.̃ xx . ſoł.

Hanc t̃rã tenuit Goduiñ hõ Toſti comitis.7 dare potuit.

In Chambeltone teñ Turſtiñ   *IN CLISTONE HVND.*

de rege . ii . hid̃.7 iiii . part̃e uni uirg̃ miñ . T̃ra . ē

una car̃ 7 dĩm . In dñio . i . hid̃ .7 i . uirg̃.7 iii.part

uni uirg̃.7 ibi eſt una car̃ . Ibi . ii . uiłłi 7 uñ bord̃

h̃nt dĩm car̃ . p̃tū . i . car̃ .7 dĩm . Silua . xx . porc̃.

Vał xxx . ſoł.7 ualuit . T.R.E.̃ xl . ſoł . Hanc t̃rã tenuer̃

iii . ſoch̃i.7 cui uoluer̃ dare 7 uend̃e potuer̃.

.XLVII.   ҉ TERRA GISLEB̃TI FILIJ SALOMOÑ. *IN CLISTONE HVND.*

ʍ G̃ISLEBERT filius Salomonis teñ Malpteſſelle

de rege . p̃ iiii . hid̃ ſe defd̃ in Bedeforde ſcire . T̃ra . ē

iiii . car̃ . In Herefortſcire ipſa uilla ſe defd̃ p̃ . iii.

hid̃ 7 una uirg̃ . T̃ra . ē . iii . car̃ . Int totū . vii . car̃ ſuꝗ.

In dñio . v . hidæ.7 iii . car̃.7 adhuc . ii . poſſ fieri . Ibi . v.

uiłłi h̃nt . ii . car̃.7 iiii . bord̃.7 ii . ſerui . P̃tū . vii . car̃ . Silua

.cc . porc̃.7 de c̃ſuetudine ſiluæ . x . ſoł . Vał 7 ualuit . vi . lib.

T.R.E.̃ x.lib̃ . Hoc ʍ tenuit Leuuiñ cilt teigñ.R.E.

7 in hoc ʍ fuer̃ . iiii . ſoch̃i . ii . hid̃ tenuer̃.7 cui uoluer̃

uend̃e potuer̃.   *IN WILGA HVND.*

In Flãmereſh̃a teñ Giſleb̃t vii . hid̃ 7 dĩm . T̃ra . ē . viii.

ʍ car̃ . In dñio . iiii . hide.7 ibi ſuꝗ . iii . car̃.7 iiii . uiłłi h̃nt

iiii . car̃ . Ibi . vi . bord̃ . p̃tū . iiii . car̃ . Vał c . ſoł . Q̇do recep.̃

xii . lib̃.7 tntd̃ T.R.E. Hoc ʍ.vi . ſoch̃i tenuer̃.7 uend̃e potuer̃.

.XLIX.   ҉ TERRA ALBERTI LOTHARIENS̃ *IN MANESHEVE HVND.*

ʍ A̧LBERTVS Lotherenſis teñ de rege *CELGRAVE* . p̃ . viii . hid̃

7 ii . partib̃ uni uirg̃ ſe defd̃ . T̃ra . ē . x . car̃ . In dñio . iii . caru

catæ træ.7 ibi ſunt . ii . car̃ . Ibi xiii . uiłłi h̃nt . viii . car̃ . Ibi

iiii . bord̃.7 vi . ſerui . P̃tū . viii . car̃ . Silua . l . porc̃ . Valet

This land has been laid waste; but when Thurstan acquired it
the value was 10s; before 1066, 20s.
Godwin, Earl Tosti's man, held this land; he could grant.

In CLIFTON Hundred

4   In CAMPTON Thurstan holds 2 hides less the fourth part of 1 virgate
from the King. Land for 1½ ploughs. In lordship 1 hide, 1 virgate
and three parts of a virgate; 1 plough there.
2 villagers and 1 smallholder have ½ plough.
Meadow for 1½ ploughs; woodland, 20 pigs.
The value is 30s; before 1066, 40s.
3 Freemen held this land; they could grant and sell to
whom they would.

48   LAND OF GILBERT SON OF SOLOMON

In CLIFTON Hundred

1   M. Gilbert son of Solomon holds MEPPERSHALL from the King. It answers
for 4 hides in Bedfordshire. Land for 4 ploughs. In Hertfordshire
this village answers for 3 hides and 1 virgate. Land for 3 ploughs.
In total, 7 ploughs. In lordship 5 hides; 3 ploughs there;
a further 2 possible.
5 villagers have 2 ploughs. 4 smallholders and 2 slaves.
Meadow for 7 ploughs; woodland, 200 pigs; from the customary
dues of the woodland, 10s.
The value is and was £6; before 1066 £10.
Young Leofwin, a thane of King Edward's, held this manor.
In this manor were 4 Freemen; they held 2 hides; they could sell
to whom they would.

In WILLEY Hundred

2   M. In FELMERSHAM Gilbert holds 7½ hides. Land for 8 ploughs.
In lordship 4 hides; 3 ploughs there.
4 villagers have 4 ploughs. 6 smallholders.
Meadow for 4 ploughs.
Value 100s; when acquired £12; as much before 1066.
6 Freemen held this manor; they could sell.

49   LAND OF ALBERT OF LORRAINE

In MANSHEAD Hundred

1   M. Albert of Lorraine holds CHALGRAVE from the King. It answers for 8
hides and 2 parts of 1 virgate. Land for 10 ploughs. In lordship 3
carucates of land; 2 ploughs there.
13 villagers have 8 ploughs. 4 smallholders and 6 slaves.
Meadow for 8 ploughs; woodland, 50 pigs.

vii . lib. Q̇do recep̃.᷑ vi . lib. 7 tntd T.R.E . Hoc Ⓜ tenuit
ifdẽ Albt. T.R.E. 7 cui uoluit dare potuit.   ⎡HVND.᷑

Ⓜ Ipſe Albt teñ OTONE . ꝑ x . hiđ ſe defđ. IN RADBERNESTOC
Tra. ẽ xi. car. In dñio. ii . hidæ . 7 ibi. iii . car. Ibi . xx . uilli
hñt. vii . car. 7 viii. poſſet fieri. Ibi . vi . ſerui . p̃tu . v . car.
Silua . cccc . porc . Val . x . lib . Q̇do recep̃.᷑ viii . lib . T.R.E.᷑
x . lib 7 xv . ſol. Hoc Ⓜ tenuit Almar hõ Tofti . 7 uende pot.᷑

In Effeltone teñ Albt . iii . hiđ . Tra . ẽ . v . car. In dñio una
hida. 7 ibi . ii . car. Ibi . vii . uilli . cũ . iii . car. 7 iiii . ſerui.
p̃tu . iii . car. Silua . c . porc. Val . xl . ſol. Q̇do recep̃.᷑ xx.
ſol. T.R.E.᷑ xlv . ſol. Hoc Ⓜ fuit 7 eft mẽbrũ de Otone.
Almar tenuit hõ Tofti comitis. IN WILGA HVND

In Sernebroc teñ Albt. ii . hiđ 7 iiii . part uni uirg.᷑
Tra. ẽ. iii . car. In dñio . i . hida. 7 ibi . ii . car. 7 iiii . uilli cũ
una . car. Ibi . iiii . borđ. 7 iiii . ſerui. 7 uñ moliñ . xvi . ſol.
p̃tu. ii . car. Silua . xl . porc. Val . l . ſol. Q̇do recep̃.᷑
xxx. ſol. T.R.E.᷑ lx . ſol. Hanc tra tenuit Algar hõ Edid
reginæ. 7 cui uoluit dare potuit.

.L. D AVID de Argentomo teñ In Rifelai . i . hiđ de rege.
TERRA DAVID DE ARGENT.᷑ IN STODENE HVND.
Tra. ẽ. i . car. ſed ibi non. ẽ. Ibi uñ uills. 7 iii . borđ.
Val. x . ſol. Q̇do recep̃.᷑ xx . ſol. T.R.E.᷑ fimilit.᷑ Hanc
tra tenuit Homdai hõ Heraldi . 7 cui uoluit uende potuit.
217 a

.LI. R ADVLFVS de infula teñ de rege jn Stratone . iiii.
TERRA RADVLFI DE INSVLA. IN BICHELESWADE ⎡HVND.᷑
hiđ. ꝑ uno Ⓜ. Tra . ẽ . viii . car. Ibi ſunt vii . 7 viii . poteft
fieri. Ibi . x . uilli 7 ii. borđ. p̃tu. iiii . car. Int totũ ual
xii . lib. Q̇do recep̃.᷑ iiii . lib. T.R.E.᷑ c . ſol. Hoc Ⓜ tenuit
Stigand archiep̃s.

Value £7; when acquired £6; as much before 1066.
Albert also held this manor before 1066; he could grant to whom he would.

In REDBORNSTOKE Hundred

2 M. Albert holds WOOTTON himself. It answers for 10 hides.
Land for 11 ploughs. In lordship 2 hides. 3 ploughs there.
20 villagers have 7 ploughs; an eighth possible. 6 slaves.
Meadow for 5 ploughs; woodland, 400 pigs.
Value £10; when acquired £8; before 1066 £10 15s.
Aelmer, Earl Tosti's man, held this manor; he could sell.

3 In SHELTON Albert holds 3 hides. Land for 5 ploughs.
In lordship 1 hide; 2 ploughs there.
7 villagers with 3 ploughs; 4 slaves.
Meadow for 3 ploughs; woodland, 100 pigs.
Value 40s; when acquired 20s; before 1066, 45s.
This manor is and was a member of Wootton. Aelmer,
Earl Tosti's man, held it.

In WILLEY Hundred

4 In SHARNBROOK Albert holds 2 hides and the fourth part of 1
virgate. Land for 3 ploughs. In lordship 1 hide; 2 ploughs there.
4 villagers with 1 plough. 4 smallholders and 4 slaves.
A mill, 16s; meadow for 2 ploughs; woodland, 40 pigs.
Value 50s; when acquired 30s; before 1066, 60s.
Algar, Queen Edith's man, held this land; he could grant
to whom he would.

50   LAND OF DAVID OF ARGENTON

In STODDEN Hundred

1 David of Argenton holds 1 hide in RISELEY from the King.
Land for 1 plough; but it is not there.
1 villager and 3 smallholders.
Value 10s; when acquired 20s; before 1066 the same.
Honday, Earl Harold's man, held this land; he could sell
to whom he would.

51   LAND OF RALPH DE L'ISLE   217 a

In BIGGLESWADE Hundred

1 M. Ralph de L'Isle holds 4 hides in STRATTON from the King as
one manor. Land for 8 ploughs. 7 there; an eighth possible.
10 villagers and 2 smallholders.
Meadow for 4 ploughs.
In total, value £12; when acquired £4; before 1066, 100s.
Archbishop Stigand held this manor.

ꝏ Ipſe Radulf⁹ ten̄ Pichelefuuade..p.x.hiđ ſe defđ.

Tra.ē.x.caꝛ.In dn̄io.v.hiđ 7 dim̄.7 iii.caꝛ ibi ſuꝰ.

Ibi.vii.uiłłi cū.vii.caꝛ.7 x.borđ.7 iii.ſerui.7 ii.molini

de.xlvii.ſoł.p̄tū.x.caꝛ.7 v.ſoliđ de feno.Vał.xvii.

liƀ.Q̷do recep̄.xv.liƀ.T.R.E.x.liƀ.Hoc ꝏ tenuit

Stigand archieps.7 ibi.ii.ſocħi dimiđ hiđ habueꝛ.

quā dare 7 uende potueꝛ.

ꝏ In Holme ten̄ iſđ Radulf⁹.ii.hiđ.Tra.ē.v.caꝛ.7 ibi

ſunt.Ibi.vi.uiłłi.p̄tū.i.caꝛ.Vał.xl.ſoł.Q̷do recep̄.

xxx.ſoł.T.R.E.xl.ſoł.Hoc ꝏ tenuit Stigandus

arcħ.7 ibi.iii.ſocħi.ii.uirg tre habueꝛ.7 uende potueꝛ.

In Wardone ten̄ iſđ Radulf⁹ IN WICHESTANESTOV HD̄.

de rege.i.uirg 7 dim̄.H̄ tra jacet in Bichelefuuade.

7 ibi eſt ap̄pciata.7 qui eā.T.R.E. tenuit nec uendere

nec dare potuit ſine licentia ej⁹ qui Bichelefuuade ten̄.

.LII. TERRA GOZELINI BRITONIS. IN MANESHEVE HVND̄.

ꝏ Gozelin⁹ brito ten̄ de rege in Poteſgraue.vii.hiđ

7 dim̄ ꝑ uno ꝏ.Tra.ē.vii.caꝛ 7 dim̄.In dn̄io.iii.hiđ.

7 ibi ſunt.iii.caꝛ.Ibi.iii.uiłłi hn̄t.ii.caꝛ.7 aliæ.ii.7 dim̄

pot fieri.Ibi.vi.borđ.7 iii.ſerui.P̄tū.v.caꝛ.Vał.l.

ſoł.Q̷do recep̄.c.ſoł.T.R.E.x.liƀ.Hoc ꝏ.iiii.teigni

tenueꝛ.7 cui uolueꝛ tā ſuā dare 7 uendere potueꝛ.

Ipſe Gozelin⁹ ten̄ Gledelai   IN DIM̄ HVND STANBVRGE.

ꝑ.ii.hiđ 7 dim̄.Tra.ē.i.caꝛ.7 ibi ſunt.iiii.boues.7 uñ

moliñ.xvi.ſoł.p̄tū.i.caꝛ.Silua.c.porc.Vał 7 ualuit

xx.ſoł.T.R.E.xl.ſoł.Hanc tā tenuit Wigot uenator

regis.E.7 cui uoluit uende potuit.   ꝼ HVND̄.

.LIII. TERRA JVDITÆ COMITISSÆ. IN RADBORGESTOC

ꝏ Jvdita comitiſſa ten̄ in Meldone.v.hiđ.7 i.uirg 7 dim̄.

7 Moniales de Elneſtou tenent de ea in elemoſina.Tra

ē.v.caꝛ.In dn̄io.ii.caꝛ.7 vii.uiłłi hn̄t.iii.caꝛ.Ibi.ii.

217 a

2 M. Ralph holds BIGGLESWADE himself. It answers for 10 hides.
　　Land for 10 ploughs. In lordship 5½ hides; 3 ploughs there.
　　7 villagers with 7 ploughs; 10 smallholders; 3 slaves.
　　2 mills at 47s; meadow for 10 ploughs; 5s from hay.
　　Value £17; when acquired £15; before 1066 £10.
　　Archbishop Stigand held this manor.　2 Freemen had ½ hide
　　which they could grant and sell.

3 M. In HOLME Ralph also holds 2 hides. Land for 5 ploughs; they are there.
　　6 villagers.
　　Meadow for 1 plough.
　　Value 40s; when acquired 30s; before 1066, 40s.
　　Archbishop Stigand held this manor. 3 Freemen had 2 virgates
　　of land; they could sell.

In WIXAMTREE Hundred
4 In (Old) WARDEN Ralph also holds 1½ virgates from the King.
　This land lies in Biggleswade; it is assessed there. Before 1066
　the holder could neither sell nor grant without the permission of
　the holder of Biggleswade.

52　　LAND OF JOCELYN THE BRETON

In MANSHEAD Hundred
1 M. Jocelyn the Breton holds 7½ hides in POTSGROVE from the King as one
　　manor. Land for 7½ ploughs. In lordship 3 hides; 3 ploughs there.
　　3 villagers have 2 ploughs; another 2½ possible.
　　6 smallholders and 3 slaves.
　　Meadow for 5 ploughs.
　　Value 50s; when acquired 100s; before 1066 £10.
　　4 thanes held this manor; they could grant and sell their land to
　　whom they would.

In the Half-Hundred of STANBRIDGE
2 Jocelyn holds (Nares) GLADLEY himself for 2½ hides.
　Land for 1 plough; 4 oxen there.
　A mill, 16s; meadow for 1 plough; woodland, 100 pigs.
　The value is and was 20s; before 1066, 40s.
　Wigot, King Edward's Huntsman, held this land; he could sell
　to whom he would.

53　　LAND OF COUNTESS JUDITH

In REDBORNSTOKE Hundred
1 M. Countess Judith holds 5 hides and 1½ virgates in MAULDEN the nuns of
　　Elstow hold from her, in alms. Land for 5 ploughs. In lordship 2 ploughs.
　　7 villagers have 3 ploughs. 2 slaves.

ſerui.7 ı.moliñ.ııı.ſolid. P̊t̃u.v.car̃.Silua.c.porc̃.

Val.ʟx.ſol.Q̨do recep̃.ıııı.lib̃.T.R.E.vıı.lib̃.Hoc

m̃ tenuit Aluuold teign regis.E.7 ibi uñ ſocħs dim̃ uirg̃

habuit.7 cui uoluit dare potuit.

In Houſtone teñ Hugo de Judita comitiſſa dim̃ hid̃.

Tra.e̅.ı.car̃.7 ibi eſt.7 ıı.bord̃.7 ſilua.xxv.porc̃.Val

7 ualuit.x.ſol.T.R.E.xıı.ſol.Hanc tr̃a Lepſi tenuit

hõ Toſti com̃.7 cui uoluit dare 7 uende potuit.

m̃ Ipſa comitiſſa teñ *WINESSAMESTEDE*.7 moniales teñ

de ea.p ııı.hid̃ ſe defd̃.Tra.vı.car̃.In dñio.ıı.car̃.

Ibi.xı.uilli hñt.ıııı.car̃.7 xı.bord̃.7 ı.ſeru.p̃t̃u dim̃

car̃.Val.vıı.lib̃.7 vı.ſol.Q̨do recep̃.xʟ.v.ſol.T.R.E.

x.lib̃ 7 x.ſol.Hoc m̃.tenuer̃.vııı.ſocħi.7 dare 7 uende

potuer̃.Judita com̃ ded̃ S̃ ᴍᴀʀɪᴀᴇ de Elneſtou in elemo

ſina.ſed ſoca jacuit ſẽp in Cameſtone.

m̃ *ELNESTOV*.p.ııı.hid̃ 7 dim̃ ſe defd̃.Moniales S̃ ᴍᴀʀɪᴀᴇ

tenent de.J.comit̃.Tra.e̅.vıı.car̃.In dñio.ıı.car̃.7 xıııı.

uilli hñt.v.car̃.Ibi.xı.bord̃.7 ıııı.ſerui.7 ı.moliñ

de.xxıııı.ſol.p̃t̃u.ıııı.car̃.Silua.ʟx.porc̃.Val.c.ſol.

217 b

Q̨do recep̃.xʟ.ſol.T.R.E.x.lib̃.Hoc m̃ tenuer̃.ıııı.

ſocħi.hõẽs regis.E.fuer̃.tr̃a ſua dare 7 uende potuer̃.

ſed in Cameſtone jacuit ſẽp ſoca eoʒ

m̃ *CAMESTONE* p x.hid̃ ſe defd̃.Tra.e̅ xx.car̃.Comitiſſa

tenet.In dñio.ıı.hide.7 ibi.ıııı.car̃.7 xvııı.uilli hñt

xıı.car̃.7 adhuc ıııı.poſſ fieri.Ibi xıı.bord̃.7 vııı.ſerui.

7 uñ moliñ de.v.ſolid.p̃t̃u.xx.car̃.Silua.cc.porc̃.

7 de paſtura.ıı.ſol.In totis ualentijs ual xvııı.lib̃.Q̨do

recep̃.xxıı.lib̃.T.R.E.xxx.lib̃.Hoc m̃ tenuit Guert

comes.7 ibid̃.ıı.teigni.ıı.hid̃ 7 dim̃.7 ı.uirg̃ 7 dimid̃

habuer̃.7 cui uoluer̃ dare 7 uende potueruñ.

1 mill, 3s; meadow for 5 ploughs; woodland, 100 pigs.
Value 60s; when acquired £4; before 1066 £7.
  Alfwold, a thane of King Edward's, held this manor. A Freeman
had ½ virgate; he could grant to whom he would.

2 In HOUGHTON (Conquest) Hugh holds ½ hide from Countess Judith.
Land for 1 plough; it is there.
  2 smallholders.
  Woodland, 25 pigs.
The value is and was 10s; before 1066, 12s.
  Leofsi, Earl Tosti's man, held this land; he could grant and
sell to whom he would.

3 M. The Countess holds WILSHAMSTEAD herself and the nuns from her.
It answers for 3 hides. Land for 6 ploughs. In lordship 2 ploughs.
  11 villagers have 4 ploughs. 11 smallholders and 1 slave.
  Meadow for ½ plough.
Value £7 6s; when acquired 45s; before 1066 £10 10s.
  8 Freemen held this manor; they could grant and sell.
Countess Judith gave it to St. Mary's of Elstow in alms; but the
jurisdiction always lay in Kempston.

4 M. ELSTOW answers for 3½ hides. The nuns of St. Mary's hold it from
Countess Judith. Land for 7 ploughs. In lordship 2 ploughs.
  14 villagers have 5 ploughs. 11 smallholders and 4 slaves.
  1 mill at 24s; meadow for 4 ploughs; woodland, 60 pigs.
Value 100s; when acquired 40s; before 1066 £10.   217 b
  4 Freemen held this manor. They were King Edward's men.
They could grant and sell their land; but their jurisdiction
always lay in Kempston.

5 M. KEMPSTON answers for 10 hides. Land for 20 ploughs. The Countess
holds it. In lordship 2 hides. 4 ploughs there.
  18 villagers have 12 ploughs; a further 4 possible.
    12 smallholders and 8 slaves.
  1 mill at 5s; meadow for 20 ploughs; woodland, 200 pigs;
    from pasture 2s.
Total value £18; when acquired £22; before 1066 £30.
  Earl Gyrth held this manor. There also 2 thanes had 2½ hides
and 1½ virgates; they could grant and sell to whom they would.

In Boleheſtre ten̄ Hugo dim̄ hidā *In Stoden Hvnd.*

de comitiſſa.Tra.ē.ı.car̄.7 ibi.ē.cū.ıı.bord̄.P̊tū

ıııı.bob.Silua.xx.porc̄.Val.x.ſol.Q̊do recep̄.̓

v.ſol.T.R.E.̓xıı.ſol.Hanc t̄rā tenuit Almar̄ teign̄

regis.E.7 dare 7 uend̄e   potuit.

In Acheleia.ten̄ Milo criſpin de comit̄.ı.hid̄.Tra.ē

ı.car̄ 7 dim̄.Vna car̄.ibi.ē.7 dim̄ pot̄ fieri.Ibi.ıɪɪ.

bord̄.7 p̊tū.ı.car̄.Val 7 ualuit.x.ſol.T.R.E.̓xx.ſol.

Hanc t̄rā tenuit Goduin hō Heraldi.7 uend̄e potuit.
                         comitis.

In Blacheſhou ten̄ Oſb̄n *In Dim̄ Hvnd de Bvchelai.*

de comitiſſa.ıı.hid̄ 7 dim̄.Tra.ē.ıııı.car̄.In dn̄io.ı.car̄.

7 vı.uill̄i hn̄t.ıɪɪ.car̄.Ibi.ıɪɪ.bord̄.7 ıɪɪ.ſerui.7 dim̄

molin̄ de.x.ſol.p̊tū.ı.car̄.Silua.c.porc̄.Val 7 ua

luit ſēp.ʟx.ſol.Hoc m̄) Leueua tenuit.hō regis.E.

7 uendere 7 dare potuit cui uoluit.

In Brunehā ten̄ Hugo de comit̄.ıı.hid̄.Tra.ē.ıı.car̄.

7 ibi ſunt.7 v.uill̄i 7 ıı.bord̄.7 ı.molin̄ de.xʟ.ſol

7 c.anguillis.De feudo q̄d̄ē comitiſſæ.ē.ſ; n̄ jacet in hac

tra.p̊tū.ıı.car̄.Val.xx.ſol.Q̊do recep̄ 7 T.R.E.̓x.ſol.

Hanc t̄rā tenuit Goduin hō Heraldi.7 uend̄e potuit.
                         coin

In Stachedene ten̄ Hugo de comit̄.ı.hid̄.Tra.ē.ı.

car̄.7 ibi eſt.7 ıı.uill̄i 7 ıı.bord̄.Silua.xʟ.porc̄.

Val 7 ualuit.x.ſol.T.R.E.̓xx.ſol.Hanc t̄rā.ıı.ſochi

hōēs regis E.tenuer̄.7 cui uoluer̄ uend̄e potuer̄.

In Falmereſhā ten̄ Giſleb̄t de comitiſſa *In Wilga Hvnd.*

ıɪɪ.hid̄ 7 dim̄.Tra.ē.ıɪɪ.car̄.In dn̄io.ı.car̄.7 ıı.uill̄i

cū.ı.car̄.7 alia pot̄ fieri.Ibi.ıııı.bord̄.7 unū molin̄

de.x.ſol.P̊tū.ı.car̄.Val.ıɪɪ.lib̄.Q̊do recep̄.̓c.ſol.

7 tn̄td̄.T.R.E.Hanc t̄rā tenuit Alli teign̄ regis.E.

In STODDEN Hundred

6   In BOLNHURST Hugh holds ½ hide from the Countess. Land for 1 plough;
it is there, with
> 2 smallholders.
> Meadow for 4 oxen; woodland, 20 pigs.

Value 10s; when acquired 5s; before 1066, 12s.
> Aelmer, a thane of King Edward's, held this land; he could grant and sell.

7   In OAKLEY Miles Crispin holds 1 hide from the Countess.
Land for 1½ ploughs; 1 plough there; ½ possible.
> 3 smallholders.
> Meadow for 1 plough.

The value is and was 10s; before 1066, 20s.
> Godwin, Earl Harold's man, held this land; he could sell.

In the Half-Hundred of BUCKLOW

8   In BLETSOE Osbern holds 2½ hides from the Countess.
Land for 4 ploughs. In lordship 1 plough.
> 6 villagers have 3 ploughs. 3 smallholders and 3 slaves.
> ½ mill at 10s; meadow for 1 plough; woodland, 100 pigs.

The value is and always was 60s.
> Leofeva, King Edward's man, held this manor; she could sell
and grant to whom she would.

9   In BROMHAM Hugh holds 2 hides from the Countess. Land for 2 ploughs;
they are there.
> 5 villagers and 2 smallholders.
> 1 mill at 40s and 100 eels; it is of the Countess' Holding,
>   but it does not lie in this land. Meadow for 2 ploughs.

Value 20s; when acquired and before 1066, 10s.
> Godwin, Earl Harold's man, held this land; he could sell.

10   In STAGSDEN Hugh holds 1 hide from the Countess. Land for 1 plough;
it is there.
> 2 villagers and 2 smallholders.
> Woodland, 40 pigs.

The value is and was 10s; before 1066, 20s.
> 2 Freemen, King Edward's men, held this land; they could sell
to whom they would.

In WILLEY Hundred

11   In FELMERSHAM Gilbert holds 3½ hides from the Countess.
Land for 3 ploughs. In lordship 1 plough;
> 2 villagers with 1 plough; another possible. 4 smallholders.
> 1 mill at 10s; meadow for 1 plough.

Value £3; when acquired 100s; as much before 1066.
> Alli, a thane of King Edward's, held this land.

In Radeuuelle ten̅ Hugo de feudo comitiſſæ.ıı.hıd̅
7 ıı.uirg̅ 7 dim̅.Tra.e̅.ı.car̅ 7 dim̅.7 ibi ſuɳ̅.Ibi un̅
uitⅼs 7 ı.bord̅ 7 un̅ ſeruus.p̊tu̅.ı.car̅.Val̅.xx.ſolid̅.
Q̸do recep̅:́x.ſol̅.T.R.E:́xʟ.ſol̅.Hanc tr̅a tenuit
Toui huſcarle regis.E.

Gislebt̅ de bloſſeuile ten̅ de comitiſſa Hareuuelle.
ᵱ x.hid̅.ſe deſd̅.Tra.e̅.xvı.car̅.In dn̅io.ııı.car̅ poſ̅s
fieri.una.e̅ ibi.7 x.uitⅼi cu̅.vıı.car̅.7 adhuc.vı.poſ̅s
fieri.p̊tu̅.vı.car̅.Silua.cc.porc̅.7 un̅ molin̅ de xxxvı.
ſol̅ 7 vııı.den̅.7 cc.anguitⅼ.Int totu̅ ual̅.vı.lib̅.Q̸do
recep̅:́xvı.lib̅.T.R.E:́xx.lib̅.Hoc ◌̄Ɔ tenuer̅.ııı.teigni
regis.E.7 cui uoluer̅ uendere potuer̅.

In Sernebroc ten̅ Hugo de comitiſſa.ııı.uirg̅ træ.
Tra.e̅.ı.car̅.7 ibi eſt.Ibi un̅ uitⅼs.7 ı.bord̅.p̊tu̅.ı.car̅.
Val̅.x.ſol̅.Q̸do recep̅:́v.ſol̅.T.R.E:́xx.ſol̅.Hanc
tr̅a tenuit Ouiet ho̅ regis.E.7 potuit dare cui uoluit.

217 c

In *HVND* de Bereforde ten̅ Osbn̅.ıı.hid̅ 7 ııı.uirg̅.
Tra.e̅.ııı.car̅.In dn̅io.ıı.car̅.7 ııı.uitⅼi cu̅.ı.car̅.
Ibi.ıı.bord̅ 7 un̅ ſeru̅.P̊tu̅.ı.car̅.Silua.cc.porc̅.Val̅
xʟ.ſol̅.Q̸do recep̅:́x.ſol̅.T.R.E:́ʟ.ſol̅.Hanc tr̅a tenuit
Vlfech Stirman regis.E.7 uende̅ potuit.

In Potone ten̅ Hugo de comitiſſa dim̅ uirg̅ træ.Tra
e̅.ı.car̅.7 ibi.e̅.cu̅.ı.bord̅.Val̅ 7 ualuit.v.ſol̅.T.R.E:́
ıı.ſol̅.Hanc tr̅a tenuit coⅿ Toſti.in Potone ſuo ◌̄Ɔ.

In Stratone ten̅ Fulcher̅ *IN BICHELESWADE HD̅*.
de pariſio.ııı.uirg̅ 7 dim̅ de comitiſſa.Tra.e̅.ıı.car̅.
In dn̅io.ı.car̅.Ibi un̅ uitⅼs 7 v.bord̅.p̊tu̅.ı.car̅.
Val̅.vııı.ſol̅.7 ualuit.T.R.E:́xx.ſol̅.Hanc tr̅a
tenuit Aluuin ho̅ regis.E.7 uendere potuit.

12 In RADWELL Hugh holds 2 hides and 2½ virgates from the Countess'
Holding. Land for 1½ ploughs; they are there.
   1 villager, 1 smallholder and 1 slave.
   Meadow for 1 plough.
Value 20s; when acquired 10s; before 1066, 40s.
   Tovi, one of King Edward's Guards, held this land.

13 Gilbert of Blosseville holds HARROLD from the Countess. It answers for 10
hides. Land for 16 ploughs. In lordship 3 ploughs possible; 1 there;
   10 villagers with 7 ploughs; a further 6 possible.
   Meadow for 6 ploughs; woodland, 200 pigs; a mill at 36s 8d
     and 200 eels.
In total, value £6; when acquired £16; before 1066 £20.
   3 thanes of King Edward's held this manor; they could sell
to whom they would.

14 In SHARNBROOK Hugh holds 3 virgates of land from the Countess.
Land for 1 plough; it is there.
   1 villager and 1 smallholder.
   Meadow for 1 plough.
Value 10s; when acquired 5s; before 1066, 20s.
   Wulfgeat, King Edward's man, held this land; he could grant
to whom he would.

In the Hundred of BARFORD
15 Osbern holds 2 hides and 3 virgates. Land for 3 ploughs.   217 c
   In lordship 2 ploughs;
   3 villagers with 1 plough; 2 smallholders and 1 slave.
   Meadow for 1 plough; woodland, 200 pigs.
Value 40s; when acquired 10s; before 1066, 50s.
   Wulfheah, King Edward's steersman, held this land; he could sell.

16 In POTTON Hugh holds ½ virgate of land from the Countess.
Land for 1 plough; it is there, with
   1 smallholder.
The value is and was 5s; before 1066, 2s.
   Earl Tosti held this land in Potton, his manor.

In BIGGLESWADE Hundred
17 In STRATTON Fulchere of Paris holds 3½ virgates from the Countess.
Land for 2 ploughs. In lordship 1 plough.
   1 villager; 5 smallholders.
   Meadow for 1 plough.
The value is and was 8s; before 1066, 20s.
   Alwin, King Edward's man, held this land; he could sell.

In Holme teñ Fulcher de com̄ . dim̄ hiđ . Tra dim̄
car̄ . 7 ibi . ē dim̄ car̄ . p̄tū dim̄ car̄ . Ibi uñ uiłłs.
Vał 7 ualuit . vii . soł . T.R.E. x . soł . Hanc tr̄a
tenuit Aluuin hō regis . E . 7 dare 7 uende potuit.
In eađ teneñ . ii . hōēs de comitiſſa . i . uirḡ . Tra . ii .
boƀ . 7 ibi ſunt . Vał 7 ualuit ſēp . v . soł . Hanc tr̄a
tenuit Goduin hō regis . E . 7 uende potuit.

(I) Ipſa comitiſſa Judita IN DIM̄ HD DE WENESLAI.
teñ POTONE . p x . hiđ ſe defđ . Tra . ē . xii . car̄ .
In dn̄io . iii . hide 7 dim̄ . 7 ibi ſunt . iii . car̄ . Ibi . xviii.
uiłłi 7 ii . ſocħi cū . viii . car̄ . 7 ix . pot fieri . Ibi
xiii . borđ 7 iii . ſerui . 7 i . moliñ . v . ſolidoꝝ . p̄tū
xii . car̄ . Paſtura ad pec uillæ . Int totū uał . xii . liƀ .
Qđo recep̄ . c . soł . T.R.E. xiii . liƀ . Hoc M̄ tenuit
rex Edw . 7 fuit com̄ Toſti . Ibiđ fuer̄ . iiii . ſocħi
qui habuer̄ . i . hiđ 7 i . uirḡ . 7 cui uoluer̄ dare potuer̄ .

In Sudtone teñ Torchil . i . hiđ 7 dim̄ . Tra . ē . i . car̄ 7 dim̄ .
Vna car̄ ibi . ē . 7 dim̄ pot fieri . Ibi . iiii . borđ . P̄tū . i . car̄
7 dim̄ . 7 xvi . deñ . Vał x . soł . Qđo recep̄ . viii . soł . T.R.E.
xx . soł . Hanc tr̄a . iii . ſocħi tenuer̄ . 7 uende potuer̄ .
In eađ teñ Leuegar dim̄ hiđ . Tra . ē dim̄ car̄ . 7 ibi eſt .
P̄tū dim̄ car̄ . 7 xii . deñ . Vał . v . soł . Qđo recep̄ . 7 T.R.E.
x . soł . Iſte q̄ nc̄ tenet tenuit . hō regis fuit . 7 uende pot .
In eađ teñ Robt̄ . iii . uirḡ 7 dim̄ . Tra . ē . i . car̄ . ſƷ ñ ſuɴt
niſi . ii . boūes . P̄tū . i . car̄ . Vał . viii . soł . 7 ualuit . T.R.E.
x . soł . Hanc tr̄a . ii . ſocħi tenuer̄ . 7 uende potuer̄ .

In Sudtone ten
Aluuin de Juđ com
. i . hiđ . Tra . ē . i . car.
Ibi ſł . iiii . borđ.
7 pt̄ . i . car.
Vał . viii . ſolđ.
Sex ſocħi tenuer̄
; đire 7 uende potuer̄.

Ibi . iii . niſi . ii . boūes P̄tū . i . car̄.
borđ.

In HOLME Fulchere holds ½ hide from the Countess.
Land for ½ plough; ½ plough there.
   Meadow for ½ plough.
   1 villager.
The value is and was 7s; before 1066, 10s.
   Alwin, King Edward's man, held this land; he could grant and sell.

9   In the same (village) 2 men hold 1 virgate from the Countess.
Land for 2 oxen; they are there.
The value is and always was 5s.
   Godwin, King Edward's man, held this land; he could sell.

In the Half-Hundred of WENSLOW
0 M. Countess Judith holds POTTON herself. It answers for 10 hides.
Land for 12 ploughs. In lordship 3½ hides; 3 ploughs there.
   18 villagers and 2 Freemen with 8 ploughs; a ninth possible.
    13 smallholders and 3 slaves.
   1 mill, 5s; meadow for 12 ploughs; pasture for the village livestock.
In total, value £12; when acquired 100s; before 1066 £13.
   King Edward held this manor; it was Earl Tosti's.
There were 4 Freemen who had 1 hide and 1 virgate; they could grant
to whom they would.

21   In SUTTON Thorkell holds 1½ hides. Land for 1½ ploughs; 1 plough
there; ½ possible.
   4 smallholders.
   Meadow for 1½ ploughs, and 16d too.
Value 10s; when acquired 8s; before 1066, 20s.
   3 Freemen held this land; they could sell.

22   In SUTTON Alwin holds 1 hide from Countess Judith.
Land for 1 plough.
   3 smallholders.
   Meadow for 2 ploughs.
Value 8s.
   6 Freemen held it; they could grant and sell.

23   In the same (village) Leofgar holds ½ hide. Land for ½ plough;
it is there.
   Meadow for ½ plough and 12d.
Value 5s; when acquired and before 1066, 10s.
   The present holder held it; he was the King's man; he could sell.

24   In the same (village) Robert holds 3½ virgates. Land for 1 plough,
but there are only 2 oxen.
   3 smallholders.
   Meadow for 1 plough.
The value is and was 8s; before 1066, 10s.
   2 Freemen held this land; they could sell.

In ead teneǥ Sueting 7 Robt.ɪ.uirg̃ t̃ræ 7 dimið.

T̃ra.ɪɪɪɪ.bob.7 ibi funt.P̃tũ.ɪ.car̃.7 uñ borð.Val.ɪɪɪɪ.

fol 7 ualuit.T.R.E. v, fol. Hanc t̃ra Eduuard tenuit.

h̃o Abbis S Albani.7 uendere potuit *IN DIM HVND*

In Sudtone teñ Turbt.ɪɪ.hið de comitiffa.T̃ra.ẽ

ɪɪ.car̃.In dñio.ɪ.car̃.7 ɪɪɪɪ.borð cũ.ɪ.car̃.p̃tũ.ɪɪ.car̃.

Val 7 ualuit.xx.fol.T.R.E. xxv, fol.Hanc t̃ra.ɪɪ.fochi

tenuer̃.7 uende potuer̃.

In ead teñ Goduin.ɪɪɪ.uirg̃ de comitiffa.T̃ra.ẽ.ɪ.car̃.

fed m̃ non.ẽ.Val.ɪɪɪ.fol.Qdo recep̃. vɪ.fol.T.R.E. x.fol.

Hanc t̃ra Vlmar tenuit h̃o Ordui.7 uende potuit.

In ead teñ Ederic dim̃ hið.T̃ra.ẽ dim̃ car̃.7 ibi.ẽ.cũ

uno uilto.p̃tũ dim̃ car̃.Val 7 ualuit.v.fol.T.R.E. x.

fol.Ifte q̃ tenet tenuit, h̃o regis fuit.7 uendè potuit.

217 d

☧ In Hatelai.teñ Jud comitiffa.ɪɪɪ.hið 7 ɪɪ.uirg̃ 7 dim̃ p̃ uno

☧.T̃ra.ẽ.vɪ.car̃ 7 dim̃.In dñio.ɪ.hið 7 dim̃ uirg̃.7 ibi.ɪɪ.car̃.

Ibi.vɪɪɪ.uilti.cũ.ɪɪɪɪ.car̃ 7 dim̃, Ibi.vɪɪɪ.borð.7 p̃tũ.ɪɪ.car̃.

Silua.ɪɪɪɪ.porc.Val.vɪ.lib,7 v.fol.Qdo recep̃. c.fol.T.R.E.

vɪ.lib.Hoc ☧ Tofti com̃ tenuit.7 jacet in Potone ☧ p̃po

comitiffæ.7 ibi q̃dã fochs unã uirg̃ habuit.potuit

dare 7 uendere.7 ad alterũ dñm recedere.

☧ Rannulf fr̃ Ilgerij teñ de comitiffa Euretone. p̃.v,

hið fe defð.T̃ra.ẽ.v.car̃.Ibi funt.ɪɪ.car̃.7 ɪɪɪ.poffuǥ

fieri.Ibi.ɪɪɪɪ.uilti.7 v.borð.p̃tũ.ɪ.car̃.Val.ɪɪɪ.lib.

Qdo recep̃. c.fol.7 tntð.T.R.E.Hoc ☧ com̃ Tofti tenuit.7 ja

cuit in Potone ☧ p̃po comitiffæ. *IN HVND DE WICHESTANESTOV.*

In Sudgiuele teñ Hugo de comitiffa.ɪ.hið.T̃ra.ẽ.ɪɪ.car̃.7 ibi

25 In the same (village) Sweeting and Robert hold 1½ virgates of land.
Land for 4 oxen; they are there.
　Meadow for 1 plough.
　1 smallholder.
The value is and was 4s; before 1066, 5s.
　Edward, the Abbot of St. Alban's man, held this land; he could sell.

In the same Half-Hundred

26 In SUTTON Thorbert holds 2 hides from the Countess.
Land for 2 ploughs. In lordship 1 plough;
　4 smallholders with 1 plough.
　Meadow for 2 ploughs.
The value is and was 20s; before 1066, 25s;
　2 Freemen held this land; they could sell.

27 In the same (village) Godwin holds 3 virgates from the Countess.
Land for 1 plough, but it is not there now.
Value 3s; when acquired 6s; before 1066, 10s.
　Wulfmer, Ordwy's man, held this land; he could sell.

28 In the same (village) Edric holds ½ hide. Land for ½ plough;
it is there, with
　1 villager.
　Meadow for ½ plough.
The value is and was 5s; before 1066, 10s.
　Its holder held it; he was the King's man; he could sell.

29 M. In (Cockayne) HATLEY Countess Judith holds 3 hides and 2½ virgates
as one manor. Land for 6½ ploughs. In lordship 1 hide   217 d
and ½ virgate; 2 ploughs there.
　8 villagers with 4½ ploughs. 8 smallholders.
　Meadow for 2 ploughs; woodland, 4 pigs.
Value £6 5s; when acquired 100s; before 1066 £6.
　Earl Tosti held this manor. It lies in Potton, the Countess'
own manor. A Freeman had 1 virgate; he could grant and sell,
and withdraw to another lord.

30 M. Ranulf brother of Ilger holds EVERTON from the Countess. It answers
for 5 hides. Land for 5 ploughs; 2 ploughs there; 3 possible.
　4 villagers; 5 smallholders.
　Meadow for 1 plough.
Value £3; when acquired 100s; as much before 1066.
　Earl Tosti held this manor. It lay in Potton, the Countess' own manor.

In the Hundred of WIXAMTREE

31 In SOUTHILL Hugh holds 1 hide from the Countess. Land for 2 ploughs;
they are there.

funt.Ibi.iii.uilli.⁊ iii.borđ.⁊ un̂ ſeru̅.p̃tu̅.ii.car̓.Silua
lx.porc̓.Val.xxx.ſol.Qₓdo recep̃⸴xl.ſol.T.R.E⸴⁓lx.ſol.
Hanc t̃ra tenuit Tuffa ho̅ comitis Wallef.⁊ uendé potuit.
In Hergentone ten̂ canonici⸴de Bedeforde de comitiſſa. .iii.hidas
T̃ra.e̅.iii.car̓.⁊ ibi ſunt.⁊ vi.uilli ⁊ iiii.borđ.p̃tu̅.ii.car̓.
Val.xxx.ſol.Qₓdo recep̃⸴xx.ſol.T.R.E⸴⁓xl.ſol.Hanc t̃ra
tenuit Azelin ho̅ comitis Toſti.n̅ potuit neqₓ uendé fine dare
licentia illius qui cameſtone m̅ com̅ tenuit.
In Chernetone ten̂ H̨ugo de comitiſſa.iii.hiđ ⁊ una̅ uirg̓
⁊ tciā par̅ uni̅ uirg.T̃ra.e̅.iiii.car̓.⁊ ibi ſunt.Ibi ſunt
xii.uilli.⁊ iii.borđ ⁊ iii.ſerui.P̃tu̅.i.car̅.Val.xl.ſol.Qₓdo
recep̃⸴xx.ſol.T.R.E⸴⁓xl.ſol.Hanc t̃ra tenuit Azelin ho̅
Toſti com̅.n̅ potuit dare ⱡ uendé fine licentia eĵ q̓ Cameſton
In Cochepol ten̂ Hugo de comitiſſa.i.uirg̓ træ. ⌐tenuit.
H̃ t̃ra.xxx.den̅ ual ⁊ ualuit se̅p.Hanc tenuit Wluuin̂
ho̅ regis.E.⁊ cui uoluit uendere potuit.
In Blunhā.ten̂ abb ⸰S̃ Edmundi dim̅ hiđ de comitiſſa.
T̃ra.e̅.i.car̅.⁊ ibi eſt.p̃tu̅.i.car̅.Val.xx.ſol.Qₓdo recep̃⸴
x.ſol.T.R.E⸴⁓xx.ſol.Hanc t̃ra ho̅.R.E.tenuit.⁊ uendé pot̓.
In Cliſtone ten̂ Aluuin̂ de comitiſſa *IN CLISTONE HVNĐ*.
.i.hiđ.T̃ra.e̅ dim̅ car̅.⁊ ibi eſt.p̃tu̅ dim̅ car̅.Val ⁊ ualuit
v.ſol.T.R.E⸴⁓x.ſol.Hanc t̃ra Vluric̅ ho̅ regis.E.tenuit.
⁊ uendere potuit.   maiſnil   ⌐HVNĐ.
.LIIII. ▞TERRA Vxoris hvgon̂ De Grent̓ *In Radborgestoch*
        ▞uxor. H. de grentemaiſnil
        ▞DELIZ ten̓ de rege dim̅ hiđ in Eſeltone.T̃ra.e̅ dim̅
car̓.⁊ ibi.e̅.p̃tu̅ dim̅ car̅.Silua.vi.porc̓.Ibi un̂ borđ.
Val.vi.ſol.⁊ ualuit.T.R.E⸴⁓x.ſol.Hanc t̃ra tenuit Goduin̂
ho̅ Guert comitis.⁊ cui uoluit dare potuit.

    3 villagers; 3 smallholders and 1 slave.
    Meadow for 2 ploughs; woodland, 60 pigs.
Value 30s; when acquired 40s; before 1066, 60s.
    Tuffa, Earl Waltheof's man, held this land; he could sell.

32 In HARROWDEN the Canons of Bedford hold 3 hides from the Countess.
Land for 3 ploughs; they are there.
    6 villagers and 4 smallholders.
    Meadow for 2 ploughs.
Value 30s; when acquired 20s; before 1066, 40s.
    Azelin, Earl Tosti's man, held this land; he could neither grant nor sell
without the permission of the holder of the Earl's manor of Kempston.

33 In CARDINGTON Hugh holds 3 hides and 1 virgate and the third part
of 1 virgate from the Countess. Land for 4 ploughs; they are there.
    12 villagers, 3 smallholders and 3 slaves.
    Meadow for 1 plough.
Value 40s; when acquired 20s; before 1066, 40s.
    Azelin, Earl Tosti's man, held this land; he could not grant or
sell without the permission of the holder of Kempston.

34 In COPLE Hugh holds 1 virgate of land from the Countess.
The value of this land is and always was 30d.
    Wulfwin, King Edward's man, held it; he could sell to whom he would.

35 In BLUNHAM the Abbot of St. Edmund's holds ½ hide from the Countess.
Land for 1 plough; it is there.
    Meadow for 1 plough.
Value 20s; when acquired 10s; before 1066, 20s.
    A man of King Edward's held this land; he could sell.

In CLIFTON Hundred
36 In CLIFTON Alwin holds 1 hide from the Countess. Land for ½ plough;
it is there.
    Meadow for ½ plough.
The value is and was 5s; before 1066, 10s.
    Wulfric, King Edward's man, held this land; he could sell.

54   LAND OF HUGH OF GRANDMESNIL'S WIFE

In REDBORNSTOKE Hundred
1 Adelaide, wife of Hugh of Grandmesnil, holds ½ hide in SHELTON
from the King. Land for ½ plough; it is there.
    Meadow for ½ plough; woodland, 6 pigs.
    1 smallholder.
The value is and was 6s; before 1066, 10s.
    Godwin, Earl Gyrth's man, held this land; he could grant
to whom he would.

In Ouſtone teñ Ernald de Adeliz . iiii . hid 7 dim ꝑ uno ꝳ.

Tra . ē . vi . car . In dñio . ii . car . 7 xi . uilli 7 vii . bord cū . iii .

car 7 dim . 7 adhuc dim pot fieri . Ibi . iii . ſerui . Ptū . ii . car .

Silua . cc . xxv . por . De hac tra teñ uñ ſochs . i . hid . Val . iiii . lib .

Qdo recep:́ lx . ſol . T.R.E:́ viii . lib . Hoc ꝳ tenuer . iii . ſochi .

qui tra ſua dare 7 uendere uoluer . In hac ead reclamat

Adeliz ꝑdicta dim uirg . 7 xxx . acs int ſilua 7 planū ſup

Hugoñe de belcap . 7 hoēs de hund portaƷ teſtimoniū

qd h̄ terra jacuit T.R.E. cū alia tra q̃ teñ Adeliz . 7 ille qui

hanc tra tenuit potuit dare uel uende cui uoluit . Hanc

tra Radulf̄ injuſte occupauit . qdo uicecomes fuit.

ꝳ Ipſa Adeliz teñ Cerlentone . *IN WICHESTANESTOV HD.*

ꝑ x . hid . ſe defd . Tra . ē . x . car . In dñio . v . hid . 7 ibi . ii . car .

7 adhuc . iii . poſſuƷ fieri . Ibi . xvi . uilli 7 ix . bord cū . v . car .

Ibi . ii . ſerui . 7 uñ moliñ . xxx . ſol . ꝑtū . x . car . Silua . xvi .

porc . Int totū ual . x . lib . Qdo recep:́ viii . lib . T.R.E:́ xii .

lib . Hoc ꝳ tenuit rex Edw . 7 fuit Toſti comitis . H̄ tra

fuit Berew de potone T.R.E . ita qd null inde ſeparare

[ꝳ Juditæ comit] ⎡ſpotuit.

ꝳ In Mildentone teñ Iuo dapifer de gent hugon *IN STODEN HVND.*

iii . hid 7 una uirg ꝑ uno ꝳ . Tra . ē . iiii . car . In dñio . ii . car .

7 viii . uilli cū . ii . car . Ibi uñ ſeruus . 7 i . moliñ . xx . ſolidoȝ .

ꝑtū . ii . car . Silua . xl . porc . Val . lx . ſol . 7 ualuit . T.R.E:́

iiii . lib . Hoc ꝳ tenuit Goduin hō Borret . 7 uende potuit.

.L.V. TERRA VXORIS RADVLFI TAILLEB *IN MANESHEVE HD.*

AZELINA femina Radulfi tallgeboſc teñ de rege

in Badeleſdone . i . hid 7 dim . Tra . ē car 7 dim . Vna ibi . ē

7 dim poteſt fieri . Ibi . ii . uilli 7 uñ bord . ꝑtū . i . car . Val

7 ualuit . xx . ſol . T.R.E:́ xl . ſol . Hanc tra tenuer . ii .

ſochi . Anſchill 7 Aluuin . 7 cui uoluer uende potuer.

2   In HOUGHTON (Conquest) Arnold holds 4½ hides from Adelaide,
as one manor. Land for 6 ploughs. In lordship 2 ploughs.
   11 villagers and 7 smallholders with 3½ ploughs;
      a further ½ possible. 3 slaves.
   Meadow for 2 ploughs; woodland, 225 pigs.
   1 Freeman holds 1 hide of this land.
Value £4; when acquired 60s; before 1066 £8.
   3 Freemen held this manor; they could grant and sell their land.
   In the same (village) the said Adelaide claims from Hugh of
Beauchamp ½ virgate and 30 acres of wood and open land.
The men of the Hundred bear witness that before 1066 this land
lay with the other land which Adelaide holds, and the holder of
this land could grant or sell to whom he would. Ralph Tallboys
appropriated this land wrongfully, when he was Sheriff.

In WIXAMTREE Hundred

3   M. Adelaide holds CHALTON herself. It answers for 10 hides. Land for 10
ploughs. In lordship 5 hides; 2 ploughs there; a further 3 possible.
   16 villagers and 9 smallholders with 5 ploughs.
   2 slaves; 1 mill, 30s; meadow for 10 ploughs; woodland, 16 pigs.
In total, value £10; when acquired £8; before 1066 £12.
   King Edward held this manor; it was Earl Tosti's. This land
was an outlier of Potton, Countess Judith's manor, before 1066,
so that no one could separate it from it.

218 a

In STODDEN Hundred

4   M. In MILTON (Ernest) Ivo, Hugh of Grandmesnil's Steward, holds 3 hides
and 1 virgate as one manor. Land for 4 ploughs. In lordship 2 ploughs;
   8 villagers with 2 ploughs.
   1 slave; 1 mill, 20s; meadow for 2 ploughs; woodland, 40 pigs.
The value is and was 60s; before 1066 £4.
   Godwin, Burgred's man, held this manor; he could sell.

55   LAND OF RALPH TALLBOYS' WIFE

In MANSHEAD Hundred

1   Azelina, wife of Ralph Tallboys, holds 1½ hides in BATTLESDEN
from the King. Land for 1½ ploughs; 1 there; ½ possible.
   2 villagers and 1 smallholder.
   Meadow for 1 plough.
The value is and was 20s; before 1066, 40s.
   2 Freemen, Askell and Alwin, held this land; they could sell
to whom they would.

M̄ Ipſa Azelina teñ Hocheleia . p x . hiđ ſe defđ . Tᵍra
ē . viii . caῖ . In dñio . v . hidæ . 7 ibi ſunt . ii . caῖ . Ibi xiii.
uilli 7 xi . borđ cū . vi . caῖ . p̄tū . iiii . caῖ . Silua . c . porᶜ.
Inꞇ toꞇ ual 7 ualuit . viii . liɓ . T.R.E.ꞓ xii . liɓ . Hoc M̄ tenuit
Anſchill . T.R.E. 7 uendᵉ potuit . IN FLICTHA HVND.
In Cainou teñ Turſtiñ de Azelina . i . hiđ . Tᵍra . ē . ii . caῖ.
In dñio . i . 7 uñ uills h̄ aliā . Ibi . iii . borđ . 7 p̄tū . i . caῖ.
7 Silua . c . porᶜ . Val . xx . ſol . Q̃do recep̄ ꞓ x . ſol . T.R.E.ꞓ
xx . ſol . Hanc tᵍrā tenuit Vluric ſocħ regis . E . 7 cui uoluit
dare 7 uendere potuit . IN BEREFORDE HVND.
In Wiboldeſtonẹ teñ Judichel . v . uirg 7 dim de Azelina
Tᵍra . ē . i . caῖ . 7 ibi . ē . cū uno uillo 7 ii . borđ . p̄tū dim caῖ.
Val . x . ſol . Q̃do recep̄ ꞓ v . ſol . T.R.E.ꞓ xxx . ſol . Hanc tᵍrā te
nuit Almar h̄o Vlmari . 7 potuit uendᵉ 7 dare cui uoluit.
In Aieuuorde teñ Brodo . i . hiđ IN BICHELESWADE HVND.
de Azelina . Tᵍra . ē . i . caῖ . 7 ibi . ē . cū uno borđ p̄tū . i . caῖ.
Val 7 ualuit ſēp . x . ſol . H̄ tᵍra . ē de maritagio . Hanc te
nuit iſđ Brodo . 7 cui uoluit uendᵉ potuit. ꞓ HVND.
M̄ In Hatelai teñ Azelina de maritagio IN WENESLAI
ſuo . v . hiđ 7 una uirg 7 dim . Tᵍra . ē . viii . caῖ . In dñio . i . hiđ
7 i . uirg . 7 ibi . ii . caῖ . Ibi . viii . uilli 7 iiii . borđ . cū . vi . caῖ.
Ibi . uñ ſerú 7 i . moliñ . xviii . ſolidoᵹ . p̄tū . ii . caῖ . Silua
iiii . porᶜ . 7 de redđ . iii . ſol . Inꞇ toꞇ ual . vi . liɓ . Q̃do re
cepit ꞓ c . ſol . T.R.E.ꞓ vi . liɓ . Hoc M̄ tenuit Vlmar teigñ

2   M. Azelina holds HOCKLIFFE herself. It answers for 10 hides.
Land for 8 ploughs. In lordship 5 hides; 2 ploughs there.
13 villagers and 11 smallholders with 6 ploughs.
Meadow for 4 ploughs; woodland, 100 pigs.
In total, the value is and was £8; before 1066 £12.
Askell held this manor before 1066; he could sell.

In FLITT Hundred

3   In CAINHOE Thurstan holds 1 hide from Azelina. Land for 2 ploughs.
In lordship 1.
1 villager has the other. 3 smallholders.
Meadow for 1 plough; woodland, 100 pigs.
Value 20s; when acquired 10s; before 1066, 20s.
Wulfric, a Freeman of King Edward's, held this land; he could
grant and sell to whom he would.

In BARFORD Hundred

4   In WYBOSTON Iudichael holds 5½ virgates from Azelina.
Land for 1 plough; it is there, with
1 villager and 2 smallholders.
Meadow for ½ plough.
Value 10s; when acquired 5s; before 1066, 30s.
Aelmer, Wulfmer's man, held this land; he could sell and grant
to whom he would.

In BIGGLESWADE Hundred

5   In EYEWORTH Brodo holds 1 hide from Azelina. Land for 1 plough;
it is there, with
1 smallholder.
Meadow for 1 plough.
The value is and always was 10s.
This land is of her marriage portion. Brodo also held this land;
he could sell to whom he would.

In WENSLOW Hundred

6   M. In (Cockayne) HATLEY Azelina holds 5 hides and 1½ virgates of her
marriage portion. Land for 8 ploughs. In lordship 1 hide
and 1 virgate; 2 ploughs there.
8 villagers and 4 smallholders with 6 ploughs. 1 slave.
1 mill, 18s; meadow for 2 ploughs; woodland, 4 pigs;
and from its payments 3s.
In total, value £6; when acquired 100s; before 1066 £6.

regis.E.7 ibi fuer̄ ıı.ſocħi hōes eŷ.ıı.uirḡ 7 dim̄ habuer̄.

7 cui uoluer̄ dare 7 uendĕ potuer̄. *In Wichestanestov*

In Stanford teñ Rogerı.ıı.hiđ de Azelina. *HVND.*

7 ħ eſt de ſuo maritagio.Tra.ē.ıı.car̄.In dn̄io.ı.car̄.7 ıı.uıłłi

7 un̄ borđ cū.ı.car̄.p̊tū.ıı.car̄.Silua.xxx.porc̄.7 ı.molin̄

xııı.ſoł 7 ıııı.den̄.Vał.lx.ſoł.Q̣do recep̄.xx.ſoł.T.R.E.

lx.ſoł.Hanc tr̄a tenuer̄.ıı.ſocħi.7 cui uoluer̄ dare potuer̄.

In Wardone teñ Walter monacħ dimiđ hiđ de Azelina.

7 ħ eſt de ſuo maritagio.Tra.ē dim̄ car̄.ſ; n̄ eſt ibi.Vn̄ borđ

ibi eſt.p̊tū dim̄ car̄.Silua.xl.porc̄.Vał.x.ſoł.Q̣do re

cep̄.7 T.R.E.xx.ſoł.Hanc tr̄a tenuit Goding hō Edrici

calui.7 cui uoluit dare potuit. *In Clistone hvnd.*

In Haneſlauue teñ Widrus.ı.hiđ 7 ııı.uirḡ de Azelina.

Tra.ē.ıı.car̄.7 ibi ſunt.Duo uıłłi.7 ıı.borđ.7 ıı.ſerui.p̊tū

ıı.car̄.Vał.xxx.ſoł.Q̣do recep̄.xx.ſoł.T.R.E.xxx.ſoł.

Hanc tr̄a tenuit Anſcħıłł.7 fuit Bereuuiche de Stodfald

T.R.E.Hanc tr̄a clam̄ Hugo de belcāp ſup Azelinā.dice⸝s

eā habere injuſte.nec ejus dotē unquā fuiſſe.

In ead̄ uilla teñ Bernarđ.ı.hiđ de Azelina.Tra.ē.ı.car̄.

7 ibi.ē.7 ııı.uıłłi.p̊tū.ı.car̄.Vał 7 ualuit.xxııı.ſoł.T.R.E.

xxvııı.ſoł.Hanc tr̄a tenuer̄.ıı.ſocħi hōes Anſcħilli.7 cui

uoluer̄ dare potuer̄.

In Chicheſana teñ.ııı.ſocħi.ııı.hiđ de Azelina.de dote

ſua.Tra.ē.ıı.car̄.Vna.ē ibi.7 alia poteſt fieri.p̊tū.ıı.car̄.

Silua.xx.porc̄.Vał 7 ualuit.xx.ſoł.T.R.E.xxv.ſoł.

Hoc ꝳ tenuer̄.ıııı.ſocħi.7 cui uoluer̄ dare 7 uendĕ potuer̄.

Wulfmer, a thane of King Edward's, held this manor. 2 Freemen, his men, were there; they had 2½ virgates; they could grant and sell to whom they would.

In WIXAMTREE Hundred

7 In STANFORD Roger holds 2 hides from Azelina. It is of her marriage portion. Land for 2 ploughs. In lordship 1 plough;
2 villagers and 1 smallholder with 1 plough.
Meadow for 2 ploughs; woodland, 30 pigs; 1 mill, 13s 4d.
Value 60s; when acquired 20s; before 1066, 60s.
2 Freemen held this land; they could grant to whom they would.

8 In (Old) WARDEN Walter the monk holds ½ hide from Azelina. It is of her marriage portion. Land for ½ plough; but it is not there.
1 smallholder.
Meadow for ½ plough; woodland, 40 pigs.
Value 10s; when acquired and before 1066, 20s.
Goding, Edric the Bald's man, held this land; he could grant to whom he would.

In CLIFTON Hundred

9 In HENLOW Widder holds 1 hide and 3 virgates from Azelina.
Land for 2 ploughs; they are there.
2 villagers, 2 smallholders and 2 slaves.
Meadow for 2 ploughs.
Value 30s; when acquired 20s; before 1066, 30s.
Askell held this land. It was an outlier of Stotfold before 1066.
Hugh of Beauchamp claims this land from Azelina, stating that she has it wrongfully, and that it was never in her dowry.

10 In the same village Bernard holds 1 hide from Azelina.
Land for 1 plough; it is there.
3 villagers.
Meadow for 1 plough.
The value is and was 23s; before 1066, 28s.
2 Freemen, Askell's men, held this land; they could grant to whom they would.

11 In CHICKSANDS 3 Freemen hold 3 hides from Azelina, of her dowry.
Land for 2 ploughs; 1 there; another possible.
Meadow for 2 ploughs; woodland, 20 pigs.
The value is and was 20s; before 1066, 25s.
4 Freemen held this manor; they could grant and sell to whom they would.

In ead uilla ten̄ Walteri . i . hid de Azelina . 7 h̄ eſt de ej̄
maritagio . Tra . ē . i . car̄ . 7 ibi eſt . p̄tū . i . car̄ . Silua . L.
porc̄ . 7 i . molin̄ de . x . ſol . Va ⁓ ⁓ ⁓ ⁓ xx . ſol . T.R.E.⸍
xxx . ſol . Hanc tr̄a tenuit Sueteman . hō Vlmeri ᴅᴇ
Etone . 7 cui uoluit dare potuit.

In Standone ten̄ Engeler . ii . hid 7 dim̄ de Azelina.
Tra . ē . ii . car̄ 7 dim̄ . In dn̄io . ii . car̄ . 7 iii . bord cū dim̄ car̄.
Ibi . ii . ſerui . p̄tū . ii . car̄ 7 dim̄ . Val LX . ſol . Q̄do recep̄⸍
xL . ſol . T.R.E.⸍ iiii . lib̄ . Hanc tr̄a tenuit Vlmar de Etone
teign̄ . R.E. 7 ibi . v . ſochi hōes ej̄d Vlmari fuer̄ . 7 dare
7 uend̄e potuer̄ cui uoluer̄.

.LVI. ⌐TERRA BVRḠSIV̄ DE BEDEF. *IN DIM̄ HVND DE BOCHELAI.*
In *BIDEHA* ten̄ Oſgar de bedeford . i . uirḡ træ de rege.
Tra . ē . ii . bob̃ . Val 7 ualuit ſēp . ii . ſol . Ipſe qui n̄c tenet
tenuit T.R.E. 7 potuit dare cui uoluit.

In ead uilla ten̄ Goduin̄ burgenſis de rege . i . hid 7 iiii.ᵗᵃ
part uni uirḡ . Tra . ē . i . car̄ . 7 ibi eſt . p̄tū . i . car̄ . Valet
7 ualuit ſēp . x . ſol . Dimidiā hidā de hac tr̄a iſte qui n̄c
ten̄ tenuit . T.R.E. quā potuit dare cui uoluit. Dimidiā
ū hidā 7 iiii.ᵗᵃ parte uni uirḡ emit poſtq̄ rex.W.in anglia
uenit . ſ̧ nec regi nec alicui inde ſeruitiū fecit . nec
de ea liberatorem habuit . Sup eund̄ hōem reclamat
Wils ſpech . i . uirḡ 7 iiii.ᵗᵃ part uni uirḡ . quæ ſibi libata
fuit 7 poſtea p̄didit.

In ead uilla ten̄ Orduui burgenſis de rege . i . hid . 7 iii.ᶜⁱᵃ
parte dimidiæ hid . Tra . ē . i . car̄ . 7 ibi . ē . Ibi . ii . uiłłi.
7 i . bord . p̄tū . i . car̄ . Val 7 ualuit ſēp . x . ſol . Dim̄ hid 7 iiii.ᵗᵃ part . i . uirḡ

12 In the same village Walter holds 1 hide from Azelina. It is of   **218 b**
her marriage portion. Land for 1 plough; it is there.
    Meadow for 1 plough; woodland, 50 pigs; 1 mill at 10s.
The value is and was 20s; before 1066, 30s.
    Sweetman, Wulfmer of Eaton's man, held this land; he could
grant to whom he would.

13 In STONDON Engelhere holds 2½ hides from Azelina.
Land for 2½ ploughs. In lordship 2 ploughs;
    3 smallholders with ½ plough.
    2 slaves; meadow for 2½ ploughs.
Value 60s; when acquired 40s; before 1066 £4.
    Wulfmer of Eaton, a thane of King Edward's, held this land. 5
Freemen, this Wulfmer's men, were there; they could grant and sell
to whom they would.

56   LAND OF THE BURGESSES OF BEDFORD

In the Half-Hundred of BUCKLOW
1 In BIDDENHAM Oscar of Bedford holds 1 virgate of land from the King.
Land for 2 oxen.
The value is and always was 2s.
    Its present holder held it before 1066; he could grant
to whom he would.

2 In the same village the burgess Godwin holds 1 hide and the fourth
part of 1 virgate from the King. Land for 1 plough; it is there.
    Meadow for 1 plough.
The value is and always was 10s.
    Before 1066 the present holder held ½ hide of this land which he
could grant to whom he would. But he bought ½ hide and the fourth
part of 1 virgate after King William came to England, but he did not
do service for it to the King or to anyone else; and he did not have a
deliverer for it. William Speke also claims from him 1 virgate and the
fourth part of 1 virgate, which was delivered to him; but he lost it later.

3 In the same village the burgess Ordwy holds 1 hide and the third
part of ½ hide from the King. Land for 1 plough; it is there.
    2 villagers and 1 smallholder.
    Meadow for 1 plough.
The value is and always was 10s.

de hac t̃ra tenuit T.R.E.iſdē qui nc̄ tenet.7 potuit

dare cui uoluit. Vnā uirg̃ ū in uadimonio tenuit

T.R.E.7 adhuc tenet.ut hōes de hoc hund̄ teſtantur.

Idem ipſe emit.1.uirg̃.7 iiij.part uni uirg̃ poſtq̃ rex

W.in Anglia uenit.7 nec regi nec alicui ſeruitiū redd̄.

In ead̄ uilla ten̄ Vlmar̃ burgenſis de rege.ii.partes

unius uirg̃.Tra.ē.i.boui.Val̄ 7 ualuit sēp.xii.den.

Iſtemet tenuit.T.R.E.7 potuit dare cui uoluit.

In WILGA HVND̃.

In Heneuuich ten̄ Eduuard̃ dim̄ hid̄ de rege.Tra.ē

dim̄ car̃.Ibi.ii.boues ſuɉ.7 i.bord̄.Val̄ 7 ualuit

v.ſol̄.T.R.E.́x.ſol̄.Hanc t̃ra tenuit pat̃ huj̃ hōis.

7 uend̄e potuit.T.R.E.Hanc rex.W.in elemoſina

eid̄ conceſſit.unde 7 breuē regis h̃t.7 teſtimon̄ de hund̄.

In Scernebroc ten̄ Almar̃ dim̄ uirg̃ de rege.

Tra.ē dim̄ car̃.ſ; ibi non.ē.Val̄ 7 ualuit.ii.ſol̄.T.R.E.́

.v.ſol̄.Hanc t̃ra pat̃ ejd̄ hōis tenuit.7 rex.W.ei

p̃ breuē ſuū reddidit.   *In WICHESTANESTOV HD̄.*

In Biſtone ten̄ Godmund̄ de rege.iii.uirg̃.Tra.iii.bob̄

7 ibi ſunt.P̃tū.iii.bob̄.Val̄ 7 ualuit.v.ſol̄.T.R.E.́

x.ſol̄.Iſtemet tenuit.T.R.E.7 cui uoluit uend̄e potuit.

In Hanſlau ten̄ Alric̃ de rege.i.uirg̃. *In CLISTONE HD̄.*

Tra.ē.ii.bob̄.7 ibi ſunt.p̃tū.ii.bobȝ.Val̄ 7 ualuit

ſemp.ii.ſol̄.Iſtemet tenuit T.R.E.7 uendere potuit.

In Alriceſei ten̄ q̃dā p̃bendari̊ regis.Vlſi.duas

partes uni̊ uirg̃ de rege.

Before 1066 the present holder held ½ hide and the fourth part of 1 virgate of this land; he could grant to whom he would. But he held 1 virgate in pledge before 1066 and still holds it, as the men of this Hundred testify. He also bought 1 virgate and the fourth part of 1 virgate after King William came to England; he does not pay service to the King or to anyone.

4 In the same village the burgess Wulfmer holds 2 parts of 1 virgate from the King. Land for 1 ox.
The value is and always was 12d.
He held it himself before 1066; he could grant to whom he would.

In WILLEY Hundred

5 In HINWICK Edward holds ½ hide from the King.
Land for ½ plough. 2 oxen there.
1 smallholder.
The value is and was 5s; before 1066, 10s.
Before 1066 his father held this land; he could sell.
King William assigned it to him, in alms, for which he has the King's writ and the witness of the Hundred.

6 In SHARNBROOK Aelmer holds ½ virgate from the King.
Land for ½ plough; but it is not here.
The value is and was 2s; before 1066, 5s.
His father held this land. King William returned it to him through his writ.

In WIXAMTREE Hundred

7 In BEESTON Godmund holds 3 virgates from the King.
Land for 3 oxen; they are there.
Meadow for 3 oxen.
The value is and was 5s; before 1066, 10s.
He held it himself before 1066; he could sell to whom he would.

In CLIFTON Hundred

8 In HENLOW Alric holds 1 virgate from the King.
Land for 2 oxen; they are there.
Meadow for 2 oxen.
The value is and always was 2s.
He held it himself before 1066; he could sell.

9 In ARLESEY a prebendary of the King, Wulfsi, holds 2 parts of 1 virgate from the King.

ITERRA p̄positoʒ ^{REGIS} 7 ELEMOSINAR̄ *In maneshevē* ^{TRVND.}

In Eurefot tenet Herƀt p̄fect regis dimidiā hidā.

7 In Woberne. iii . uirg træ. 7 in Potefgraue . i . hiđ.

Has . iii . tras ten in miniflerio regis . quæ n̄ jacuer̄ ibi

T.R.E. fed ex quo Radulf ^{tallgebofc.} uiceconi fuit . dicit fe eas ħa

buiffe p conceffione regis . Ibi . ē un uitts . Int tot ual

vi . fot. Q̨do recep̄: xx . fot . T.R.E. fimilit . Hanc trā

v . fochi regis. E . tenuer̄. 7 cui uoluer̄ uende potuer̄.

In eađ Potefgraua ten q̨đā equari regis dim hiđ.

Tra . ē dim car̄. 7 ibi eft . Vat 7 ualuit . v . fot . T.R.E:

x . fot. Hanc trā tenuit Ofuui ħo comitis Tofti. 7 cui

uoluit dare potuit.

.I. In Preftelai ten p̄fect regis . i . hiđ. Tra . ē . i . car̄. Ibi

un uitts . P̊tū . i . car̄ . Silua . xx . porc . Vat. v . fot. Q̨do

recep̄: x . fot. T.R.E: xxx . fot. Hanc trā tenuer̄. iiii . teigni.

7 cui uoluer̄ dare 7 uende potuer̄. *In ratborgeftoc hđ.*

.II. In Meldone ten q̨đā p̄fect regis dimiđ hiđ . Tra . ē dim

car̄. 7 ibi eft . cū . ii. uittis . p̄tū dim car̄ . Vat 7 ualuit

iii . fot. T.R.E: x . fot. Hanc trā . ii . fochi regis . E . tenuer̄.

7 cui uoluer̄ dare potuer̄. *In bicheleſwade hvnđ.*

.III. In Tamifeforde ten Aluuin p̄fect. i . hidā. 7 iiii . part

unius uirg. Tra . ē . i . car̄. 7 ibi eft . cū . iii . uittis. p̄tū

dim car̄. Vat 7 ualuit. xx . fot. T.R.E: xxvii. fot. Hanc

trā tenuer̄. vi . fochi. 7 cui uoluer̄ uende potuer̄.

.IIII. In Edeuuorde ten Aluuin p̄fect regis. ii . hiđ 7 dim.

Tra . ē . ii . car̄. 7 ibi funt . cū . ii . uittis . Vat 7 ualuit ſēp

xxx . fot. Hoc Ꝏ tenuit Branting ħo regis. E. 7 uende

.V. In Holme ten Aluuin p̄fect regis . i . hiđ ⌠ potuit.

7 dim . Tra . ē car̄ 7 dim . Ibi eft . i . car̄. 7 dim poteſt

7] LAND OF THE KING'S REEVES, [BEADLES] AND ALMSMEN 218 c

In MANSHEAD Hundred

1 In EVERSHOLT Herbert, a reeve of the King's, holds ½ hide;
in WOBURN 3 virgates of land; in POTSGROVE 1 hide. He holds
these three lands in the King's Administration; they did not lie
there before 1066, but since Ralph Tallboys was Sheriff; he states
that he has had them by the King's assent.
1 villager.
In total, value 6s; when acquired 20s; before 1066 the same.
5 Freemen of King Edward's held this land; they could sell
to whom they would.

2 Also in POTSGROVE a groom of the King's holds ½ hide.
Land for ½ plough; it is there.
The value is and was 5s; before 1066, 10s.
Oswy, Earl Tosti's man, held this land; he could grant
to whom he would.

3 i In PRIESTLEY a reeve of the King's holds 1 hide. Land for 1 plough.
1 villager.
Meadow for 1 plough; woodland, 20 pigs.
Value 5s; when acquired 10s; before 1066, 30s.
4 thanes held this land; they could grant and sell to whom they would.

In REDBORNSTOKE Hundred

3 ii In MAULDEN a reeve of the King's holds ½ hide. Land for ½ plough;
it is there, with
2 villagers.
Meadow for ½ plough.
The value is and was 3s; before 1066, 10s.
2 Freemen of King Edward's held this land; they could grant
to whom they would.

In BIGGLESWADE Hundred

3 iii In TEMPSFORD Alwin the reeve holds 1 hide and the fourth part
of 1 virgate. Land for 1 plough; it is there, with
3 villagers.
Meadow for ½ plough.
The value is and was 20s; before 1066, 27s.
6 Freemen held this land; they could sell to whom they would.

3 iv In EDWORTH Alwin, a reeve of the King's, holds 2½ hides.
Land for 2 ploughs; they are there, with
2 villagers.
The value is and always was 30s.
Branting, King Edward's man, held this manor; he could sell.

3 v In HOLME Alwin, a reeve of the King's, holds 1½ hides.
Land for 1½ ploughs; 1 plough there; ½ possible.

fieri.Ibi.ii.uilli.Val 7 ualuit sẽp.xx.fol.Hanc trã

tenueꝝ Aluric̟ 7 Lemar̟ bedelli.7 uendere potueꝝ.

.VI. In Sudtone ten Aluuin̟.i.uirg̟ 7 dim̟.Val 7 ualuit

iiii.fol.T.R.E.´v.fol.Hanc tram.ii.fochi tenueꝝ.
  or

7 cui uolueꝝ dare 7 uendere potueꝝ.

Has.vi.terras appofuit Rad talgebofc in minifte

rio regis.q̇do uicecomes fuit.n̄ eni fueꝝ ibi.T.R.E.

Qui eas nc̄ habȩꝫ´.c̄ceffione regis tenent.fic̄ dn̄t.

In Stradlei ten̟ p̄fect̟ de hund *IN FLICTHA HVND*.

ii.part uni uirg̟ ad op̟ regis.quæ m̄ jacent in Lintone

Ꝏ regis.fed n̄ jacueꝝ ibi.T.R.E.Bondi ftalꝛ̟ appofuit

in hoc Ꝏ.7 Radulf̟ tallgebofc appofitas ibi inuenit.

Tra.e̅ dim car̟.Val 7 ualuit.v.fol.T.R.E.´x.fol.

Hanc trã tenuit Vlmar̟ pƀr.7 cui uoluit dare potuit.

In Sudtone ten̟ Aluuin̟.i.hid.*IN WENESLAI HVND*.

In dn̄io.i.car̟.7 iii.borđ cū.i.car̟.p̄tū.ii.caꝝ.7 xii.

den̟.Val 7 ualuit.xx.fol.T.R.E.´x.fol.De hac

tra iftemet tenuit.iii.uirg̅.7 q̇dā Eduuard̟.i.uirg̟.

potueꝝ dare 7 uendȩ cui uolueꝝ.*IN WILGE HVND*.

In Carlentone ten̟ Chelƀt̟.iii.uirg̟ 7 dim̟.Tra.e̅ ad

unã caꝝ.7 ibi eft cū.ii.uillis 7 iii.borđ.p̄tū.i.caꝝ.

Val.x.fol.Q̇do recep̟´duas ores.T.R.E.´x.fol.

De hac tra tenuit iftemet.i.uirg̟.hō fuit Edid reginæ

7 cui uoluit dare potuit.Duas uirg̟ ū 7 dim̟ occupauit.

unde nec libatorȩ nec aduocatū inuenit.quã trã

tenuit Alli teign̟.E.regis.

In Wimentone tenȩꝫ´.v.fꝝs cū matre fua.iii.uirg̟ de dū.

218 d

Tra.e̅.i.car̟.f; n̄ eft ibi.Val.iii.fol.T.R.E.´xv.fol.Hanc

trã tenuit Lant pat̟ eoꝛ.7 dare 7 uendȩ potuit.

2 villagers.

The value is and always was 20s.

Aelfric and Leofmer, beadles, held this land; they could sell.

3 vi In SUTTON Alwin holds 1½ virgates.

The value is and was 4s; before 1066, 5s.

2 Freemen held this land; they could grant and sell to whom they would.

Ralph Tallboys put these six lands in the King's Administration when he was Sheriff, for they were not there before 1066.

The present holders hold them by the King's assent, as they state.

In FLITT Hundred

4   In STREATLEY the reeve of the Hundred holds 2 parts of 1 virgate for the King's work. They now lie in (the lands of) the King's manor of Luton, but they did not lie there before 1066. Bondi the Constable put them in this manor and Ralph Tallboys found them put there. Land for ½ plough.

The value is and was 5s; before 1066, 10s.

Wulfmer the priest held this land; he could grant to whom he would.

In WENSLOW Hundred

5   In SUTTON Alwin holds 1 hide; In lordship 1 plough;

3 smallholders with 1 plough.

Meadow for 2 ploughs and 12d too.

The value is and was 20s; before 1066, 10s.

He held 3 virgates of this land himself; one Edward, 1 virgate; they could grant and sell to whom they would.

In WILLEY Hundred

6   In CARLTON Ketelbert holds 3½ virgates. Land for 1 plough; it is there, with

2 villagers and 3 smallholders.

Meadow for 1 plough.

Value 10s; when acquired 2 *ora*; before 1066, 10s.

He held 1 virgate of this land himself; he was Queen Edith's man; he could grant to whom he would. However, he appropriated 2½ virgates for which he found neither deliverer nor patron. Alli, a thane of King Edward's, held this land.

7   In WYMINGTON 5 brothers with their mother hold 3 virgates from (her) dowry. Land for 1 plough; but it is not there.   218 d

Value 3s; before 1066, 15s.

Their father, Lank, held this land; he could grant and sell.

In Coldentone teñ Alric Wintremelc *IN BEREFORD HD.*

dim hiđ de rege. Tra. ē dim cař. 7 ibi eſt. p̃tū. III. boƀ.

Val 7 ualuit sẽp. V. ſoł. Iſte qui nc̄ teñ tenuit. T.R.E.

hõ regis. E. fuit. 7 potuit dare cui uoluit. Quā poſtea

canonicis S Pauli ſub. W. rege dedit. 7 ut poſt mortē

ſuā habent omīno c̄ceſſit. *IN WICHESTANESTOV HD.*

In Stanford teñ Alric de rege. IIII. part uni uirǥ.

Tra. ē dimiđ boui. 7 ibi ē ſemibos. Val 7 ualuit. XII. deñ.

Iſdē teñ qui tenuit. T.R.E. 7 potuit dare cui uoluit.

In eađ uilla teñ Ordui 7 IIII. part uni uirǥ. Tra. III. boƀ.

7 ibi ſuɴ. p̃tū. III. boƀ. Val 7 ualuit sẽp. IIII. ſoł. Iſtemet

tenuit T.R.E. hõ regis fuit. 7 cui uoluit uendē potuit.

In Biſtone teñ Aluuin. I. uirǥ 7 dim. Tra. ē dim cař.

Ibi. II. borđ. Val. XII. deñ. Q̇do recep̃. IIII. ſoł. T.R.E.

. X. ſoł. H̄ tra appoſita. ē in miniſterio regis. ubi non

fuit. T.R.E. ſʒ dot qui eā tenuit 7 dare 7 uendē potuit.

In Weſcota. teñ Ordui. I. uirǥ *IN RADBVRNESTOC HD*

de rege. Tra. ē dim cař. Ibi ſunt. V. boues. cū. I. borđ

7 I. ſeruo. Val 7 ualuit. V. ſoł. T.R.E. x. ſoł. Iſtemet tc̄

tenuit. hõ regis fuit. 7 uendē potuit. *IN STODEN HVND*

In Dene teneɴ. XI. ſochi Wiłłi regis. VII. uirg træ

7 IIII. partē uni uirǥ. Tra. ē. III. cař 7 dim. 7 ibi ſunt.

Val 7 ualuit sẽp. XXX. ſoł. Hanc tra tenueř. T.R.E. idē ipſi

qui nc̄ teneɴ ſochi. 7 cui uolueř dare potueř. Hanc tra

appoſuit Rad in miniſterio regis. ubi non fuit. T.R.E.

In eađ uilla teñ Goduuidere de Bedeford dim uirǥ

de rege. 7 ual 7 ualuit sẽp. XII. deñ. Iſtemet tenuit

T.R.E. 7 potuit inde facere qđ uoluit.

In BARFORD Hundred

8 In GOLDINGTON Alric Wintermilk holds ½ hide from the King.
Land for ½ plough; it is there.
    Meadow for 3 oxen.
The value is and always was 5s.
    The present holder held it before 1066; he was King Edward's
man; he could grant to whom he would. Later he gave it to the
Canons of St. Paul's under King William, and assented that they
should have it altogether after his death.

In WIXAMTREE Hundred

9 In STANFORD Alric holds 4 parts of 1 virgate from the King.
Land for ½ ox; half an ox is there.
The value is and was 12d.
    The present holder held it before 1066; he could grant
to whom he would.

10 In the same village Ordwy holds 4 parts of 1 virgate.
Land for 3 oxen; they are there.
    Meadow for 3 oxen.
The value is and always was 4s.
    He held it himself before 1066; he was the King's man;
he could sell to whom he would.

11 In BEESTON Alwin holds 1½ virgates. Land for ½ plough.
    2 smallholders.
Value 12d; when acquired 4s; before 1066, 10s.
    This land was put in the King's Administration, where it was
not before 1066; but Dot who held it could both grant and sell.

In REDBORNSTOKE Hundred

12 In 'WESTCOTTS' Ordwy holds 1 virgate from the King.
Land for ½ plough; 5 oxen there, with
    1 smallholder and 1 slave.
The value is and was 5s; before 1066, 10s.
    He held it himself then; he was the King's man; he could sell.

In STODDEN Hundred

13 In DEAN 11 Freemen of King William's hold 7 virgates of land and
the fourth part of 1 virgate. Land for 3½ ploughs; they are there.
The value is and always was 30s.
    The same Freemen who now hold this land also held it before
1066; they could grant to whom they would.
    Ralph put this land in the King's Administration, where it
was not before 1066.

14 In the same village Godwy Dear of Bedford holds ½ virgate
from the King.
The value is and always was 12d.
    He held it himself before 1066; he could do what he would with it.

In Hanefeld teñ Saiet . I . uirg̊ de ſoca regis . Tra . e̅
di̅m cař . 7 ibi . e̅ . Val 7 ualuit . v . ſol . T.R.E.ʹx . ſol.
Iſtemet tc̅ tenuit . 7 potuit inde facere qđ uoluit.

In eođ Stoden hund teñ Turgot 7 mat ej̊ de rege
di̅m hiđ . Tra . e̅ . I . cař . 7 ibi eſt . cu̅ uno uiłło 7 II . borđ.
Silua . IIII . porc̊ . Val 7 ualuit . x . ſol . T.R.E.ʹxII . ſol.
Hanc tr̅a tenuit pat̊ huj̊ Turgoti . teign̊ regis fuit.
7 tr̅a ſua̅ dare 7 uendĕ potuit.

In Mildentone teñ q̊da̅ bedełł regis di̅m̊ uirg̊ de
rege . Tra . e̅ . II . bob̊ . Val 7 ualuit . xII . den̅ . Hanc tr̅a
tenuit pat̊ ej̊ qui nc̅ tenet . 7 cui uoluit dare potuit.

In Brimeha̅ teñ Oſiet . I . uirg̊ IN DI̅M HD̅ DE BVCHELAI.
7 II . part uni uirg̊ . Tra . e̅ . I . cař . 7 ibi . e̅ . p̊tu̅ di̅m cař.
Val . x . ſol . T.R.E.ʹv . ſol . Iſtemet tc̅ tenuit . 7 dare potuit.

In Toruei teñ Aluuin de rege tcia̅ part̅e IN WILGE HD̅.
de di̅m hida . Tra . e̅ . II . bob̊ . 7 ibi ſunt . Val 7 ualuit . III . ſol.
Iſtemet tenuit . T.R.E. 7 potuit facere de ea qđ uoluit . ※

In eođ hund teñ Oſiet regis p̅fect di̅m hiđ de rege.
Tra . e̅ di̅m cař . 7 ibi eſt . Val 7 ualuit se̅p . III . ſol . Hanc
tr̅a tenuit . I . ſoch̅s . T.R.E . que̅ rex . W . cu̅ tra hac p̅dicto
p̅fecto c̅omdauit . ut qua̅diu iuueret uictu̅ 7 ueſtitu̅ ei
In Wimtone . teñ Turchiłł de rege . I . hida̅ . ꝭ p̅beret.
Tra . e̅ . I . cař . 7 ibi . e̅ . Val 7 ualuit . v . ſol . T.R.E.ʹx . ſol.
Iſtemet tc̅ tenuit . 7 cui uoluit uendĕ potuit.

※ Rex u̅ . W . ſibi poſtea in elemoſina c̅ceſſit . unde ꝑ anima
regis 7 regina̅
o̅mi edđa . II . feria miſsa̅ p̅ſoluit.

15   In *HANEFELD* Saegeat holds 1 virgate, of the King's jurisdiction.
Land for ½ plough; it is there.
The value is and was 5s; before 1066, 10s.
    He held it himself then; he could do what he would with it.

16   Also in the Hundred of STODDEN Thorgot and his mother hold ½ hide
from the King. Land for 1 plough; it is there, with
    1 villager and 2 smallholders.
    Woodland, 4 pigs.
The value is and was 10s; before 1066, 12s.
    This Thorgot's father held this land; he was a thane of the King's;
he could grant and sell his land.

17   In MILTON (Ernest) a beadle of the King's holds ½ virgate from the King.
Land for 2 oxen.
The value is and was 12d.
    The present holder's father held this land; he could grant to
whom he would.

In the Half-Hundred of BUCKLOW
18   In BROMHAM Osgeat holds 1 virgate and 2 parts of 1 virgate.
Land for 1 plough; it is there.
    Meadow for ½ plough.
Value 10s; before 1066, 5s.
    He held it himself then; he could grant.

In WILLEY Hundred
19   In TURVEY Alwin the priest holds the third part of ½ hide from
the King. Land for 2 oxen; they are there.
The value is and was 3s.
    He held it himself before 1066; he could do what he would with it.

(continued below, directed by transposition signs to its proper place.)

20   In the same Hundred Osgeat, a reeve of the King's holds ½ hide
from the King. Land for ½ plough; it is there.
The value is and always was 3s.
    A Freeman held this land before 1066. King William commended
him to the said reeve with this land, so that as long as lived he should
provide food and clothing for him.

21   In WYMINGTON Thorkell holds 1 hide from the King. Land for 1 plough;
it is there.
The value is and was 5s; before 1066, 10s.
    He held it himself then; he could sell to whom he would.

(57,19 continued, directed by transposition signs to its proper place.)

But King William later granted it to him in alms, for which he performed
mass every week on Mondays for the souls of the King and the Queen.

BEDFORDSHIRE HOLDINGS
ENTERED ELSEWHERE IN THE SURVEY

The Latin text of these entries is given in the county volumes concerned

In HERTFORDSHIRE

1   **LAND OF THE KING**   132 b

In the Half-Hundred of HITCHIN ...   132 c

E1   5   King William holds WESTONING. It answers for 5 hides.
Land for 14 ploughs. In lordship 2 hides; 2 ploughs.
16 villagers with 3 smallholders have 5 ploughs;
a further 5 possible.
4 slaves; meadow for 7 ploughs; pasture for the village
livestock; woodland, 400 pigs, and 3s too.
Earl Harold held this manor; it lay and lies in Hitchin (lands);
but the obligations of this manor lay in Bedfordshire before 1066,
in the Hundred of Manshead. It is and always was a manor there;
since 1066 it has not met the King's tax.

13   **LAND OF ST. PAUL'S, LONDON**   136 b

In DACORUM Hundred

E2   1   The Canons of London hold KENSWORTH. It answers for 10 hides.
Land for 10 ploughs. In lordship 5 hides; 2 ploughs there;
a further 3 possible.
8 villagers with 3 smallholders have 2 ploughs; a further 3
possible.
3 slaves; pasture for the livestock; woodland, 100 pigs, and
from the payments of the woodland 2s.
Total value 70s; when acquired 100s; before 1066 as much.
Young Leofwin held this manor from King Edward.

19   **LAND OF ROBERT D'OILLY**   137 d

[In the Half-Hundred of HITCHIN]

E3   2   In POLEHANGER Martell holds ½ hide from Robert d'Oilly.
Land for 1 plough; it is there, with
2 cottagers and 2 slaves.
Meadow for 1 plough; woodland, 2 pigs.
The value is and was 10s; before 1066, 20s.
Aelfric, Earl Waltheof's man, held this land; he could sell.

21   **LAND OF ROBERT OF TOSNY**   138 a

In DACORUM Hundred

E4   2   In BARWYTHE Baldric holds 5 hides from Robert. Land for 3
ploughs. In lordship 2; a third possible.
3 villagers, with a priest and a Frenchman, with 4 smallholders.
Meadow for 1 plough; pasture for the village livestock;
woodland, 100 pigs.
In total, value 40s; when acquired 30s; before 1066, 60s.
Oswulf son of Fran held this land; he could sell to whom he
would.

2   LAND OF THE BISHOP OF LINCOLN   203 d

LEIGHTONSTONE Hundred ...

E5 9   In PERTENHALL Alwin had 1 virgate of land taxable.
Land for ½ plough.

K   This land is situated in Bedfordshire, but it pays tax
and service in Huntingdonshire. The King's officers
claim it for his work.

Value before 1066 and now 5s.

William holds it from Bishop Remigius and ploughs
there, together with his lordship.

13   LAND OF WILLIAM OF WARENNE   205 c

[KIMBOLTON Hundred]

E6 3 S. In SWINESHEAD 3½ hides taxable. Land for 4 ploughs.
Jurisdiction.

Now 1 Freeman, 7 villagers and 5 smallholders.

Meadow, 16 acres; woodland pasture 1 league long and
4 furlongs wide.

Value 40s.

Eustace holds from William.

19   LAND OF EUSTACE THE SHERIFF   206 a

KIMBOLTON Hundred

E7 11 M. In SWINESHEAD Fursa had ½ hide taxable. Land for ½ plough,
with full jurisdiction.

Now 1 villager.

Meadow, 3 acres; woodland pasture 1 league long and 1
furlong wide.

Value before 1066, 15s; now 6s.

Ralph holds from Eustace.

D   DECLARATIONS OF THE SWORN MEN   208 a

E8 14   The men of the County testify that King Edward gave   208 b
SWINESHEAD to Earl Siward, with full jurisdiction, and so
Earl Harold had it; moreover that (its men) paid tax in the
Hundred, and went with them against the enemy.

E9 16   Of Alwin Devil's 1 virgate of land in PERTENHALL,
King Edward had the jurisdiction.

ABBREVIATIONS used in the notes.
BCS ... Birch *Cartularium Saxonicum.* DB .. Domesday Book. DBB ... Maitland
Domesday Book and Beyond. DG ... H.C. Darby and G. H. Versey *Domesday Gazetteer.*
EPNS ... English Place-Name Society Survey (Bedfordshire, unless otherwise indicated).
KCD ... Kemble *Codex Diplomaticus.* MS ... Manuscript. OEB ... G. Tengvik *Old
English Bynames*.* PNDB .. O. von Feilitzen *The Pre-Conquest Personal Names of
Domesday Book*.* VCH ... Victoria County History, Bedfordshire, Volume 1.
*Nomina Germanica, Uppsala, Volumes 3 and 4.

The manuscript is written on leaves, or folios, of parchment (sheepskin), measuring about
15 inches by 11 (38 bv 28 cm), on both sides. On each side, or page, are two columns,
making four to each folio. The folios were numbered in the 17th century, and the four
columns of each are here lettered a,b,c,d. Chapter numbers and titles are in red ink, and
sections are normally distinguished by initial capitals, outlined in red. Many Hundred and
place names are written in capitals, scored through in red, normally represented by Farley
with italic capitals. Farley's principal variants from this convention are, in place names,
neither capitals nor scored in the MS, 23,16; scored, but not in capitals, 24,9; 26,1; 27,1;
40,3; 41,2; in capitals, but not scored, 23,14; and HVND at 2,2, in capitals but not scored
in the MS. Deletion is normally marked by underlining.
 The MS has more minor careless mistakes in Bedfordshire than in many counties,
chiefly the misspelling, omission or repetition of words and occasionally of phrases. The
overall total of hides is however independently confirmed (see note below), and there is
no reason to suppose serious or frequent error in other figures.

BEDFORDSHIRE. *Bedefordscire* in red at the top of each page, over both columns. The
Shire emerged from the district assigned to the maintenance of the Danish army of Bedford
in the late 9th century, but was formally organised later, probably about 1008 (see
Warwicks. 1,6 note). In the 'County Hidage' (Maitland DBB 475), held to have been
drafted not much later, it is entered at 1200 hides; the 1086 hides also total approximately
1200. The external boundary may therefore have been little changed. It was however
artificial in 1086, dividing a dozen manors and parishes, several of which were not reunited
until the 19th century. The gains however roughly balance the losses, and the total surface
area did not greatly differ from that of the modern county, about 300,000 acres.

B   HIDES. The hide was the unit of measurement of land, of productivity, of extent,
         or of tax liability, and contained four virgates. Governments tried to standardise
         the hide at 120 acres, but incomplete revision left hides of widely different
         extent in different areas (see Sussex, Appendix). In Bedfordshire (32,14; 39,3),
         as occasionally elsewhere, woodland was sometimes measured by the hide. If the
         Bedfordshire hides regularly included all productive land, they might have been
         standardised at 120 acres, 1200 of them accounting for a little under half the
         total area of the Shire.
         BISHOP REMIGiUS. Of Lincoln.
         VALUE. *Valet* normally means the sums due to lords from their lands.
         100s. DB uses the English currency system, in force until 1971. The pound
         contained 20 shillings, each of 12 pence, and the abbreviations £.s.d. preserved
         the DB terms *librae, solidi, denarii.* DB often lists smaller sums in multiples of
         shillings rather than of pounds, as here. 100s means £5.
L 40   LOVETT. Old French *louet,* wolf-cub, OEB 363; distinct from English *Levet* (20,1).
L 50   ARGENTON. Or, less probably, Argentan, OEB 69.
1,1a   HUNDRED. As in some other Shires, the Bedfordshire Hundreds are normally
         entered in the same order in each chapter. The order is Manshead and Stanbridge
         (interchangeable), Redbornstoke, Stodden, Flitt, Bucklow, Willey, Barford,
         Biggleswade, Wenslow, Wixamtree and Clifton. Apart from marginal insertions,
         the main variants are ch. 23, where Hugh of Beauchamp's lordship land and his
         men's lands are separately listed, and his last four lordship manors (13-16), are also a
         separate list, possibly an addition; and ch. 57, also in three successive lists, which
         do not however relate to the three categories of the chapter title. See also 48,2;
         54,4; 57, notes.

30 HIDES. 47 with those of 1b, 43 without 1c. The commonest figures are multiples of 5 hides, the old English basis for military and other obligations; e.g., Berks., B 10.

LAND FOR . . PLOUGHS. An estimate of the arable, probably earlier than 1066.

MEADOW FOR . . PLOUGHS. For the oxen who pull the plough, reckoned at eight.

DOG DUES. Payments replacing the obligation to feed and kennel the King's hounds.

IVO TALLBOYS increased the payments of the King's three *dominica maneria*, evidently those which had been King Edward's; to each of them his brother Ralph, the Sheriff, added manors which had not been King Edward's. Ivo was a magnate, later Steward to William II, and survived till about 1115. He is chiefly remembered as an outstanding commander in the King's siege of Hereward and the English earls in Ely in 1069, and as an enemy to the monks of Crowland. Ralph acquired most of the numerous manors of Askell of Ware, but exchanged Ware (see Index of Places) with Hugh of Grandmesnil for various Bedfordshire lands. He died before 1086, and most of his lands passed to Hugh of Beauchamp, but some went to his widow, his daughter and his niece, married to Ranulf son of Ilger. His heirs and the two Hughs disputed many items of the inheritance; see ch.23, and also Hertfordshire, especially EB 3, note.

1,1b   HIDES . . PLACED. Probably including Eggington,Stanbridge and Billington, not named in DB, since 47 hides is over large for Leighton Buzzard on its own.

1,1c   BISHOP WULFWY. Of Dorchester-on-Thames, died 1067; under his successor, Remigius, the see was transferred to Lincoln.

1,2   MANSHEAD HUNDRED. Luton was later in Flitt Hundred, but not in DB; it was therefore presumably in Manshead in 1086, probably in Woodcroft Hundred before 1066 (1,4 note). Dunstable was a deserted Roman ruin, not yet resettled.

1,3   HOUGHTON. MS clearly *HOVSTONE;* unclear in Farley's print.

1,4   QUEEN EDITH. Wife of King Edward, daughter of Earl Godwin.
       WOODCROFT HUNDRED. Otherwise unknown. Evidently merged in Manshead and Stanbridge, both of which were much above the normal size of other Hundreds (1,5 note 'ANOTHER HUNDRED').. The meeting place was presumably *Wodecroft* in Luton, last recorded in 1372, EPNS 160; the Hundred therefore probably included Luton.
       INCREASE IT GAVE HIM. Or possibly 'he gave'.

1,5   PLACED. *Apposuit* Accidentally repeated, and deleted.
       5 HIDES. Perhaps those of Caddington.
       ANOTHER HUNDRED. The occasions of transfers from one Hundred to another are rarely noted in DB, though transfers were plainly frequent. EPNS maps later changes, and DB entries point to earlier changes. As in other midland Shires, Bedford's 1200 hides probably originally meant twelve Hundreds, each of 100 hides. There were still twelve Hundreds in 1086, but not of 100 hides each. Three are in several entries termed Half-Hundreds, Stanbridge, Bucklow and Wenslow. By 1086, Wenslow had cut Biggleswade into two separated portions, but the two portions together totalled 100 hides; as in Flitt, compensation after a boundary change is a likely explanation. Precise figures for 1086 cannot be had without close analysis, but a provisional count, to the nearest hide, suggests the main areas of change. Four Hundreds retained their assessment, Stodden and Biggleswade with 100 hides each, Flitt with 97 and Clifton with 99. Five other Hundreds are entered at 501 hides between them, Manshead (167) and Stanbridge (109), both well over their formal rating, with the former Hundred of Woodcroft, and with Redbornstoke (116) and Wixamtree (109). Willey (104) and Barford (93), with the Half-Hundreds of Wenslow (45) and Bucklow (55), total 297 hides, the equivalent of three Hundreds. The grand total of these hides, 1194, is virtually unchanged, but the internal boundaries had evidently been drastically rearranged; beyond the obvious inference that the larger part of Woodcroft was assigned to Manshead and Stanbridge, there is no evident explanation of the nature, date or purpose of these changes. It is possible that analysis of landholding in and before 1066 may suggest some of the reasons.

2,2   HOLDING. *De fedo,* MS error for *de feudo,* meaning the Bishop's entire Holding. *In feudo* is occasionally used in DB for land held by a special grant, sometimes for life, see Sussex 11,8 note.

2,3   FREEMEN. See Appendix.

2,5   BEFORE 1066. Farley *TR..; TRE* is legible beneath a MS blot.

2,6   BUCKLOW. The MS is blotted. Read *Boch[el]ai...Stach[eden]e...p[ot].* See 3,4 note.
       7 SMALLHOLDERS. MS *vii;* Farley, in error, *vi.*

2,8 WIMUND. Probably of Tessel, see 23,37.

ALFWOLD. See 15,2.

2,9 VILLAGERS. As a general term, including Freemen and smallholders.

3,3 5 PLOUGHS. The MS is difficult to read; probably *v car.*

3,4 BEFORE 1066. MS blotted, facing 2,6. Read *[T]RE...v. [so]chi,* and, in 3,5, *d[api]fer.*
The stop after *v,* before *[so]chi,* is clear in the MS.

3,6 EASTON. See *Inquisitio Eliensis* 66a, columns 1-2 (ed. Hamilton p.166) *in comitatu
Huntedonie Spalduuic...7 Ber. Estou, Estune, Bercheham* (In Huntingdonshire
Spaldwick and the outliers (Long) Stow, Easton and Barham). The places adjoin each
other; see Hunts., Appendix. See also Hunts. D 19 'The County testifies that the third
part of ½ hide which lies in Easton (*Estone*) and pays tax in Bedfordshire belongs to
Spaldwick, the Abbot of Ely's manor'; Eustace had annexed it in 1071. Spaldwick
was in Hunts., but Easton paid tax in Bedfordshire. The eleven entries for Easton total
9½ hides. It may have been a ten-hide manor, the other half-hide being a portion of
the Spaldwick outlier which Eustace had not annexed.

In 1881 Airy emended *Estone* to *Westen,* wasteland, and therefore located it on
'the high clay table of Little Staughton', which was 'one of a series of *Westens*', including
Westoning, similarly emended'. In 1904 Round (VCH 213-215) properly rejected this
etymology (with which he parallelled Airy's derivation of *Segresdone* (Shirdon) from
'sacristan') and the consequent location; he suggested the obvious Easton, noting that
William of Warenne's Honour of Kimbolton later retained 1 hide of Easton, where in
1086 he had held over 2 hides (Bedfordshire, 17,4-7). But the identification with Little
Staughton was repeated by EPNS 20 in 1926, adding 'sic', and by DG, without
qualification.

The Domesday manor was clearly larger than the later parish. In proportion to the
acreage, ploughs and assessed ploughs were both four times as numerous as in the
neighbouring parishes of Staughton, which include the DB manors of Dillington and
Perry. Easton therefore probably included part of Great Staughton, now in Hunts., and
all or part of Little Staughton, now in Beds. It might have consisted of scattered
portions, but since such separate outliers are normally individually recorded in Beds.,
it is here mapped as a single area, with uncertain bounds, separated from Tilsworth by
the Honour and former Hundred of Kimbolton, in Hunts.

3,8 BLEADON. The Bishop of Coutances also exchanged Tyringham and Clifton (Raynes)
(Bucks. 5,10; 18...145 b,c) for *Bledone.* The only place named in DB with the same or
similar spelling (Old English *bleo dun,* 'blue', or coloured, hill) is Bleadon in Somerset,
with which VCH identified it, followed by DG. But Bleadon was held by the Bishop
of Winchester before and after 1066 (Somerset 2,3... 87 d), whereas all the lands which
the Bishop of Coutances received had been held by men of the King, except Tyringham,
held by two thanes, one of them a man of Earl Waltheof, whose lands fell to the King
on his execution, the other without a named lord. *Bledone* should therefore be a manor
formerly held by the King or his men. There are two main alternative possibilities,
either a variant spelling of Blewbury or Blewburton (*bleo byrig dune*) (Berks
151-2), a manor of King Edward's and King William's (Berks. 1,5... 56 d), or a lost
place. Since the lands which the Bishop received lay close together, about the junction
of Beds., Bucks., and Northants., DB may have omitted a King's manor in this area.
Elsewhere the text occasionally refers to a manor not listed in the Survey.

3,9 NEWTON BROMSHOLD. See also Northants.

4   LAND OF THE BISHOP OF COUTANCES   220 c
                               . . .
20 From the Bishop himself William holds 2 hides less ½ virgate in   220 d
    NEWTON (Bromshold). Land for 2 ploughs. In lordship 2 ploughs;
          8 villagers and 6 smallholders with 2 ploughs.
          Woodland 2 furlongs long and 1 furlong wide.
    The value was 20s; now 40s.
    Azor held it before 1066.
The whole parish is now in Northants.; DB enters only a small part in Beds.

3,10 4 HIDES. Possibly in Chellington, not named in DB, but held by Geoffrey's heirs, VCH 225.

3,11 TURVEY. MS *Tornai* for *Torvai;* so also 24,23 and 32,3.

3,17   RUSHDEN. See also 22,2 and Northants.

        [35]   LAND OF WILLIAM PEVEREL   225 d
        [In HIGHAM Hundred]
        1a William Peverel holds HIGHAM (Ferrers)...
        1b In RUSHDEN 6 hides. Land for 12 ploughs.
            19 Freemen have them.
            A mill at 10s; meadow, 30 acres. ...
        1g [Countess] Gytha held it, with full jurisdiction.
           The Freemen of Rushden, Irchester and Raunds were Burgred's men; for this
           reason Bishop Geoffrey (of Coutances) claims their homage *(hominationem)*.
Beds. 3,17 had been held by one of Burgred's men, Beds. 22,2 by one of Countess
Gytha's, who was William Peverel's predecessor elsewhere. Rushden is now wholly in
Northants. See also 32,5 and 42,1 (Podington and Farndish).
OXEN. *Terra bobus* (dative), but *pratum bouum* (genitive).

4,2   WILLIAM'S FATHER. Evidently one of the Normans who held from King Edward
    before 1066.

4,3   PIGS. *Porc* accidentally repeated, but not deleted.

4,5   VALUE...6s. MS *vi sol;* the *i* is thinner and fainter than the *v,* but is clear and distinct;
    Farley, in error, *v sol.*

6   ST. EDMUND'S. Bury St. Edmunds.

6,1   ORDWY held more land in Biddenham, 56,3.
    BOROUGH REEVE. Rarely recorded in DB.

6,2   KINWICK. EPNS 109.

7,1   STANWICK. See also Northants.
        6   LAND OF ST. PETER'S OF PETERBOROUGH ...   221 b
        17 The Church itself holds 1 hide and 1 virgate of land in STANWICK.   221 c
           Land for 3 ploughs. In lordship 2 ploughs, with 1 slave;
             8 villagers and 4 smallholders with 1 plough and 2 oxen.
           A mill at 20s; meadow 8 acres.
           The value was 40s; now 100s.
    Two-thirds of Stanwick was in Beds. in 1086; it is now all in Northants.
    PLOUGH IRON. Primarily for plough-shares; from the woodland, where the fuel was;
    iron was forged more easily there than by hauling timber to the village.

8,9   VALUE. Added in smaller lettering.

10,1   CARUCATE. Not the *carucata* of the Danish Shires. Here equivalent to 'Land for 1
    plough', as in the Exon. DB and other comparable records. In the Home Counties,
    used of lordship land, probably exempt from the King's tax. See Hunts., B 18; B 21
    and Hurstingstone Hundred entries, where additional 'Land for ploughs' and *carucatae*
    are equated with each other, but distinguished from *inland* in 6,19. Interlinear
    corrections there and in Middlesex 24,1 (where the note, from line 2, *carucatae,* onward,
    should be deleted) suggest that DB was itself in some doubt as to when *carucae,*
    ploughs, and when *carucatae* should be written for the abbreviated *car.*

12,1   CADDINGTON. See also Herts.
        13   LAND OF ST. PAUL'S, LONDON   136 b
        In DACORUM Hundred...
        2   The Canons hold CADDINGTON themselves. It answers for 10 hides.
           Land for 10 ploughs. In lordship 4 hides; 1 plough there;
           a further 3 possible.
             22 villagers have 6 ploughs. 5 smallholders; 2 slaves.
             Pasture for the livestock; woodland, 100 pigs and 2s too.
             Total value 110s; when acquired £6; before 1066 as much.
           (Young) Leofwin held this manor from King Edward.
    The parish of Caddington was not reunited until 1897, when the Hertfordshire portion,
    together with the adjoining parish of Kensworth, also held by Leofwin (E 2), was
    transferred to Bedfordshire.
        About 1053 (KCD 920) Leofwin's father, Edwin of Caddington, bequeathed
    Watford, where Leofwin held Bushey (Herts. 33,2), to St. Alban's, and 'to my son
    Leofwin' Sundon, Caddington, Streatley (Beds. 24,18), (Cockayne) Hatley, *Pirian,*
    Putnoe and Barley (Herts. 29,1). DB enters other 1066 lay holders for Sundon, Hatley

and Putnoe, and Leofwin's lands at Beeston and Meppershall are not named in his father's will. A few years later 'Leofwin of Caddington' was one of the witnesses to Oswulf's grant of Studham to St. Albans (Beds. 26,1 note). He was a King's thane, possibly identical with Leofwin, Earl Harold's man, in Herts.

13,1   BIDDENHAM. Added in the margin.

14   ERNWIN. MS *Ernui* for *Ernuuin.*

14,1   ERNWIN THE PRIEST. He also held in Notts., Lincs., and the future Lancashire.

   PLOUGH. Half a plough there, but no inhabitants mentioned, as in several smaller Bedfordshire holdings. '½ plough possible' omitted.

15   COUNT EUSTACE. Of Boulogne, brother-in-law of King Edward.

15,2   ALFWOLD. *Adeloldus,* Aethelwold. But he is plainly identical with *Aluuoldus,* Alfwold of Stevington (2,8), and therefore with Alfwold of 15,1; 4-7.

15,6   PLOUGHS. 'Land for 5 ploughs' omitted.

16,2   BATTLESDEN. In all, 11 hides; with its neighbour, Chalgrave, 9 hides, a total of 20 hides.

16,5   DUNTON. *Domtone,* MS error for *Donitone.*

16,9   MILL 3s 3d. The abbreviation above *iii solid* is *[tri]um.*

17   WILLIAM OF WARENNE. A prominent magnate, created Earl of Surrey by William II; died 1088.

   DELIVERER. The *liberator* handed over land on the King's behalf, and freed it from other claims.

17,2   TILBROOK. Now in Huntingdonshire.

   SO THAT. The cumbersome phrase is unusual. Very many Freemen and others in DB are said to have had the right, before 1066, to 'withdraw', either without qualification, sometimes equated with *alodium,* 'freehold', or 'to another lord'. Here, as commonly in Beds., they are not said to have been subject to any lord. Normally, the Commissioners, or their clerk, transcribed the phrase without comment; the wording suggests that on this occasion they asked 'the men of the Hundred' to explain its meaning.

   HUGH (OF) BEAUCHAMP...RALPH TALLBOYS. See 1,1a note, Ivo Tallboys, and 23,7 note.

17,3   KIMBOLTON. Formerly a Hundred, in 1086 the centre of William of Warenne's Honour, in Huntingdonshire, jutting into Bedfordshire between Tilbrook and Easton. *Hanefelde* evidently lay close to the Shire boundary in this area.

   OBLIGATIONS. *Warras,* from *werian,* defend, guard, be wary of; probably including both the King's *geld* and liability for military service. Not to be confused with *Waras,* Ware in Hertfordshire (23,7ff.), probably a plural of *waer,* weir, EPNS Herts. 206.

17,4   ASKELL. Of Ware, see 1,1a Ivo Tallboys and 23,7 notes.

   COLMWORTH. See 23,38.

   SHERIFFDOM. Since in 1086 each Shire had its Sheriff *(vicecomes),* but only two had an Earl *(comes),* DB often uses *vicecomitatus* for *comitatus,* county.

17,5   COMMENDED. An unusually explicit definition of *commendatio;* see 23,17; 57,20.

17,7   GODRIC. Possibly a MS error for *homo Godrici vicecomitis,* a man of Godric the Sheriff; see 23,25.

18,1   BOSCOMBE. In Wiltshire. He was William's predecessor in other counties.

20,1   WULFWARD. Wulfward White, a magnate of King Edward's, Arnulf's predecessor in several other counties.

   LEOFED. *Levet,* perhaps *Leofede,* PNDB 322 *(Luvede);* or *Levid, quedam femina* (Essex 30,44...62 a), see PNDB 312; or a misspelling of *Leviet* (Leofgeat).

20,2   EDWARD WHITE. *Uuit* is a frequent byname, used by a number of different unrelated people. But since Edward held from Arnulf, he may have been a relative of Wulfward, (20,1); if so, his is a rare instance of an Old English family name. It is however possible that the interlinear correction was added against the wrong name, intended for Wulfward.

   THE 3 ABOVE. Those of 21,12.

   LISOIS. Of Moutiers. His courage and initiative forced the passage of the Aire in William's campaign against York in 1069, Ordericus 4,7.

22,1   TILSWORTH. MS *Pileworde* mistakes Old English 'thorn' (Th) for P; the return which DB here transcribed was therefore written by a clerk familiar with Old English letters.

22,2   MALET. Normally a byname. The personal name was perhaps omitted.

   COUNTESS GYTHA. Widow of Earl Ralph of Hereford, William Peverel's predecessor elsewhere; different from her namesake, wife of Earl Godwin and mother of King Harold.

23,1	KEYSOE. See also Hunts.	
	13 LAND OF WILLIAM OF WARENNE...	205 c

13   LAND OF WILLIAM OF WARENNE...   205 c

2 S.   In KEYSOE Aellic, 3 virgates of land taxable. Land for 6 oxen. Jurisdiction.
     1 Freeman and 7 smallholders.
     Meadow, 4 acres; woodland pasture 50 acres.

29   LAND OF THE KING'S THANES...   207 c

LEIGHTONSTONE Hundred

2   In KEYSOE Alwin had 1 virgate of land taxable, with full jurisdiction.
Land for 2 oxen. It lies in Bedfordshire, but it pays tax in Huntingdonshire.
Now he holds it himself from the King and has
     1 villager, with 2 oxen in a plough.
Value before 1066, 16d; now the same.

   DB reports a total of 5 hides and 1 virgate of Keysoe in Bedfordshire; it may be that the record omitted a statement that William of Warenne's 3 virgates also 'lay in Bedfordshire'. It is probably that the Huntingdonshire taxable hide lay in the north of the manor, adjoining Pertenhall (E 9).

23,5   CHAINHALLE. VCH 237 suggests Channel's End (TL 11 57), apparently on the similarity of the modern name, but queries it because Channel's End is in Barford Hundred; and is followed by DG, without the query. EPNS map gives it as an alternative name for Ravensden, but omits it from its text. Presumably the editors (Mawer and Stenton, in 1926) had some evidence to support this identification; but the relevant EPNS records were lost or destroyed during the war. Its position in the text places it in Bucklow Hundred, which Ravensden adjoins.

23,7   GOLDINGTON HIGHFIELDS. 2½ miles north-west of Goldington, separated from it by Putnoe.
WARE. Ralph received in all (see Index of Places) 22 hides and 3 virgates in exchange for Ware, assessed at 24 hides; but their combined value was much less than the value of Ware. See 1,1a Ivo Tallboys, note.

23,15   AKI. *Achi,* here and in 23,38, may be a mistake for *Aschil,* but since Hugh held much land that had not been Askell's, Aki may be a separate person.

23,16   WHEN ACQUIRED. i.e., by Hugh.

23,17   COMMENDED. See 17,5 and 57,20 notes.

23,22   THERE WAS 1 FREEMAN. MS *fuerunt* for *fuit* ('were' for 'was'); see 23,53.

23,27   BLETSOE. Here and in 53,8 in Bucklow. Geographically, in 1086, Bletsoe should have been in Willey, Radwell in Bucklow, with the Ouse as Hundred boundary. The anomaly may be the result of a transfer, see 1,5 note.

23,31   OSBERN. MS Osbert for Osbern, see 23,27; 44,2; 46,1 notes.

23,36   HIDES. MS *car,* underlined for deletion, emended to *hid(as).*

23,48   HOO. In Wootton (49,2), which Aelmer held; EPNS 86.

23,50   IN THE SAME VILLAGE. Repeated 23,51-55.

23,53   HELD. MS *tenuit,* probably a MS error for *tenet,* holds, as in 23,22 above.

24,2   FUGLO. MS *Suglo,* in error, PNDB 256. The text was evidently transcribing a return which used small-letter hooked 's', easily confused with 'f'.

24,5   OATS FROM THE WOODLAND. Presumably from clearings in the woodland.

24,9   THEY ALL. Evidently some names have been omitted, probably of Freemen.

24,11   BROOM. The marginal addition is placed against the wrong Hundred.

24,13   WESTCOTTS. By Wilshamstead, formerly balancing Eastcotts, the parish centred on Cotton End, TL 08 45; EPNS 86 and 91.

   PLOUGH IRON. See 8,1 note.

24,15   SMALLHOLDERS and slaves here entered after resources.

24,17   HOLD. The MS omits *de* and repeats *ten(et).*

24,18   SOMEONE. *Quidem,* probably for a word or name illegible in the return transcribed.
MARRIAGE PORTION. DB distinguishes *maritagium,* provided by the bride's father, from *dos,* the dowry provided by the husband; see also ch. 55.

24,19   MILTON ERNEST. With this entry, Milton Ernest makes 10 hides, as does Milton Bryan in Manshead Hundred. Milton Ernest is in Stodden; but it is possible that a portion of its lands lay across the Ouse, in Willey, and that the Hundred heading is inserted after, instead of before, the entry, as occasionally in other counties.

PLOUGH POSSIBLE. The MS probably omitted *pot(est) fieri* after *vill.*

25,1 PASSWATER. French *passe l'eau,* hence English Paslow, Parslow, etc., OEB 386.

25,11 FRENCHMEN. *Franci,* probably for the more usual *francigenae,* rather than 'freemen'.

25,14 THANE OF THE KING'S. The MS probably omitted *E(dwardi)* after *regis.*

26,1 STUDHAM. Granted to St. Albans (KCD 945) shortly before 1066 by Oswulf and his wife, Aethelida. The named witnesses are Bishop Wulfwy, Bondi the Constable, Burgred and his son Edwin, Godric *'tribunus',* Alstan the Sheriff and Leofwin of Caddington (12,1 note). Aethelida had inherited Studham from her first husband Wulfsi. She and Oswald retained its use for their lives, and the Abbot provided timber to build a church in Studham 'in honour of our Lord Jesus Christ and St. Alban'. St. Albans did not acquire the land, presumably because Oswulf lived until the Conquest, and the medieval church was dedicated to the Virgin.

27,1 EDLESBOROUGH. See also Bucks.

> 22   LAND OF GILBERT OF GHENT   149 d
>
> In YARDLEY Hundred
>
> 1 M.   Gilbert of Ghent holds EDLESBOROUGH. It answers for 20 hides.
> Land for 14 ploughs. In lordship 10 hides; 4 ploughs there.
> 26 villagers with 4 smallholders have 10 ploughs.
> 10 slaves; 2 mills at 15s 4d; meadow for 4 ploughs; woodland, 400 pigs.
> Total value £13; value before 1066 £14.
> Ulf, a thane of King Edward's, held this manor; he could sell.

The two thirds of the manor in Bucks. presumably included the village; the Beds. portion would therefore be in the south-east of the modern parish. The village is now all in Bucks.
10d. MS probably omits *den(arii),* but might intend 110 shillings.

30,1 SON OF FAFITON. So Hunts. 25,1.

HORN. MS *Horim,* in error; see Middlesex 4,11.

32,5 PODINGTON. See also Northants.

> [35]   LAND OF WILLIAM PEVEREL   225 d
> 1a William Peverel holds Higham (Ferrers)...
> 1g In PODINGTON ½ hide in jurisdiction *(de soca).*
>   4 villagers with 1 plough.

See also Beds. 3,17 and 42,1 (Rushden and Farndish).
The larger part of Podington was in Beds., and the whole parish now is.

32,6 PLOUGHS. 'Another plough possible' omitted.

32,10 THANE. MS *Steignus* for *Teignus.*

32,14 ½ HIDE OF WOODLAND. Woodland is occasionally measured by the hide elsewhere, e.g. Essex 24, 1-2 (42a); see Sussex, Appendix. The other half of the Southill woodland is entered at 39,3.

35,2 SHIRDON. EPNS 17.

38,1 SUDBURY. EPNS 59.

39,1 VIRGATE. The figure is omitted; 1 virgate completes a 10 hide manor.

40,1 MORCAR. See 1, 2b.

LUTON. MS *Lintone* for *Luitone,* as also in 57,4; EPNS 156.

40,2 £7. Probably a MS error for *vii sol.*

40,3 PLOUGHS. '2 ploughs possible' omitted.

42,1 FARNDISH. See also Northants.

> [35]   LAND OF WILLIAM PEVEREL   225 d
> 1a William Peverel holds HIGHAM (Ferrers)...
> 1f In FARNDISH 3 virgates of land in jurisdiction *(de soca).*
>   Land for 1 plough; 2 Freemen have it.

See also 3,17 and 32,5 (Rushden and Podington). The whole of the parish is now in Beds.

43 THE FIGURE is clear in the MS, smudged in Farley's print.

44,2 OSBERN. MS Osbert for Osbern, as in 23,31; 46,1.

44,4 ELVEDON. EPNS 17.

46,1 A MILL. Resources entered before people, as occasionally elsewhere.

OSBERN. MS Osbert for Osbern, as in 23,31; 44,2.

RALPH... GAVE TRIBUTE. Canute is said to have ruled that if a landholder was more than four days overdue with his payments, whoever came forward and paid might have the land (Heming *Chartularium Ecclesiae Wigornensis* 1, 278); VCH 207.

46,2   BEFORE 1066. TRE accidentally repeated in the MS.

47,4   2 HIDES LESS. *et* accidentally inserted in the MS.

48,1   MEPPERSHALL. See also Herts.

40   LAND OF GILBERT SON OF SOLOMON   142 a

1   Gilbert son of Solomon holds MEPPERSHALL. It answers for 3 hides
     and 1 virgate.
         3 villagers and 4 cottagers.
     This land is assessed in Bedfordshire with (his) other land.
     Leofwin, a thane of King Edward's, held this land.

The manor was divided by the county boundary, and Polehanger, to the north, was in
Herts. This area may have been detached; or the eastern end of Stondon and Shillington
may have been included in the manor, with a boundary as here mapped, marked uncertain.
GILBERT. Elsewhere he held only 30 acres, at Felsted (Essex 73,1...96 b).
YOUNG LEOFWIN. See 12,1 note.

48,2   WILLEY HUNDRED. The normal Hundred order is here reversed, perhaps because
Meppershall was Gilbert's principal residence.
PLOUGHS. '1 plough possible' omitted.

49,1   ALBERT. Chaplain to King Edward and King William.

50,1   HONDAY. PNDB 292.

52,2   GLADLEY. Now in Heath and Reach parish, to which it may correspond.
MILL. No population is recorded, as often on small holdings, but rarely on one of this
size. The omission may be accidental, as that rectified by a marginal addition in 53,24.

53,8   MAN...SHE. *Homo* here includes woman.

53,15   OSBERN HOLDS. Perhaps Sudbury, with which this holding would make 3 hides,
VCH 258, citing *Feudal Aids,* 1,15,33.
10s. The mark over the *x,* shown in Farley as the abbreviation normally written above
the 'm' of marginal manor, is more probably a flourish at the end of *recep(it).*

53,16   POTTON. Entered out of Hundred order. The entry is also contradictory; lands
described as 'held in Potton' should not normally include Potton itself. The holding
may be a half virgate in Barford, belonging to Potton.

53,17   PLOUGH. Either 1 villagers' plough, or 1 plough possible, omitted.

53,21   SUTTON. Smaller lettering is used, to 56,4.

53,30   EVERTON. See also Hunts.

24   LAND OF RANULF BROTHER OF ILGER   207 b

TOSELAND Hundred

1 M.   In EVERTON Ingward had 7 hides taxable. Land for 18 ploughs.
     Now in lordship 2 ploughs;
         19 villagers and 12 smallholders who have 9 ploughs.
         A priest and a church; meadow, 15 acres; underwood, 40 acres.
     Value before 1066 £10; now £7.
     Ranulf brother of Ilger holds from the King.

The larger part of the manor was in Hunts., but the parish is now in Beds. The modern
parish is however somewhat small for so large a manor, and the Hunts. manor may
have included at least the detached part of Tetworth parish, and the strip of Cambridge-
shire that divides Tetworth.

53,32   HOLDER OF KEMPSTON. Not named, perhaps because of uncertainty. Kempston
(53,5) is entered as held by Tosti's brother Gyrth; it may have passed to him on Tosti's
exile in 1065. It is possible that the abbreviation *com* refers to Countess Judith, as
1086 holder of Kempston, but, with one exception (53,3), her name is written as
comit or *comitissa,* not *com.*

54,1   MEADOW. Resources before people, see 46,1.

54,4   MILTON ERNEST. Out of Hundred order. Not said to be held of Adelaide, but by her
husband's steward. It was perhaps intended as a separate chapter, see VCH 260-1.

55,1   WIFE. *Femina,* not implying widow, but interchangeable with *uxor; uxor* is used in
the chapter title of Azelina, who was a widow, but in the Landholders' list *femina* is
used both of Azelina, and of Adelaide, whose husband was living.

55,2   HOCKLIFFE. Possibly in Stanbridge Half-Hundred, since the parish lies south and
west of Watling Street.

55,5	MARRIAGE PORTION. See 24,18 note; compare e.g. 56,11 *de dote,* dowry.
56,3	HIDE. The total and the details of this holding disagree by a fraction of a virgate. Both figures make Biddenham just under 10 hides.
57	REEVES. The Hundred order is here is three consecutive lists, 1-5 (including 3 i-vi grouped together on their own); 6-11; and 12-21). Of the three categories in the chapter title, Reeves are named in 1-5 and 20-21; a Beadle in 17; and an almsman in 19.
	BEADLE. An unpopular lesser official with minor police functions.
57,1	ADMINISTRATION. *Ministerium Regis.* The phrase is unusual. It does not here carry any generalised meaning of 'service' or 'use', but is confined to lands which the King, as in other counties, distributed in small holdings to various beneficiaries, usually former public servants of various kinds.
57,4	REEVE OF THE HUNDRED. Rarely recorded in DB.
	LUTON. *Lintone* for *Luitone;* see 40,1.
	BONDI. One of the few English notables who retained lands and office for some time after 1066. He was probably Sheriff of Bedfordshire, before Ralph Tallboys.
57,5	PLOUGHS. 'Land for 2(?) ploughs' omitted.
57,3	ORA. Literally an ounce. A unit of currency still in use in Scandinavia. Reckoned at either 16d, as probably here, or at 20d.
57,7	LANK. PNDB 309 (rather than the alternative 'Land').
57,8	ST. PAUL'S. Probably of London.
57,9	4 PARTS. So the MS, as in 57,10. The zig-zag abbreviation over *part* normally abbreviates *partes; parte,* with a line above the *e,* is normal for *partem,* with *tam* added above *iiii* to indicate *quartam.* The usage is not however always consistent, and, since Beds. DB has more scribal errors than most counties, a mistake for 'fourth part' is possible.
	HALF OX. The probable meaning is a half share in an ox; the other share is not reported.
57,12	WESTCOTTS. See 24,13.
57,14	GODWY DEAR. OEB 343.
57,20	COMMENDED. See 17,5 note. In this instance, the Freeman was doubtless aged.
E 5	MARGINAL K. For *Klamor,* claim.
E 6	MARGINAL S. For *Soca,* Jurisdiction.

APPENDIX

Associations of Freemen *(sochemanni)* were numerous in Bedfordshire before 1066, except in the extreme south, and on the lands of the King and of English churches. Elsewhere some 600 *sochemanni* held about a third of the land, rising to two thirds in some Hundreds, with an average of over half a hide each, a range from a single acre to nearly two hides. Only a dozen of them held their land individually, but more than half of them in groups of between eight and twenty-four persons. Only a few are said to have held from lords. But by 1086 the total had been reduced to about 100, all of whom held from lords.

Similar groups on a similar scale are reported throughout the east midland Shires, of Cambridge and Northampton, Leicester and Nottingham, and especially Lincoln. Elsewhere these associations survived in greater numbers for some centuries, but freedom from lords is most marked in the Bedfordshire Survey. *Sochemanni* were somewhat less numerous in Derbyshire and Yorkshire, but plentiful in Norfolk and its borders; there however their different and varied status requires discussion in the county volumes. They are also entered in smaller numbers in Kent and Surrey, in Buckinghamshire, Huntingdonshire, Hertfordshire and Middlesex, where the average value was twice as large as in Bedfordshire; but groups are fewer and smaller in these counties.

Throughout DB, except in East Anglia, the terms *liber homo* and *sochemannus* are mutually exclusive; where one is plentiful, the other is rare or absent. The difference in meaning in Bedford-shire is clearly stated in the Stanford entry (23,9); of four *sochemanni,* three were *liberi,* but the fourth could neither grant nor sell. The *liber homo* was free to sell his land; most *sochemanni* could 'grant or sell', and most of them were therefore also *liberi.*

The terms overlap, but had different meanings. Though DB enters tens of thousands of *sochemanni,* the word is rare and late in earlier documents. Shortly before 1066 King Edward granted to Westminster land at Eversley in Hampshire, held by four named men, including his brewer and one of his guards, described as *mine fre socne men* (Harmer *Anglo-Saxon Writs* 85 = KCD 845). The corresponding DB entry (Hants. 8,1...43 c) reports that *quattuor liberi homines tenuerunt de rege E in alodium,* 'four free men held from King Edward in freehold'. To King Edward they were both 'free' and also *socnemen;* in Hampshire DB uses only *liberi,* and does not use *sochemanni* or *socnemen.* Elsewhere the distinction may often be verbal; DB selects one of two adjectives that describe different rights of the same individual.

The term *sochemannus* clearly derives from *soca*, jurisdiction, and the profits arising therefrom. Several entries describe this jurisdiction. At Wandsworth (Surrey 21,3) 'Six *soche manni* held from King Edward...There were two Halls...it answered for 12 hides'. These were men of substance, with two hides apiece, and also 'free' to sell ('go where they would' in the idiom of the Surrey Survey); the 'Hall' gave them the jurisdiction normal in a manor. But when smaller men lacked halls, their absence was sometimes worthy of remark; in Kent (5,181...11 a), before 1066, two *sochemanni* had held half a yoke *sine aulis et dominiis*, without halls and lordships. Such men, as in Bedfordshire, had no lord but the King, and are sometimes termed *sochemanni regis*. But others also sometimes had some jurisdiction; on one Ramsey holding (Hunts. 6,3) the Abbot had the larger fines, the *sochemanni* the lesser fines. These and other entries argue that the root meaning is a man who exercised jurisdiction and received its profits, not a man subject to jurisdiction; for in the numerous places described as *soca* of northern manors, in their jurisdiction and subject to their halls, the inhabitants are not *sochemanni*. But the right to exercise limited jurisdiction implies exemption from comparable jurisdiction by others, by the Hundred court, or the lord, or both. *Sochemanni* enjoyed a restricted Franchise or Liberty; and many or most were also *liberi*, free to sell. Those who held only a few acres had little occasion for halls and jurisdiction, as in the Kentish entry, but it is probable that they inherited or acquired the exemptions attached to their name. It is also probable that the numerous *liberi homines* who held manors before 1066 also exercised some jurisdiction over their villagers. Both words describe men whose status and average holdings placed them above the villager, though many individuals among them held less land than some villagers. The differences between them are partly of substance, partly of terminology, partly regional; they cannot be seen more clearly until the information from all counties is examined and compared. Because the terms overlap, and sometimes describe the same persons, the *sochemannus*, with his Franchise, is here translated as 'Freeman', the *liber homo* as 'free man'.

It is however clear that the term *sochemannus* was relatively recent in 1066, abundant and long-lived in areas settled by the Danes in the 9th century, infrequent and in decline elsewhere. Since it is found in areas far removed from Danish influence, it is unlikely to describe a status originated by the Danes. It more probably derives from an older status, which was progressively reduced by English rulers of the 10th and 11th centuries, but which throve and prospered in Danish areas, and thereby acquired a new general name.

INDEX OF PERSONS

Familiar modern spellings are given when they exist. Unfamiliar names are usually given in an approximate late 11th century form, avoiding variants that were already obsolescent or pedantic. Spellings that mislead the modern eye are avoided where possible. Two, however, cannot be avoided: they are combined in the name of 'Leofgeat', pronounced 'Leffyet', or 'Levyet'. The definite article is omitted before bynames, except where there is reason to suppose that they described the individual. The chapter numbers of listed landholders are printed in italics.

Acard of Ivry	23,17	Alfward Bellrope	25,1
Adelaide wife of Hugh	*54*	Alfward	24,6; 23
of Grandmesnil		Alfwold of Stevington	2,8. 15,1-2; 4-7
Aelfeva	18,5	Alfwold	3,17. 34,2. 53,1
Aelfled	10,1	Earl Algar	23,20
Aelfric Small	24,16. 25,3	Algar	49,4
Aelfric the Beadle	57,3 v	Alli	47,1. 53,11. 57,6
Aelfric of Flitwick	25,2	Alric Wintermilk	57,8
Aelfric	3,15; 17. 24,15.	Alric the priest	23,25
	25,3. E 3	Alric son of Goding	24,2; 6-7
Aellic	23,1 note	Alric	16,1. 21.8. 25,1.
Aelmer of Hoo	23,48		32,15. 56,8. 57,9
Aelmer	23,42. 25,2. 49,2; 3.	Alstan of Boscombe	18,1-4; 6-7
	53,6. 55,4. 56,6	Alstan	23,52
Aethelwulf the	40,3	Alwin Devil	4,2; 6-8. E 5; 16
Chamberlain		Alwin Horn	30,1
Aki (Askell?)	23,15; 38	Alwin Sack	4,5
Albert of Lorraine	*49*	Alwin the priest	57,19
Alfred of Lincoln	*31. 32,7*	Alwin the reeve	57, 3 iii-vi; 5
Alfsi of Bromham	23,28-29	Alwin brother of Bishop	16,4
Alfsi	2,1. 47,1	Wulfwy	

Alwin	3,9; 13. 18,7. 21,7. 23,1 note. 28,2. 35,2. 41,2. 44,2; 4. 53,17-18; 22; 36. 55,1. 57,11	Fulchere of Paris	16,7. 24,25-26. 53,17-18
		Fursa	E 7
		Geoffrey of Trelly	3,4; 10
		Geoffrey	4,1
Ambrose	22,1	Germund	16,8
Canon Ansfrid	13,2	Giffard, see Walter	
Ansgot of Rochester	2,2-3	Count Gilbert, see Richard	
Ansketel the priest	23,9	Gilbert of Blosseville	53,15
Arnold	54,2	Gilbert of Ghent	27
Arnulf of Ardres	15,1-2; 4-6	Gilbert son of Solomon	48. 29,1
Arnulf of Hesdin	20	Gilbert	53,11
Asgar the Constable	1,5	Glew	31,1
Askell (of Ware), see also Aki	17,4. 23,1-3; 5-6; 11-13; 22; 24; 27; 33; 42; 44; 52. 55,9-10	Godfrey	4,1; 3
		Goding, see Alric	
		Goding	55,8
Askell	18,5. 55,1-2	Godmer	18,3
Augi	17,4-6	Godmund	3,8. 56,7
Auti	23,20	Godric the Sheriff	23,25
Azelin	53,32-33	Godric	4,1; 3. 17,7
Azelina wife of Ralph Tallboys	55	Godwin the burgess	56,2
		Godwin Frambold	31,1. 32,7. 46,2. 47,2
Azor	43. 2,4		
Bald, see Edric		Godwin son of Leofwin	24,9
Baldric	26,1. E 4	Godwin	18,2. 23,13. 29,1. 47,3. 53,7; 9; 19; 27. 54,1; 4
Abbot Baldwin of (Bury) St Edmund's	6,1		
Basset, see Richard, William		Godwy Dear	57,14
Bellrope, see Alfward		Godwy	15,3
Bernard	18,6. 23,45. 24,21. 55,10	Golderon	24,20
		Grimbald	41,1
Black	17,6	Gross, see William	
Bondi the Constable	57,4	Gunfrid of Chocques	37
Branting	23,55. 57,3 iv	Gunfrid	23,51
Brictric	19,1; 3. 32,2	Earl Gyrth	53,5. 54,1
Brodo	55,5	Countess Gytha	3,17 note. 22,2
Burgred, see also Wulfsi	2,4. 3,1-7; 9;13-17. 25,6. 54,4	Earl Harold	23,4. 35,2. 50,1. 53,7; 9. E 1, 8
Butler, see Hugh		Henry son of Azor	43
Crispin, see Miles		Herbert the reeve	57,1
David of Argenton	50	Herbert son of Ivo	2,6-9
Dear, see Godwy		Herfast	16,3. 24,6; 8; 29-30
Devil, see Alwin			
Domnic	21,11	Honday	50,1
Dot	57,11	Horn, see Alwin Horn	
Queen Edith	1,4. 2,1. 23,28-29; 32. 49,4. 57,6	Hubald, see Hugh	
		Hubert, see Eudo	
Edric the Bald	55,8	Hugh of Beauchamp	23. 4,2. 17,2; 4; 6. 21,6; 10. 25,7. 54,2. 55,9
Edric	53,28		
Edward White	20,2		
Edward	53,25. 56,5. 57,5	Hugh Butler	35
Edwin	1,5	Hugh Hubald	44,1-4
Engelhere	53,13	Hugh of Bolbec	16,1; 3-4
Ernwin the priest	14. 4,3	Hugh of Flanders	34
Eudo the Steward, son of Hubert	21. 8, 4-5. 25,7. 28,1	Hugh of Grandmesnil, see also Adelaide	29,1. 54,1; 4
Count Eustace	15	Hugh, nephew of Herbert, son of Ivo	2.9
Eustace the Sheriff	E 6-7		
Fafiton, see Robert		Hugh	25,3; 12. 32,3; 5; 8; 12; 16 . 33,2. 53,2; 6; 9-10; 12; 14; 16; 31; 33-34
Fisher, see Osbern			
Frambold, see Godwin			
Fran, see Oswulf			
Froissart, see William		Humphrey	3,15
Fuglo	24,2; 7	Ilger, see Ranulf	
Fulbert	18,7	Ingward	53,30 note

Iudichael   55,4

Ivo, Steward of Hugh   54,4
of Grandmesnil

Ivo Tallboys   1, 1a; 2a; 3. 4,5

Ivo, see Herbert

Jocelyn the Breton   *52*

John of Les Roches   8,2. 24,12

Countess Judith   *53.* 21,1. 54,3

Ketelbert   57,6

Ketel   24,20

Lank   32,6. 57,7

Ledmer   23,47

Leofed, see Wulfward

Leofeva   23,17. 53,8

Leofgar   53,23

Leofgeat the priest   13,1

Leofgeat   23,32

Leofmer the Beadle   57,3 v

Leofmer   25,12

Leofnoth   24,20. 32,1; 3-6;
8-9. 33,1-2

Leofric son of Osmund   22,1

Leofric   4,4. 15,1. 19,3.
25,6. 34,3

Leofsi   53,2

Young Leofwin   12,1. 24,18. 25,14.
48,1. E 2

Leofwin,   8,6. 24,25. 32,10;
see also Godwin   12-13; 15. 40,3

Liboret   23,55

Lisois (of Moutiers)   21,13

Lovett, see William

Malet   22,2

Martell   E 3

Merwen   13,2

Miles Crispin   *19.* 53,7

Moding   23,32

Morcar the priest,   1,2b. 40,1-2
of Luton

Mordwing   23,44

Nigel of Aubigny   *24.* 8,2. 16,3

Nigel of Le Vast   24,9-11; 22-23

Nigel, see Robert

Norman   21,13. 23,52

Ordric   32,9

Ordwy, burgess of   6,1. 56,3
Bedford

Ordwy   53,27. 57,10; 12

Osbern Fisher   *46*

Osbern son of Richard   *44*

Osbern son of Walter   *45*

Osbern   8,5. 53,8; 15

Osbert of Breuil   23,27; 31

Osbert   32,1; 6-7

Oscar of Bedford   56,1

Osgeat the reeve   57,18; 20

Osgeat   23,56

Canon Osmund   13,1

Osmund   22,1

Oswulf son of Fran   26,1-3. E 4

Oswy   22,1. 57,2

Passwater, see Ralph

Peverel, see William

Pirot   21,14-15. 24,18;
24

Poynant, see Richard

Rainward, see William

Ralph Passwater   25,1

Ralph Tallboys,   1, 1b; 4-5. 4,2. 13,1-2.
see also Azelina   17,2; 5. 21,6. 23,7; 12;
16; 41-42; 55. 24,14.
46,1. 54,2; 57,1; 3 vi;
4; 13.

Ralph of Lanquetot   16,5-6; 8; 9

Ralph de L'Isle   *51*

Ralph   21,16. 23,19.25,4. E 7

Ranulf brother of   *29.* 53,30
Ilger

Raven   21,14-15

Reginald, see William

Reginald   23,50. 32,2; 9

Bishop Remigius   B. *4.* 1,1c. E 5
(of Lincoln)

Rhiwallon   23,34-36. 24,17.
25,7

Richard Basset   28,1

Richard Poynant   *39*

Richard Talbot   16,2

Richard son of Count   *38*
Gilbert

Richard, see Osbern

Richard   23,42

Robert d'Oilly   *28.* 19,2. E 3

Robert of Tosny   *26.* E 4

Robert (son of) Fafiton   *30*

Robert son of Nigel   29,1

Robert son of Rozelin   15,7

Robert   23,49; 54. 34,3.
39,2. 40,2. 53,24-25

Roger the priest   23,55

Roger son of Theodoric   23,41

Roger   23,48. 24,17. 55,7

Roland   21,12

Rozelin, see Robert

Sack, see Alwin

Saegeat   57,17

Saemer   24,25

Saemer the priest   22,2

Serlo of Rots   23,28-29. 25,4

Sigar of Chocques.   *36.* 3,6

Sihere, see Walter

Sihere   32,15

Earl Siward   E 8

Small, see Aelfric

Solomon the priest   28,2

Solomon, see Gilbert

Speke, see William

Starker   1,1b

Stephen   24,7

Archbishop Stigand   16,5. 39,1; 3. 51,1-3

Stori   44,1-2; 4

Sweeting   53,25

Sweetman   53,12

Talbot, see Richard

Tallboys, see Ivo, Ralph

Theodbald   21,1. 23,40. 37,1

Theodoric,   17,7
see also Roger

Thorbert   3,10. 53,26

Thorgils   3,13. 23,19.24,1-4; 19

Thorgot	57,16
Thorkell	23,18. 53,21. 57,21
Thurstan the Chamberlain	47
Thurstan	3,12. 55,3
Earl Tosti	23,47. 24,14. 44,1. 47,3. 49,2-3. 53,2; 16; 20; 29-30; 32-33. 54,3. 57,2
Tovi the priest	2,4
Tovi	46,1. 53,12
Tuffa	53,31
Ulf	27,1
Walraven	1,4
Walter Giffard	16
Walter the monk	55,8
Walter of Flanders	32. 8,2. 31,1. 32,4
Walter brother of Sihere	33
Walter, see Osbern	
Walter	18,2. 23,43; 56. 25,5-6. 55,12
Earl Waltheof	6,2. 23,17. 40,3. 53,31. E 3
Warner	23,30
Wending	23,46
White, see Edward	
Widder	55,9
Wig	35,1. 36,1
Wigot, King Edward's Huntsman	52,2
William Basset	23,26
William Froissart	23,20-21
William Gross	25,8
William Lovett	41
William Peverel	22. 3,17. 32,5. 42,1 note
William Speke	25. 17,1. 56,2
William the Chamberlain	40. 1,2b; 3
William, Steward of the Bishop of Coutances	3,5; 9
William of Cairon	4,2; 6-8. 21,5; 8-9; 17. 24,28
William of Eu	18
William of Loucelles	23,22-23
William of Warenne	17. 23,1 note. E 6
William son of Rainward	25,7
William son of Reginald	25,2
William	42. E 5
Wimund of Tessel	23,37-38
Wimund	2,8. 23,24; 33; 38
Wintermilk, see Alric	
Wulfeva	3,5
Wulfgeat	23,24. 28,1. 53,14
Wulfheah, King Edward's steersman	53,15
Wulfmer the burgess	56,4
Wulfmer, King Edward's priest	6,1
Wulfmer the priest	57,4
Wulfmer of Eaton	21,1; 5-6; 9-10; 14-15; 17. 45,1. 55,12-13
Wulfmer	53,27. 55,4-6
Wulfnoth	23,25. 25,5
Wulfric	18,5. 53,36. 55,3
Wulfsi the prebendary	56,9
Wulfsi son of Burgred	25,5
Wulfward Leofed	20,1
Wulfwin	53,34
Bishop Wulfwy	1,1c. 16,4. 24,23. 28,2. 34,2
Wynsi the Chamberlain	1,1b

Churches and Clergy. Archbishop of Canterbury ... Stigand. Bishop of Bayeux 2. 40,3. Coutances 3. 31,1. Dorchester ... Wulfwy. Durham 5. Lincoln ... Remigius. Abbess of Barking 11. Abbot of St. Alban's 23,12. 53,25. (Bury) St.Edmund's 6. 53,35. Peterborough 7. Ely 3,6 note. Ramsey 8. 19,1. 34,3. Thorney 10. Westminster 9. Canons of Holy Cross of Waltham 5,1-2. St Paul's of Bedford 13. 53,32; 35. St Paul's of London 12. 57,8. E 2. See also Ansfrid, Osmund. Church of Houghton Regis 1,3. Leighton Buzzard 4,9. Luton 1,2b. St Nicholas of Angers 24,29. Monks of St Neot's 38,1-2. See also Walter. Nuns of St Mary's of Elstow 53,1,3-4. Prebendary, see Wulfsi. Priests, see Alric, Alwin, Ansketel, Ernwin, Leofgeat, Morcar of Luton, Roger, Saemer, Solomon, Tovi, Wulfmer.

Secular Titles and Occupational Names. Beadle (bedellus)... Aelfric, Leofmer. Chamberlain (camerarius) ...Aethelwulf, Thurstan, William, Wynsi. Constable (stalre).. . Asgar, Bondi. Count (comes)...Eustace, Gilbert. Countess (comitissa)...Gytha, Judith. Earl (comes).. Algar, Gyrth, Harold, Siwald, Tosti, Waltheof. Queen (regina)... Edith. King's Huntsman (venator regis)...Wigot. Reeve (prefectus)... Alwin, Herbert, Osgeat. Sheriff (vicecomes)... Godric. King Edward's Steersman. (Stirman)...Wulfheah. Steward (dapifer)... Eudo, Ivo, William. Young (cilt)... Leofwin.

INDEX OF PLACES

The name of each place is followed by (i) the initial of its Hundred and its location on the Map in this volume; (ii) its National Grid reference; (iii) chapter and section references in DB. Bracketed figures denote mention in sections dealing with a different place. Unless otherwise stated, the identifications of EPNS and the spellings of the Ordnance Survey are followed for places in England; of OEB for places abroad. The National Grid reference system is explained on all Ordnance Survey maps, and in the Automobile Association Handbooks; the figures reading from left to right are given before those reading from bottom to top of the map. The Bedfordshire Hundreds (see 1,1 note) are Barford (Ba); Biggleswade (Bg); Bucklow Half-Hundred (Bk); Clifton (C); Flitt (F); Manshead (M); Redbornstoke (R); Stanbridge Half-Hundred (Sb); Stodden (Sd); Wenslow Half-Hundred (Ww); Willey (Wy); Wixamtree (Wx). Places entered in Hertfordshire and Huntingdonshire in DB are indexed as (He) and (Hu). Grid references beginning with the figure 9 are in the 100 kilometre grid square SP. All others are in square TL. Approximate locations are printed in italic type. Places mentioned in the notes, but not in DB, are shown on the map by open circles. Unidentified places are shown in DB spelling, in italics.

	Map	Grid	Text		Map	Grid	Text
Ampthill	R 12	03 38	24,10	Clifton	C 2	16 39	4,7. 8,6. 21,17.
Arlesey	C 6	19 36	5,2. 18,6.				24,28. 53,46
			24,30. 56,9	Clophill	F 2	08 38	24,14
Apsley Guise	M 3	94 36	23,17	Colmworth	Ba 2	10 58	23,38. (17,4).
Astwick	Bg 12	21 38	23,45-47. 32,12				(23,24)
Great Barford	Ba 9	13 52	23,36-37; 39-40	Cople	Wx 6	10 48	23,49-55. 53,34
Little Barford	Bg 1	17 56	8,5. 45,1	Cranfield	R 7	95 42	8,1
Barton-in-the-Clay	F 9	08 30	8,2	Husborne Crawley	M 4	95 36	24,1. 41,1
Barwythe	He B	02 14	E 4	*Cudessane*	C		16,8. 23,57
Battlesden	M 13	96 28	16,2. 40,2. 55,1	Dean	Sd 6	04 67	3,3. 4,1.
Bedford	Bk 10	04 49	B. (4,9. 6,1. 13.				17,1. 57,13-14
			53,32. 56	Dunstable	M 19	02 21	1,2 note
			57,14)	Dunton	Bg 6	23 44	16,5. 39,1
Beeston	Wx 7	16 48	21,12-14.	Easton	Sd 4	13 71	3,6. 4,2. 17,4-7.
			25,14. 47,3.				23,24. 35,1.
			56,7. 57,11				36,1. 44,1
Biddenham	Bk 9	02 50	4,4. 6,1. 13,1-2 .	Eaton Bray	Sb 7	97 20	2,1
			23,28. 25,4.	Eaton Socon	Ba 3	16 58	21,1.
			56,1-4				See Wulfmer.
Biggleswade	Bg 4	18 44	51,2. (51,4)	Edlesborough	Sb 9	97 19	27,1
Billington	Sb 6	94 22	1,1b note	Edworth	Bg 11	22 40	18,4. 57,3 iv
Biscot	F 13	08 23	1,5	Eggington	Sb 3	95 25	1,1b note
'Bleadon'			(3,8; 10-11)	Elstow	R 2	05 47	53,4. (53,1; 3)
Bletsoe	Bk 1	02 58	23,27. 53,8	'Elvedon'	Sd 9	06 66	44,4
Blunham	Wx 1	15 51	6,3. 21,11.	Eversholt	M 6	99 33	2,2. 23,19
			53,35				57,1
Bolnhurst	Sd 15	08 59	2,4-5. 3,8.	Everton	Ww 2	20 51	53,30
			10,1. 53,6	Eyeworth	Bg 7	24 45	25,10. 55,5
Bromham	Bk 6	01 51	15,1. 23,29.	Farndish	Wy 3	92 63	42,1. 43,1
			53,9. 57,18.	Felmersham	Wy 8	99 57	48,2. 53,11
			(23,28)	Flitton	F 3	05 35	30,1
Broom	Wx 10	17 43	24,11	Flitwick	R 16	03 34	(25,2). 41,2
Caddington	F 14	06 19	12,1	Nares Gladley	Sb 1	91 27	52,2
Cainhoe	F 4	10 36	24,15. 55,3	Goldington	Ba 10	07 50	4,5. 23,41-
Campton	C 3	12 38	16,9. 18,7. 47,4				43. 57,8
Cardington	Wx 5	08 47	23,10. 53,33	Goldington Highfields	Bk 4	05 53	23,7
Carlton	Wy 13	95 55	2,7. 24,20-21.				
			46,2. 57,6	Gravenhurst	F 7	11 35	23,21
Chainhalle	Bk 5		23,5-6	*Hanefelde*	Sd		17,3. 57,15
Chalgrave	M 15	00 27	20,2. 49,1	Harlington	M 11	03 30	24,5
Chalton	Wx 3	14 50	54,3	Harrold	Wy 11	94 56	53,13
Chawston	Ba 5	15 56	21,3.. 23,34.	Harrowden	Wx 4	06 47	14,1. 24,27.
			25,7-8				53,32
Chellington	Wy 12	95 55	3,10 note	Cockayne Hatley	Ww 4	25 49	53,29. 55,6
Chicksands	C 1	12 39	4,8. 55,11-12				
Clapham	Sd 18	03 52	19,1. (19,2)	Haynes	F 1	08 41	23,15

Place	Code	Grid	References
Heath and Reach, see Gladley			
Henlow	C 4	17 38	24,29. 32,16 55,9-10. 56,8
Higham Gobion	F 8	10 32	23,23
Hinwick	Wy 5	93 61	3,12. 25,5. 34,2. 37,1. 47,2. 56,5
Hitchin	He H	18 29	E 1
Hockliffe	M 16	97 26	55,2
Holcot	M 2	94 38	25,1
Holme	Bg 8	19 42	18,5. 23,44. 24, 26. 32,11, 51,3. 53,18-19. 57,3 v
Holwell	C 10	16 33	8,8. 9,1
Hoo, see Aelmer			
Houghton Conquest	R 9	04 41	23,14. 53,2. 54,2
Houghton Regis	M 17	01 23	1,3. (1,4)
Husborne, see Crawley			
Kempston	R 1	01 47	53,5. (53,3-4; 32-33)
Kensworth	He K	03 19	E 2
Keysoe	Sd 12	07 63	23,1. 44,3. (23,2)
Kimbolton	Hu K	09 67	(17,3)
'Kinwick'	Bg 3	18 49	6,2
Knotting	Sd 10	00 63	3,1
Langford	Bg 10	18 41	32,13. (32,10)
Leighton Buzzard	Sb 2	91 25	1,1. 4,9
Lidlington	R 10	99 38	11,1
Luton	M 20	08 21	1,2. (1,5. 40,1. 57,4)
Marston Moretaine	R 8	99 41	16,3. 24,8
Maulden	R 13	05 38	16,4. 23,13. 24, 12. 53,1. 57,3 ii
Melchbourne	Sd 8	02 65	3,2
Meppershall	C 5	13 36	48,1
Millbrook	R 11	01 38	24,9
Millow	Bg 9	23 43	5,1. 16,6. 18,3
Milton Bryan	M 10	97 30	2,3. 23,20
Milton Ernest	Sd 16	01 56	19,2. 23,26. 24,19. 32,2. 54,4. 57,17
Newton Bromshold	Sd 7	99 65	3,9
Northill	Wx 8	14 46	21,15-16. 23,56. 25,15 26,2. 53,7
Oakley	Sd 17	01 53	15,6. 32,4
Odell	Wy 7	96 58	15,4. 29,1. 47,1
Pavenham	Bk 2	98 55	8,3
Pegsdon	F 10	11 30	E 5; 9
Pertenhall	Hu P	08 65	32,5. 34,1
Podington	Wy 4	94 62	E 3
Polehanger	He P	13 37	40,1. 52,1. 57,1-2
Potsgrove	M 12	95 29	53,16. 53,20. (53,29-30. 54,3)
Potton	Ww 3	22 49	24,4. 57,3 i
Priestley	M 7	01 33	24,17
Pulloxhill	F 5	06 34	23,3. (23,6-7)
Putnoe	Bk 7	06 51	24,22. 53,12
Radwell	Wy 9	00 57	
Ravensden	Bk 5	07 54	23,5 note
Riseley	Sd 11	04 62	3,7. 4,3. 23,2; 25. 44,2. 50,1
Roxton	Ba 7	15 54	23,35 25,9
Rushden	Wy 1	95 67	3,17. 22,2
Salford	M 1	93 39	23,18
Salph	Ba 8	07 52	23,16
Sandy	Ww 1	17 49	21,6
Segenhoe	R 14	98 35	33,1
Sewell	M 18	99 22	1,4
Sharnbrook	Wy 6	99 59	3,13-16. 15,7. 23,31. 34,3. 46,1. 49,4. 53,14. 56,6
Shelton	Sd 2	03 68	3,5
Shelton	R 4	99 43	24,6-7. 49,3. 54,1
Shillington	C 9	12 34	8,7
'Shirdon'	Sd 13	09 64	35,2
Silsoe	F 6	08 35	24,16. 33,2
Southill	Wx 11	14 42	21,8. 23,8. 25,11. 32,14-15. 39,3. 53,31
Stagsden	Bk 8	98 49	2,6. 15,3. 23,4. 53,10
Stanbridge	Sb 4	96 24	1,1b note
Stanford	Wx 12	16 41	21,9-10. 23,9; 48. 25,12. 55,7. 57,9-10
Stanwick	Sd 1	98 71	7,1
Little Staughton	Sd 14		3,6 note
Steppingley	R 15	01 35	25,2
Stevington	Bk 3	98 53	15,2. (2,8)
Stondon	C 8	15 35	8,9. 55,13
Stotfold	C 7	21 36	23,12. (55,9)
Stratton	Bg 5	20 44	16,7. 32,10. 51,1. 53,17
Streatley	F 11	07 28	18,2. 23,22. 24,18. 25,3. 57,4
Studham	Sb 10	01 15	26,1
'Sudbury'	Ba 1	17 61	38,1
Sundon	F 12	04 26	18,1
Sutton	Ww 5	21 47	21,7. 53,21-28. 57,3 vi; 5
Swineshead	Hu S	05 65	E 6-8
Tempsford	Bg 2	16 53	4,6. 21,4-5. 39,2. 57,3 iii
Thurleigh	Wy 10	05 58	19,3. 23,32. 28,1-2. 32,8-9
Tilbrook	Sd 3	07 69	17,2
Tilsworth	Sb 5	97 24	22,1
Tingrith	M 8	00 32	24,3
Toddington	M 14	00 28	20,1. (25,1; 4)
Totternhoe	Sb 8	99 21	32,1. 40,3
Turvey	Wy 14	94 52	2,8. 3,11. 15,5. 23,30. 24,25. 26, 3. 32,3. 57,19
Old Warden	Wx 9	13 43	25,13. 51,4. 55,8
Ware	He	35 14	(23,7;16; 41-43; 55)

'Westcotts'	R 6	07 43	24,13. 57,12.
Westoning	M 9	02 32	E1
Wilden	Ba 4	09 55	2,9
Willington	Wx 2	11 59	23,11. (23,52)
Wilshamstead	R 5	06 43	53,3.
'Woodcroft' Hundred			1,4
Woburn	M 5	94 33	16,1. 57,1
Wootton	R 3	00 45	49,2. (49,3)
Wyboston	Ba 6	16 56	8,4. 21,2. 23,33 24,24. 38,2. 55,4
Wymington	Wy 2	95 64	25,6. 31,1. 32,6-7. 57,7;21
Yelden	Sd 5	01 66	3,4

Places not named

BARFORD Hundred 53,15.   BIGGLESWADE Hundred 24,25.   MANSHEAD Hundred 24,2.
STODDEN Hundred 57,16;20.

Places not in Bedfordshire. Indexed above.

Elsewhere in Britain.
BUCKS...Edlesborough.   HERTS...Holwell; Ware, see Askell.   HUNTS...Everton; Kimbolton;
Tilbrook.   KENT...Rochester, see Ansgot.   LINCOLN ...see Alfred.   NORTHANTS...Newton
Bromshold; Rushden; Stanwick.   WILTS...Boscombe, see Alan.
See also Index of Churches.

Outside Britain
Angers...Churches.   Ardres...Arnulf.   Argenton...David.   Aubigny...Nigel.   Bayeux...Bishop.
Beauchamp...Hugh.   Blosseville...Gilbert.   Bolbec...Hugh.   Breuil...Osbert.   Cairon...William.
Chocques...Gunfrid, Sigar.   Coutances...Bishop.   Eu...William.   Flanders...Hugh, Walter.
Ghent...Gilbert.   Grandmesnil...Hugh.   Hesdin...Arnulf.   Ivry...Acard.   Lanquetot...Ralph.
Les Roches...John.   Le Vast...Nigel.   L'Isle...Ralph.   Lorraine...Albert.   Loucelles...William.
Moutiers ...Lisois.   Oilly...Robert.   Paris...Fulchere.   Rots...Serlo.   Tosny...Robert.
Trelly...Geoffrey.   Warenne...William.

SYSTEMS OF REFERENCE TO DOMESDAY BOOK

The manuscript is divided into numbered chapters, and the chapters into sections, usually marked
by large initials and red ink. Farley however did not number the sections. References in the past
have therefore been to the page or column. Several different ways of referring to the same column
have been in use. The commonest are:

(i)	(ii)	(iii)	(iv)	(v)
152a	152	152a	152	152ai
152b	152	152a	152.2	152a2
152c	152b	152b	152b	152bi
152d	152b	152b	152b.2	152b2

The relation between Vinogradoff's notation (i), here followed, and the sections is:

209 a	B	- Landholders	213 a	23,10 -	23,18	217 a	51,1 -	53,4
b	1,1	- 1,2b	b	23,18 -	23,27	b	53,4 -	53,14
c	1,3	- 2,3	c	23,27 -	23,40	c	53,15 -	53,28
d	2,3	- 3,3	d	23,40 -	23,52	d	53,29 -	54,3
210 a	3,3	- 3,12	214 a	23,52 -	24,6	218 a	54,4 -	55,11
b	3,13	- 4,6	b	24,6 -	24,17	b	55,12 -	56,9
c	4,7	- 7,1	c	24,17 -	24,27	c	57,1 -	57,7
d	8,1	- 8,9	d	24,27 -	25,6	d	57,7 -	57,21
211 a	9,1	- 14,1	215 a	25,6 -	25,14			
b	15,1	- 16,2	b	25,14 -	30,1			
c	16,2	- 16,9	c	30,1 -	32,5			
d	17,1	- 18,1	d	32,6 -	32,16			
212 a	18,2	- 20,1	216 a	33,1 -	37,1			
b	20,1	- 21,8	b	38,1 -	42,1			
c	21,9	- 22,2	c	43,1 -	47,2			
d	22,2	- 23,10	d	47,3 -	50,1			

BARFORD Hundred
1 'Sudbury'
2 Colmworth
3 Eaton Socon
4 Wilden
5 Chawston
6 Wyboston
7 Roxton
8 Salph
9 Great Barford
10 Goldington

BIGGLESWADE Hundred
1 Little Barford
2 Tempsford
3 'Kinwick'
4 Biggleswade
5 Stratton
6 Dunton
7 Eyeworth
8 Holme
9 Millow
10 Langford
11 Edworth
12 Astwick

BUCKLOW Hundred
1 Bletsoe
2 Pavenham
3 Stevington
4 Goldington Highfields
5 *Chainhalle*
6 Bromham
7 Putnoe
8 Stagsden
9 Biddenham
10 Bedford

CLIFTON Hundred
1 Chicksands
2 Clifton
3 Campton
4 Henlow
5 Meppershall
6 Arlesey
7 Stotfold
8 Stondon
9 Shillington
10 Holwell

FLITT Hundred
1 Haynes
2 Clophill
3 Flitton
4 Cainhoe
5 Pulloxhill
6 Silsoe
7 Gravenhurst
8 Higham Gobion
9 Barton-in-the-Clay
10 Pegsdon
11 Streatley
12 Sundon
13 Biscot
14 Caddington

MANSHEAD Hundred
1 Salford
2 Holcot
3 Apsley Guise
4 Husborne Crawley
5 Woburn
6 Eversholt
7 Priestley
8 Tingrith
9 Westoning
10 Milton Bryan
11 Harlington
12 Potsgrove
13 Battlesden
14 Toddington
15 Chalgrave
16 Hockliffe
17 Houghton Regis
18 Sewell
19 Dunstable
20 Luton

REDBORNSTOKE Hundred
1 Kempston
2 Elstow
3 Wootton
4 Shelton
5 Wilshamstead
6 'Westcotts'
7 Cranfield
8 Marston Moretaine
9 Houghton Conquest
10 Lidlington
11 Millbrook
12 Ampthill
13 Maulden
14 Segenhoe
15 Steppingley
16 Flitwick

STANBRIDGE Hundred
1 Nares Gladley
2 Leighton Buzzard
3 Eggington
4 Stanbridge
5 Tilsworth
6 Billington
7 Eaton Bray
8 Totternhoe
9 Edlesborough
10 Studham

HUNTS
K Kimbolton
P Pertenhall
S Swineshead

HERTS
B Barwythe
H Hitchin
K Kensworth
P Polehanger

STODDEN Hundred
1 Stanwick
2 Shelton
3 Tilbrook
4 Easton
5 Yelden
6 Dean
7 Newton Bromshold
8 Melchbourne
9 'Elvedon'
10 Knotting
11 Riseley
12 Keysoe
13 'Shirdon'
14 Little Staughton
15 Bolnhurst
16 Milton Ernest
17 Oakley
18 Clapham

WENSLOW Hundred
1 Sandy
2 Everton
3 Potton
4 Cockayne Hatley
5 Sutton

WILLEY Hundred
1 Rushden
2 Wymington
3 Farndish
4 Podington
5 Hinwick
6 Sharnbrook
7 Odell
8 Felmersham
9 Radwell
10 Thurleigh
11 Harrold
12 Chellington
13 Carlton
14 Turvey

WIXAMTREE Hundred
1 Blunham
2 Willington
3 Chalton
4 Harrowden
5 Cardington
6 Cople
7 Beeston
8 Northill
9 Old Warden
10 Broom
11 Southill
12 Stanford

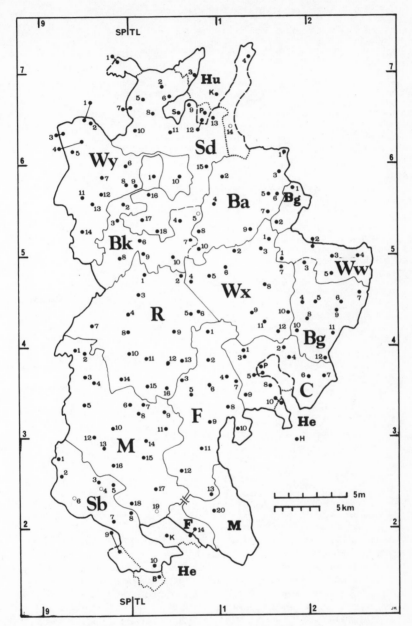

The County Boundary is marked by thick lines, continuous for 1086, dotted for modern boundaries; Hundred boundaries (1086) by thin lines, broken where uncertain.

National Grid 10-kilometre squares are shown on the map border.

Each four-figure square covers one square kilometre, or 247 acres, approximately 2 hides, at 120 acres to the hide.

TECHNICAL TERMS

Many words meaning measurements have to be transliterated. But translation may not dodge other problems by the use of obsolete or made-up words which do not exist in modern English. The translations here used are given in italics. They cannot be exact; they aim at the nearest modern equivalent.

BORDARIUS. Cultivator of inferior status, usually with a little land. *s m a l l h o l d e r*
CARUCA. A plough, with the oxen who pulled it, usually reckoned as 8. *p l o u g h*
CARUCATA. See 10,1 note. *c a r u c a t e*
DOMINIUM. The mastery or dominion of a lord *(dominus)*; including ploughs, land, men, villages, etc., reserved for the lord's use; often concentrated in a *home farm* or *demesne*, a 'Manor Farm' or 'Lordship Farm' *l o r d s h i p*
FEUDUM. See 2,2 note. *H o l d i n g*
FIRMA. Old English *feorm*, provisions due to the King or lord; a sum paid in place of these and of other miscellaneous dues. *r e v e n u e*
GELDUM. The principal royal tax, originally levied during the Danish wars, normally at an equal number of pence on each *hide* of land. *t a x*
HIDE. A unit of land measurement, see B note. *h i d e*
PRAEPOSITUS, PRAEFECTUS. Old English *gerefa*, a royal officer. *r e e v e*
SOCHEMANNUS. See Appendix. *F r e e m a n*
TAINUS, TEGNUS. Person holding land from the King by special grant; formerly used of the King's ministers and military companions. *t h a n e*
T.R.E. *tempore regis Edwardi*, in King Edward's time. *b e f o r e 1 0 6 6*
VILLA. Translating Old English *tun*, town. The later distinction between a small *village* and a large *town* was not yet in use in 1086. *v i l l a g e*
VILLANUS. Member of a *villa*, usually with more land than a *bordarius*. *v i l l a g e r*
VIRGATA. A quarter of a *hide*. *v i r g a t e*

ADDITIONS AND CORRECTIONS to volumes published earlier.

HERTFORDSHIRE

B3 and Index of Persons. *For* Wulfmer of Eton *read* Wulfmer of Eaton.
25,2. *For* [...1½ virgates] *read* [....½ virgate].
Index of Places, Elsewhere in Britain. *For* BUCKINGHAMSHIRE Eton?
read BEDFORDSHIRE Eaton Socon.

SURREY

1,8. *For* in-going *read* death duty. *Delete* note; *substitute* DEATH DUTY.
Releva, payable by the heir, normally to the King.
2,1 note. The *Domesday Monachorum* of Canterbury (ed. D C. Douglas 1944), written about 1100, reproduces much of the Kentish DB material. One list of revenues ends with the Archbishop's manors in Surrey, Middlesex, and Sussex. (p.10 folio 5v) = transcript p. 99). The Surrey entries are *Croindene de firma xxx lib & xl sol archiepiscopo. Gablum xxxiiii sol & vii d. De quodam theine xx sol. Mortelace & Heisa de firma lvi lib & xl sol archiepiscopo. Gablum lxxiiii sol & iii d.* The DM *firma* is slightly more than the DB *valet* of Croydon, but less than the *valet* of Mortlake, with Hayes (Middlesex). Under Tarring (Sussex 2 and 2,9 notes) is listed *Buresto viii lib*, evidently Burstow (TQ 31 41) EPNS Surrey 286.

MIDDLESEX

2,1-2 note. *Domesday Monachorum* enters Hayes with Mortlake (Surrey) and continues with Harrow *Herges de firma liiii lib & xx sol archiepiscopo & xxx porcos. Gablum lx & vii sol.* The *firma* is slightly less than the DB *valet*.